52954

DATE			
	DISCARD		

BAKER & TAYLOR BOOKS

Bale o' Cotton

NUMBER FORTY-THREE
CENTENNIAL SERIES OF THE
ASSOCIATION OF FORMER STUDENTS,
TEXAS A&M UNIVERSITY

Bale o' Cotton

The Mechanical Art of Cotton Ginning

KAREN GERHARDT BRITTON

TEXAS A&M UNIVERSITY PRESS

COLLEGE STATION

Library of Congress Cataloging-in-Publication Data
Britton, Karen Gerhardt, 1946–
    Bale o' cotton : the mechanical art of cotton ginning / Karen
Gerhardt Britton. – 1st ed.
        p.   cm. – (Centennial series of the Association of
Former Students, Texas A&M University ; no. 43)
    Includes bibliographical references and index.
    ISBN 0-89096-510-2 (cloth : alk. paper)
    1. Cotton gins and ginning–United States–History.
I. Title.   II. Title: Bale of cotton.   III. Series
TS1585.B75   1992
677'.2121–dc20
                                        92-14229
                                        CIP

Manufactured in the United States of America
FIRST EDITION

Dedicated to the memories of
my parents,
BERRY AND EVELYN GERHARDT,
and my mentor and friend,
SUZANNE COMER

Contents

Illustrations

Preface

In 1975, when I was researching the history of East Texas for another book, I wrote to Dr. Calvin B. Parnell, an agricultural engineer at Texas A&M University, for information about cotton gins. I knew a little about the purpose of ginning, but I had no real understanding of how gins worked. Although he was surprised by my request, Dr. Parnell responded with a mountain of printed material about ginning and commented in his letter, "It's refreshing to find a lady interested in cotton ginning." Neither of us could have guessed that eleven years later I would begin writing a complete history of cotton ginning. At the time, having that abundance of material was like diving into a wagon full of seed cotton–soft, warm, and itchy.

Perhaps the itchiness had always been there, as inevitable as fibers growing silently inside a boll. My maternal grandmother's parents, John and Mollie Lane, left the war-torn, depleted soil of Georgia in 1872 to begin a new life in the rich cotton lands of Texas' Brazos River bottom. My grandmother, Elsie Lane, was born at Port Sullivan (near Franklin in Robertson County), which was a cotton shipping point on the Brazos River. At that time John Lane owned a small cotton farm and worked as a mechanic at a local gin. Eventually the combination of flooding, a drop in the price of cotton, and his own growing family caused him to give up farming and move to Corsicana, about fifty miles south of Dallas. In Corsicana, he opened a bicycle shop and prospered well beyond the expectations of a two- or three-bale-per-season farmer.

My maternal grandfather, Jesse Owen Robinson, grew up on a cotton farm outside Howard, near Waxahachie in Ellis County, where his parents had settled in the 1880s after leaving Mississippi. He was working as the bookkeeper at the Howard gin when my mother was born in the summer of 1918. When boll weevils destroyed the cotton crop in 1920, my grandparents left Howard and went to Commerce where my grandmother, a language arts teacher, could find work, and where my grandfather, a mathematics

teacher during the school term, could finish the education that would enable him to serve as principal or superintendent in various rural school districts. In many ways the boll weevil was directly responsible for a vagabond lifestyle that did not end for my grandparents until they retired to a farm near Mexia, in Limestone County, in 1951.

My mother often recalled picking cotton as a child while visiting her grandparents' farm at Howard. She never forgot those long, hot, tedious, and painful afternoons in the fields. Filled with a sense of adventure, she became, and remained, a "city girl." At the age of eighteen, when she learned to fly a two-seater airplane, she and her copilot barnstormed half the small towns in north central Texas. One stormy afternoon they missed their target and crash-landed in a cotton field. Neither of them was hurt, but she refused to fly again.

My father's side of the family had an even closer relationship with cotton. My father's maternal great-grandfather, Dick Sanders, had owned a cotton plantation in Upshur County before the Civil War. Like many Southern gentlemen, Dick Sanders went to fight for the Confederacy and when the war ended, he walked home. My great-grandmother, a small girl at the time, often waited by a well, hoping to be the first in the family to welcome home the father she hardly remembered. As other men passed by, she would give them water and ask if they had seen him. Because they did not know if he were alive, but could not deny hope to a child, they would point behind them and say, "He's just down the road apiece." When he did return, as angry as he was proud, he dismissed all of the loyal freed men and women who had remained on the plantation, creating severe hardships for them and for his own family. Even after oilcloth was available, he insisted upon using china and crystal place settings on linen for every meal. His empire might have been gone, but he was never defeated.

My grandmother's father, Jack Craton, was a cotton farmer in Upshur County. When he hauled the season's bales to Jefferson to sell them, he spent a day or two in town, sleeping under his wagon at night, sometimes enjoying himself a bit too much. On one such occasion he forgot that his wife had asked him to bring home six yards of calico and purchased an entire bolt (about twenty yards) instead. My grandmother, Mary Craton Gerhardt, often chuckled at the memory of how tired she and her brothers and sister became of wearing identical shirts and dresses.

My paternal grandfather, Vivian James Gerhardt, was a scale engineer for the Missouri-Kansas-Texas ("Katy") Railroad and spent forty years traveling the line from Chicago to Galveston, calibrating scales for grain elevators, rice mills, and cotton gins. He applied for a patent for what would one day become truck scales, but he did not receive it because he could not furnish a model that would prove his theory.

My own childhood and adult life have not depended upon cotton for a livelihood, but cotton's influence was subtle and pervasive. I grew up in Waco, where the fragrance of crushed cottonseed wafted across the entire city at times, making us hungry even if we had just eaten. Images of the glamorous era of the Cotton Palace, a complex of exhibit buildings and fairgrounds dedicated to King Cotton, filled my father's stories of his youth. I still have a fifth-grade notebook about King Cotton—as if some internal voice kept whispering that this contained something too important to throw away, some hidden mystery that I would later unravel.

More important than that notebook were the weekends and summers spent at my grandparents' farm near Mexia. Playing on and exploring that beloved farm, I never knew that Robert Munger's gin facility in town had once been the largest in the country, or that the Hermann Focke gin down the road, toward my favorite picnic place at the lake near Fort Parker, would outlast my grandparents' ownership of that farm.

The irony of the importance of Limestone County to ginning, and to me personally, lingers. I have since found the site of the Munger complex, verified by Mr. Tom Chatham of Mexia, and the sense of elation I felt at following and proving a hunch has made all the hours of research as valuable to me as the warm memories of my childhood.

Initial inspiration for this book may have come from my family, but it is not about my family. It is about land and machinery and people, about economic enterprise, and about entire communities with their distinctive personalities and faces and voices. While writing this book I met many wonderful people, saw more of the state than I ever had before, and experienced the satisfaction of participating in active restoration projects. I learned about the music of the steam engine, and I also discovered, through oral history, a folklore which has been largely ignored. As described by ginners such as Donald Baird and mechanics such as L. V. Risinger, long days and tedious hours bred a penchant for practical jokes that, based upon the truths of human nature, were funny fifty and seventy-five years after they occurred.

I wondered what role women played in ginning. I knew that they had worked as accountants and bookkeepers, but I discovered that they had also worked on the ginning floor and some had received patents for improvements to the gin stands. Unmarried women owned and ran gins with a success rate that had nothing to do with gender. In her ideological and financial support of Eli Whitney, Catherine Greene began a tradition of female involvement in a predominantly male enterprise that has lasted for two centuries.

To my surprise, I learned that cotton and cotton ginning have earned a small but enduring place in the arts. William Faulkner's play *27 Wagons Full of Cotton* exemplifies the competition between two gins, one independent and one syndicated, in a small cotton growing area and shows the vengeance of each gin manager upon the other. This play was the basis for the movie *Baby Doll*. Horton Foote's *Places in the Heart* illustrates the critical timing needed to pick the season's first wagon load of cotton and to be the first to arrive at the gin in order to receive prize money. Foote's character Edna Spalding needed that money to save her farm from foreclosure, and the superhuman efforts of each character epitomized the day-to-day heroism of the time.

The cotton industry is depicted in Currier and Ives prints of steamboats laden with cotton bales, in Edgar Degas' 1873 portrait of New Orleans cotton brokers, and in the Jerome Kern/Oscar Hammerstein II song "Ol' Man River" composed for the musical *Showboat* in 1927.

I found that the growth of the gin manufacturing industry paralleled the nation's march toward industrialization, beginning with small firms like Whitney's that made each cotton gin by hand, and expanding until, in 1890, there were fourteen gin and auxiliary equipment manufacturers. The Chatham Machine Company of Bryan, operating between 1869 and 1899, was Texas's only gin manufacturer. The devastation of the boll weevil, the shift of the South's labor force from farms to cities, and the need for mechanical harvesting of cotton forced manufacturing to become more centralized, and by the 1950s there were only seven companies making gins and their related equipment. Today there are two primary gin manufacturers left, with some smaller firms keeping the free-enterprise system active.

Like the gin manufacturing companies, the individual gin plants also reflected the nation's change from an agrarian to an industrial culture and economy. The plantation gin was usually a single gin stand owned by a reasonably prosperous farmer who ginned his neighbors' cotton. Custom gins were owned by associations of farmers and businessmen, were generally on a westward pushing rail line, and were often the primary reason for a town's existence. Today's cooperative gins belong to investors from local associations or townships, and corporate (or syndicate) gins provide services for local cotton growers and revenue for stockholders in distant cities.

A gin plant may be a combination of old and new equipment, held together by "spit and baling wire" and made productive by the ingenuity and experience of the ginner. It may also be a sleek steel building, possibly cleaner and safer than the older installations with all of their inherent problems and dangers, but costing millions of dollars and requiring of its workers a dependence upon electronics rather than ingenuity.

Regardless of ownership or size, each gin plant was modified, improved, and expanded by technological advances to handle more and more cotton. Those technological advances fell into four stages: the invention of the gin stand itself (1793), pneumatic handling of bulk seed cotton through a mechanized system (the 1880s), the shift from manual to machine harvesting (the 1950s), and the development of modules (the 1970s). As will be seen, each stage affected the gin plant's economic and mechanical ability to produce a bale of cotton.

Once I began to conduct research for this book, I discovered that there were vast resources describing the South's cotton economy and culture and many articles filled with statistics about cotton as a world-wide economic force, but there was no single book to describe the interim steps linking seed cotton straight from the field to the textile and cottonseed mills, to the medical and automobile industries, or to world markets. This was the challenge. In terms of gathering, sorting, cleaning, and packaging, the process of turning out a bale of cotton became the perfect metaphor for researching, writing, and tying out, at best, an imperfect book.

Grading and classing will be left to readers.

It is my profound hope that readers will develop and indulge their curiosity by safely exploring gin plants or by visiting gin restoration projects. It is my heartfelt intention to provide readers with enough information to enable them to recognize the machines and to understand what appears to be a jumbled network of belts and pulleys, piping runs, and steel boxes mounted in the rafters. A lucky visitor may find a ginner who will "spin yarns" and reveal the legends, experiences, and practical jokes of a century ago. The ginning process has changed in technology, but not in principle, for two hundred years. I believe that Eli Whitney would take pride in the machine that he invented as well as in the industry that he founded.

If you walk into an old-time gin building at twilight, you will hear the creaks and groans of age, the whispers of half-forgotten passion, the echoing exclamations of joy or sorrow. You may sense remnants of a hard past that was romanticized to give it dignity and heroism, or was ostracized and ignored until it vanished. But the spirit of inventiveness smiles from every dusty corner. And the magic remains.

Acknowledgments

When I began writing this book I had only shadowy ideas and fond memories of old buildings to guide me through the work of collecting and organizing the material. It was like walking through a cotton field at twilight—I was always able to see down the row but not quite able to find my own feet. Without the help of many knowledgeable and generous individuals, I would never have found my way home.

First, I wish to express sincere thanks to Noel R. Parsons of Texas A&M University Press. He is a skilled teacher, a generous advisor, and a patient gentleman. Throughout the long and difficult circumstances of the writing, he never lost faith in the successful outcome of the project.

It would have been impossible to write the book without the help of Larry N. Jones, Museum Specialist with the Smithsonian Institution, who read every word, made the most judicious of corrections and comments, found photographs, expedited paperwork, and continually offered enthusiastic support. His sense of humor, and his sense of direction, kept the project tightly focused in spite of the writer's tendency to wander in search of new territory to explore.

Tommy M. Brown, Advertising Coordinator with Continental Eagle Corporation, and Billy Thompson, Executive Technical Coordinator with Lummus Industries, Inc., provided an overwhelming array of company records, illustrations, histories, and catalogues. Their technical assistance was an education in itself, and their confidence in my ability to interpret historical and technological advances in a field in which I had no expertise was invaluable. Both gave generously and unfailingly of their time, interest, and cooperation. I am grateful to Tommy Brown for his interest in my discovery of the Munger complex at Mexia. And I am equally grateful to Billy Thompson for accompanying me through the gin at Burton, for answering many questions, and for giving me the title "gin historian."

At the outset of the project, Donald Van Doorn of Lummus and Willie Redden of Continental offered assistance that gave the book shape and scope.

I am indebted to Alfred M. Pendleton, U.S. Department of Agriculture Cotton Ginning Engineer, who spent a great deal of time educating me in the history and mechanics of ginning and who inspired excitement about the restoration of gin plants and equipment. He shared his extensive collection of articles and photographs, and his own fine writings appear as quoted material.

Because the book was researched and organized by geography, I met many delightful and helpful individuals throughout Texas and across the Cotton Belt.

Mr. and Mrs. Lewis S. Stanford of Livingston provided insight into ginning in East Texas. It was the Stanford gin that I remembered from early childhood, and many precious but half-forgotten images became clear and powerful from newly acquired understanding.

In Central Texas, Mr. and Mrs. J. B. Vandiver of Moody explained module systems and allowed city folks with roots in McLennan County to ask many questions and take innumerable photographs. Joe Owens explained how cotton was classed, bought, and sold. Cora Lee Jones shared her special knowledge of ginning. Thomas E. Mooney of McGregor provided excellent photographs of the early days in McLennan County. Mr. and Mrs. Michael Moore of Navasota opened their home to me and kindly answered many questions.

Erma Britton found rare photographs and delightful individuals to be interviewed for the book.

Stephen C. Britton devoted many hours of professional skill to field and studio photography. His curiosity about the process of ginning and his knowledge of mechanics gave the photographs an impact they would not otherwise have had.

Thanks are due to Mr. and Mrs. Douglas Hutchinson, Frankie Jaster, Leverne Hinze, Weldon Matthies, Annie Maud Knittel Avis, Mr. and Mrs. Hank Wehring, Nell Wehring Moseley, Mr. and Mrs. Bill Shaw, and the members of Operation Restoration in Burton, Texas.

Lubbock and the South Plains provided the writer with another delightful workshop. Noel White offered details of South Plains farming, and A. O. "Bill" Kressenberg entrusted to me valuable drawings and documents and offered expert advice. A. L. Vandergriff, at different times President of Continental Gin Company and Executive Vice President of Lummus Cotton Gin Company, first told me about R. L. Munger's system ginning; from his comments about the chronology of ginning, at a critical moment in the writing, the book expanded to include a new and exciting dimension.

Sincere thanks go to O. R. Carey, Jr., who made the introductions that led to some of the finest interview material I obtained. Mr. and Mrs. Carey welcomed me into their home, and I will always think of Lubbock as a city of generous hospitality. Through Mr. Carey I met Donald Baird who told stories, loaned photographs, and brought me the gift of ginning folklore. His sense of humor pervaded every moment and made our time spent together unforgettable. His corrections to the manuscript were invaluable. I also met Jack Dempsey who, at the golden age of ninety-five, shared with me the brilliance of his wisdom and experience. Charlie F. Hunter and L. V. Risinger offered unique observations about ginning on the South Plains. Mr. Hunter told a story, included herein, that gave me the title of the book. I am especially grateful to Mr. Risinger for his description of the music of the steam engine, the poetry of the machine. It was a moment Walt Whitman would have understood and treasured, and a perfect blending of man and machine, the discovery of mechanical art as a medium of livelihood and creative expression.

Weldon Schwarz explained South Texas ginning and showed me a rare Ben Pearson spindle picker. Technical assistance was provided by Roy Childers, Calvin B. Parnell, and Robert Metzer of Texas A&M University's Agricultural Extension Service who furnished volumes of research material and photographs. Baylor University's T. Lindsay Baker, Curator of the Governor Bill and Vara Daniel Historic Village, explained many aspects of steam power and how it applied to ginning. At the onset of the project, Ted Hollingsworth showed me the Historic Village's Gullett gin stand—the first "old-timer" I had seen.

The collections and photographs of several fine libraries and museums are represented here. Sincere thanks are due to Tom Fort of the Hidalgo County Historical Museum in Edinburg, Claire Kuehn of the Panhandle-Plains Historical Museum in Canyon, Martha Utterback of The Daughters of the Republic of Texas Library at the Alamo in San Antonio, Ellen Kuniyuki Brown of the Texas Collection at Baylor University in Waco, Tommie Massey of the Melanee Smith Memorial Library in Waller, and to the fine staffs of the Houston Public Library, the Southwest Collection at Texas Tech University, the Institute of Texan Cultures, the Library of Congress, Yale University, and the Smithsonian Institution. Matthew Moye of the Westville Historic Handicrafts restoration project at Lumpkin, Georgia, and Ms. Pat Phillips of the Georgia Agrirama at Tifton kindly answered many questions and furnished printed material. Lucille Phipps provided photographs, brochures, and documents from the National Cotton Council.

Special thanks go to the Texas Cotton Ginners' Association and to the *Cotton Gin and Oil Mill Press*.

Many individuals also provided information and assistance, among them Rick Lewis, then of the Texas Historical Commission, Homer T. Fort of Midland, Mr. and Mrs. Jay Edwards of Pipe Creek, Bill Mayfield of the U.S. Department of Agriculture in Memphis, Tennessee, and H. F. Hassett of the Port City Compress Warehouse Company in Houston.

I am indebted to Lambert Wilkes, author of the module system of ginning, for his comments, insight, and interest in the project.

Mrs. Minnie Bains, Mr. and Mrs. Harris Garrett, and Mr. and Mrs. Klaus Elfeldt, all of Brookshire, Texas, gave generous help in regard to the history and preservation of the unique Cotton Gin Restaurant.

I am additionally grateful to Mr. Tom Chatham of Mexia who shared with me the very special history of the Chatham Machine Company of Bryan.

Details of cultural practices were provided by C. A. Myers of Beeville, Iva Cabrera of Houston, the late Patrick Richard of Houston, and John Richard of Lafayette, Louisiana.

Writing any book is an intensely personal journey, and I have been blessed throughout my travels by the loyalty and enthusiasm of friends and family. For almost two decades, Lianne Mercer has remained a gifted mentor, a trusted friend, and my sister in spirit. To her is extended the credit for any clarity in communication that I may have acquired.

My brothers, Berry and Dana Gerhardt, maintained constant faith and support throughout the long and frustrating process of researching and writing. No words of thanks are adequate to express my gratitude.

During the last weeks of revisions, when a technological crisis threatened the outcome of the project, Marjorie Brinegar fearlessly reproduced the manuscript, added insertions, and remained a cheerful and calm influence.

It is with singular sadness that I acknowledge the guiding influence of the late Suzanne Comer, senior editor at Southern Methodist University Press, who did not see this project come to fruition. I first approached her with the idea for a book about cotton ginning in 1987. Her primary focus was fiction, and she suggested that I contact Noel Parsons at Texas A&M University Press. Before I could do so, he wrote to me at Suzanne's recommendation. Excited about the prospect of producing a book that was a first in its field, we immediately began work.

It is clear, now, that Suzanne perceived the reality of the book long before I did, and because of her belief, indeed her assumption, that I could and must write it, I gained the confidence to make that assumption as well. Her kindness and friendship, brilliance and wit, talent and dedication are an irrevocable legacy.

And finally, I am grateful to my son Richard Britton, for his patience and understanding during all the times we could not spend together. I hope he knows, deep in his heart, that this book is for him.

Bale o' Cotton

CHAPTER ONE

Threads in the Loom

In antiquity, sometime after ancient peoples recognized the need to protect themselves by creating communities, and before they developed ways to record their thoughts, hunter/gatherers became cultivators of the land. Small groups ceased wandering from cave to cave and settled in fertile river valleys, where they built homes and planted simple crops. Whether by design or accident, these ancient peoples found a way to collect the white, fluffy fibers growing wild on trees that were taller than their own heads and to make practical use of those fibers. Scientists can only speculate on when men and women first spun cotton into thread, colored it with natural dyes, and wove it into cloth; however, for centuries cotton cloth has been prized for its softness, durability, and coolness in hot climates. As both a raw and a finished product, cotton was one of the world's first international commodities.

Cotton is a vegetable fiber of the genus *Gossypium,* a member of the *Malvaceae,* or mallow, family, and a first cousin of the hibiscus. Wild cotton grows in tropical and subtropical regions of the United States, Mexico, South America, Africa, the Arabian Peninsula, India, Australia, New Guinea, and Hawaii. Modern domesticated cotton is cultivated in the more temperate climates of Turkey, Pakistan, China, South Korea, and parts of the United States.

Although there are no fossil remains of cotton plants, scientists who have studied the taxonomy of cotton believe that the genus was successfully creating subgenera during the Cretaceous period, approximately sixty-five million years ago. New varieties were spontaneously produced as recently as eleven thousand years ago.

During the Pleistocene epoch, just before the appearance of humans, the world underwent massive climatic changes. Glaciers advanced and retreated, causing sea levels to fluctuate by as much as five hundred feet and breaking land masses into new continents with shifting coastlines. Several varieties of cotton developed seed coats that were impervious to salt water—thus protecting the seeds until they were

ready for germination—and also developed seed hairs that made flotation possible. These varieties established themselves on the constantly changing saline shorelines. Other varieties remained in place, adapting to new climates and terrains.

As the Pleistocene epoch gave way to the Recent, the earth's climate became warmer and drier. Subgenera of *Gossypium* spread throughout the Southern Hemisphere: buoyant seeds floated on the ocean, while others were carried by wind or in the fur of small animals. Moths and hummingbirds pollinated some species; one variety simply fell to the ground, usually after pollination by birds, and germinated beneath the parent plant. Scientists have traced the dispersal, evolution, and species relationships of *Gossypium,* but the prehistoric conditions under which the seeds developed such thick coats of hairs remain unknown.[1] With time, cotton adapted to a wide variety of soils, pests, and climates, thriving in coastal areas, savannas, deserts, and rain forests. Approximately one hundred species gradually developed, from bushy, low-growing shrubs to trees over six feet tall. Some boasted bright, decorative flowers; others developed silvery, reddish, or brownish fibers.

Scholars and scientists do not know how people first discovered cotton's usefulness, but bits of string and woven fibers have been identified by archeologists in excavations at Mohenjo-Daro in the Indus River Valley of what is now Pakistan. Civilization there reached its peak between 2300 and 1750 B.C., indicating that the practices of spinning thread and weaving cloth from cotton began even earlier.

Remains of a variety native to India have been found at archeological sites in ancient Nubia on the eastern coast of Africa. The plant was apparently grown or traded for its seeds to be used as animal fodder rather than its fibers for clothing. The forty-five-hundred-year-old site suggests widespread knowledge and cultivation of Old World cotton and indicates established trade routes between Africa, the Middle East, and India.[2]

Although trade routes between India and the east

Cream-colored cotton flower, related to the hibiscus. *Courtesy National Cotton Council*

coast of Africa were established early in human history, scientists cannot readily determine how cotton was cultivated or how ideas for spinning and weaving might have traveled along with the finished cloth, but there is no doubt that cotton was an easily transportable commodity with a ready market throughout the known world.

From earliest times cotton was grown, spun, dyed, and woven in India. The Hindus developed a simple technology to separate the seeds from the fibers, and an ancient hymn refers to "threads in the loom." The Holy Bible's Book of Esther mentions white, green, and blue hangings at a feast in Susa (600 B.C.). Herodotus, the Greek historian, described trees in India that had "a wool exceeding in beauty and goodness that of sheep" from which clothing was made (445 B.C.).[3]

Alexander the Great (356–323 B.C.) and his army returned from their invasion of India with clothes that were made of cotton and printed with vegetable dyes. To satisfy the demand for cotton cloth and other luxuries that soon spread throughout the West, Alexander opened trade routes to the East. Because of their strategic crossroads location, Arab traders began to dominate international trade. They set up distribution centers in the coastal cities and controlled the flow of goods throughout the Middle East.

One land route followed a northerly path across Persia (now Iran and Iraq) and traversed the Pamir Range of the Hindu Kush (Tibet) before entering China. Another route extended from Iran to western Turkey. The routes were chosen for their proximity to grass and water for camels; secret mountain trails were used for protection from attacks by rival traders.

The water routes provided the fastest, cheapest means of transporting goods. From the time that the Malaysians sailed their outriggers ahead of the monsoons, across the Indian Ocean to the coast of Africa, and introduced the spice trade to the Middle East, trade by river and ocean had been popular. One route began at the Indus River, crossed the Arabian Sea, and entered the Red Sea. At the port of Berenice on the African coast, goods were transferred onto camels and carried overland to Coptos, a city on the Nile River, then shipped down the Nile to Alexandria. Another route entered the Tigris and Euphrates rivers through the Persian Gulf; from there ships sailed to Constantinople and to port cities on the Mediterranean.[4]

As the Greek empire faded and the Roman ascended, Arab traders continued to bring Chinese silks and Indian cottons to the Middle East. Pliny, a Roman historian of the first century, saw cotton growing in Egypt and described the white fibers and the fine cloth made from them. Egyptian priests favored cotton for their clothing, but it was the more plentiful Egyptian linen that was shipped to Central Asia and Europe where less comfortable garments made of wool and animal skins had been worn for centuries. After the disintegration of the Roman Empire, the Arabs not only maintained their control of the trade routes, but also began to cultivate their own cotton and to look for markets for their goods.

For centuries the North African Arabs had coveted Spain, a lush land across the narrow Straits of Gibraltar. In A.D. 711, following the teachings of Muhammad to spread the religion of Islam, they swept into southern Spain and made Córdova their capital city. The North African invaders introduced cotton plants to Spain, and by A.D. 950, it had become a center of cotton cultivation and trade. The word *cotton* comes from the Old Spanish *cotón* which in turn is derived from the Arabic *qutun* or *qutn*. Córdoba, Sevilla, and Granada were famous for weaving and dyeing, and Barcelona, a seaport, was known for its sailcloth.

From tenth-century Spain the cotton trade gradually spread across Europe. Venice, in northern Italy, became the dominant trading center, using its strategic position on the Mediterranean to control the flow of goods from the old Alexandrian trade routes to cities in northern Europe. Venice, Italy, and Ulm, Germany, enjoyed a lively commerce in textiles and spices by 1320, and Venice and Antwerp, Belgium, shared a trade in printed cottons. Antwerp (Belgium), Bruges (Belgium), and Haarlem (The Netherlands) became major cotton ports, but only after goods had passed through Venice.

The Portuguese, who wanted a share of the commerce with the East, were in the best geographic position to outmaneuver the Venetians. Royal leadership and support from Prince Henry the Navigator led to improvements in ship building, navigational devices such as the astrolabe and compass, and ship-mounted weapons. All of these gave the Portuguese advantages over other European countries.[5] Politically unified, the Portuguese were prepared to compete with the Venetians for commercial supremacy. Bartholomeu Dias found a passage around the Cape of Good Hope in 1488, and ten years later Vasco da Gama sailed around Africa to reach trading posts on the coast of India. The Portuguese had no interest in acquiring territory, setting up colonies, and manufacturing goods, but they instead preferred to enter established systems of commerce with native peoples and/or Muslim traders. They set up coastal trading posts and quickly joined or created trading routes that extended from Africa to China and Japan. Spain, Holland, France, and England followed Portugal's lead in developing their own trading patterns, and the Venetians lost their monopoly of the European market.

By the time that Spain, competing with Portugal for its own trade route to India, was willing to sponsor Columbus's voyage, cotton cloth was a firmly established luxury, in constant demand by Europeans. Columbus was not seeking a source of cotton in his voyage southwestward and was surprised to find wild cotton growing in the West Indies. In his journal he noted that the natives presented the explorers with skeins of cotton thread, laboriously spun by hand.[6] Since Columbus knew that the best cotton cloth came from India, the islanders' gifts must have contributed to his belief that he had reached Asia.

The European explorers who followed Columbus found that the trading of cotton was as important to the New World as to the Old. Cotton had been grown, harvested, and spun in the Tehuacán Valley of Mexico since antiquity. In the Yucatán Peninsula, heart of the Mayan Empire, cotton was grown as a cash crop and exported, both as bales of lint and as finished textiles, along coastal and across inland areas.[7] Cotton was also used like paper. Messages were painted on sheets of cotton, rolled on wooden dowels like Middle Eastern scrolls, and carried by runners to recipients throughout the region.

Hernán Cortés, arriving in Mexico in 1519, was pre-sented with embroidered cotton mantles sent by the Aztec emperor Montezuma II, who believed Cortés was the god Quetzalcoatl returning home. As Cortés systematically conquered the native peoples, he encountered more than Aztec lords in feathered head-dresses, gold ornaments, and embroidered mantles. He discovered a healthy industry, based on cultivated cotton, that produced and exported some three hundred thousand bales of cotton per year from the Tehuacán Valley deep into Mayan Guatemala and beyond. In Peru, Francisco Pizarro learned that along with the mining and working of gold, the Incas were masters of the art and craft of textile design and manufacture. Ferdinand Magellan, sailing around the world, saw cotton growing in Brazil.

The origin of the first use of cotton in the New World is unknown, but bits of cotton dated as early as 2500 B.C. have been found at Huaca Prieta in Peru. One of the cultivated New World cottons, *Gossypium hirsutum L.*, was known in southern Mexico and Guatemala, while another, *Gossypium barbadense L.*, was common to northern Peru. The *barbadense* cottons, with black seeds and fibers up to 1¾ inch long, spread eastward and northward to the Caribbean. The *hirsutum* cottons, with green seeds and fibers ranging from ⅞ to 1¼ inch long, grew to the north and west as far as present-day New Mexico. The cotton plants were most likely perennial shrubs, and a few plants would have provided enough fiber to clothe a family. Varieties of these dooryard cottons were found in various climates throughout the New World.

The sixteenth century was primarily a time of discovery, but the seedlings of global commerce had been planted in Medieval Europe by traveling Flemish and Venetian traders as they exchanged spices, jewels, and cloth. Gradually, the traveling merchant began to remain at home, offering a commission to agents in faraway cities. With the development of double-entry bookkeeping and banking, international commerce became increasingly sophisticated. Another two hundred years of colonialism would pass and expanded marketing practices would be established, however, before cotton became a dominant force in global economics and ignited a technological revolution.[8]

To conduct global trade and integrate the new American colonial possessions into the European system of imports and exports, the old merchant guilds created trade associations which eventually became chartered companies. A charter, granted by the government, offered a company both protection from competitors and opportunities for trade, often as a monopoly, in distant areas. The British East India Company was chartered in 1600, followed by the Dutch East India Company two years later. These companies perceived the New World as a source of raw materials rather than a partner in reciprocal trade because of its sparse population.

The companies' primary trade partners remained in the Orient. An uncontrolled flow of gold from the New World through Spain and across Europe created an inflationary spiral—and a middle class that could now afford to pay for goods formerly offered only to the aristocracy. Caught up in a renaissance of learning and floating on an ocean of prosperity, Europeans bought Oriental spices and perfumes, clothing and carpets, and looked to the East for cultural inspiration. As the rising tide of inflation slowly began to undermine the economy and demand outstripped supply, merchants sought ways to produce more goods, at a lower cost, closer to home.

Closer to home meant Europe, in particular, England. In 1328, King Edward III of England settled a colony of Flemish weavers in Manchester. This new spinning and weaving industry required a continuous volume of imported cotton. By 1600, the Manchester textile industry had added fustian (a coarse cloth of cotton and linen, similar to today's velveteen and corduroy) and dimity (a dyed or printed, heavy cotton drapery fabric unlike today's dimity, which is lightweight and sheer) to its list of cotton goods. The trading companies prospered from increased exports, and England remained dependent upon the Middle East, India, and the Orient for its raw cotton.

Once it had been established by explorers that the northern continent of the New World had little gold and silver and was rich only in raw products such as timber and furs, England considered its colonies to be rough outposts for maintaining territorial integrity. After early attempts to cultivate cotton in New England failed, England urged its colonists to produce tobacco, indigo, sugar, and rice.

Cotton was planted at the Jamestown Colony in Virginia as early as 1607, but it was grown as a dooryard decoration rather than as a commercial crop. By 1619, the colonists were harvesting enough cotton for home use; two years later, cotton was selling for eight pence per pound. It was important as a source of thread for weaving cloth rather than as a commodity for export, but the cotton industry, like the persistent, adaptable *Gossypium* itself, now had a roothold in the northern colonies.

Tobacco, the colonists' great commercial crop, was grown so widely and so successfully that it fostered the plantation system, defined by the use of slave labor, the practice of hiring factors to sell the crop, and an economic philosophy of worldwide supply and demand, all of which later became associated with cotton. Many of the European-born colonists found the hard work of clearing land, cultivating, and harvesting crops demeaning. As a result, there were never enough freemen willing to work for wages on the plantations.

Early attempts to train North American Indians to become agricultural workers were unsuccessful. In South America many Indians had been accustomed to a rigid class structure and agricultural labor before the Europeans arrived, but the native peoples of North America were primarily hunter/gatherers with a more flexible social system and a minimal agricultural tradition. Those who were willing to become laborers for the Europeans caught their diseases and died in ever-increasing numbers, and survivors fled the European settlements. In addition the colonists, who were steadily encroaching upon tribal lands, were often attacked by native Americans and, thus, were reluctant to employ them in large groups.

European indentured servants formed a more stable labor supply. In most cases, they sold their services for periods of four to seven years in exchange for free passage to America. In return, they were to be provided food and shelter by their masters until their contracts expired. Not all indentured servants came willingly. Many were debtors, drunks, thieves, or convicts who were either sentenced to indenture or kidnapped and placed on board ships bound for the New World. Once adjusted to the freedom of the New World, these servants soon discovered opportunities to become their own masters, and they often "canceled" their contracts by disappearing into the wilderness. Whether or not they served the terms of their indenture, they entered the mainstream of colonial America, becoming shopkeepers and landowners like those they had formerly served.

The planters' solution to the problem of the agricultural labor shortage was the acquisition of African and West Indian slaves. A few slaves were brought to Virginia as early as 1619, and the first privateerload of African slaves arrived in Jamestown to be sold as agricultural workers in 1621. Excuses for the barbarity of the practice became more "creative" as it became more widespread: the African and West Indian slaves were accustomed to the warmer coastal climate and enjoyed a greater immunity to disease; they already had an agricultural tradition, having owned land individually or collectively, and knew how to work the land with skill; they could neither return to ancestral homes, as the Indians did, nor organize large-scale rebellions. After the 1670s, the colonies developed an elaborately justified legal code that made blacks slaves for life, depriving them of all legal rights, and made children inheritors of their mothers' status. At first, slaves were not imported to work in the cotton fields; they were needed on the southern tobacco plantations. Generally, one healthy slave was required to maintain three acres of tobacco, and as the demand for tobacco increased in Europe, more land was planted, and more slaves were imported.

Tobacco wore out its soil within seven years, but land was so plentiful and so cheap that when the soil no longer produced tobacco, farmers moved inland along the waterways, cleared new fields, and planted new crops. Tobacco's devastation of the soil was recognized early, and King James I (1603–25) urged colonists to diversify crops. An oversupply of tobacco in the 1640s and the resulting lower price proved the need to find other staple crops for export. The West Indies turned to the production of sugar. Rice was grown in South Carolina after 1685, and in North Carolina, indigo became important after 1740. A silk industry was attempted but did not succeed. Sheep were imported to the middle colonies, and wool was shipped to England for use in the mills.

By the mid-1600s, England's attitude toward its colonies had changed considerably. No longer outposts against the expansion of other countries into North America, the colonies were now sources of raw materials and importers of English goods. In 1660, Parliament passed the first of three Navigation Acts designed to monopolize colonial shipping and trade. In the Navigation Act of 1660, all colonial goods had to be transported in English or colonial ships; certain "enumerated articles," which included "cotton-wool," limited colonial exports to England or English colonies. The Staple Act of 1663 required that all goods (except salt for fisheries, Madeira wine, Irish servants, and horses) being exported to the colonies by European countries first pass through England. The Navigation Act of 1660, however, had placed import duties on the enumerated goods destined for England, but not on goods sold from colony to colony, and, thus, those goods were cheaper for the colonists to buy than for residents of England. Nor was there any law to prohibit the colonies' selling of goods directly to Europe. By paying no duties to European countries, colonial merchants could sell more cheaply than English merchants. The Plantation Duties Act of 1673 eliminated these earlier oversights by levying duties on all enumerated articles not destined for England, and the duties were to be collected at the plantations themselves.[9]

Planters consigned their tobacco and other crops to English merchants who sold the crops, purchased clothes and household goods that they shipped to the planters, and advanced credit when profits were lower than expected. At the same time, planters often acted as merchants for yeoman farmers who had moved inland and used the waterways to transport their tobacco to market. Planters made imported goods available to the inland farmers on credit. When the tobacco was harvested each autumn, planters could accept the tobacco as payment against the credit or could buy it outright and sell it with their own. Under the terms of the Navigation Acts, the planters also collected the required duties from the inland farmers.

By the early eighteenth century, large landholders like Robert Carter, William Byrd II, and Richard Lee II began to realize that they were in financial bondage to their agents and their slaves. The initial cost of a slave was higher than that of an indentured servant (eighteen to twenty pounds as opposed to ten to fifteen pounds), but the indentured servant might remain as few as four years, while the slave remained on the land for life; thus the investment could be amortized over a longer period of time. The planters attributed other advantages to slaveholding in order to justify its continued existence: black women would work in the fields, whereas white women would not; blacks did not demand the living conditions that Europeans did; and there was no threat of blacks entering white society. However, in years of low crop-yield, the cost to maintain slaves could outweigh profits and create a spiraling deficit.[10] A planter would then remain in bondage to his agent, who advanced credit against unsold or low-profit crops, for years.

Tremendous financial obligations to feed, clothe, and house the people needed to work depleted soil kept the planters in a state of near-bankruptcy. Planters like Robert Carter of Nomini Hall, Virginia (grandson of the earlier mentioned Robert Carter), experimented with grains, flax, hemp, and cotton. Carter was remarkable in that he hired some of his field workers, purchased and sold large amounts of wheat, flour, and cornmeal, produced bread on a commercial scale, and manufactured textiles.[11] Like many of his contemporaries, Carter recognized the decline of tobacco as the colonies' primary agricultural export, but rather than abandon his plantation and move inland, he chose to diversify and rotate his crops. Cotton had been exported from the Carolinas to other colonies by the late 1600s, and after the turn of the eighteenth century, it was grown in Georgia, Mississippi, Alabama, and Louisiana and as far north as the Chesapeake Bay area. With the rise of the Industrial Revolution in England, sparked by an increased demand for textiles, Carter and other American planters began to look at cotton as a commercial export crop.

The British East India Company continually imported quantities of cotton cloth from India and created such competition with the powerful English woolen industry, begun in the mid-1300s, that Parliament passed laws to protect woolen interests by restricting imports. It even went so far as to require that the dead be buried in woolen shrouds.[12] Such laws were not generally enforced, however. Gradually, it became clear to woolen interests and Parliament alike that the popular cotton goods were going to remain in use and that a method of economical production of cotton goods had to be found.

In spite of increasing imports, most English and colonial cloth was manufactured on looms in individual homes. The term "cottage industry" applied to the agricultural processes as well as to the spinning and weaving needed to make wool, linen, and cotton cloth. As more people moved into the cities and the middle class expanded, fewer homes manufactured their own cloth, thus increasing the demand for finished goods. English cotton cloth producers needed a manufacturing technology in order to compete successfully with woolen cloth producers.

As early as 1597, English clergyman William Lee had invented a machine to knit stockings, and during the 1600s, better ways of dyeing and finishing cloth were developed in the Netherlands. Almost another century passed, however, before the textile industry began to be mechanized. In 1733, John Kay, an inventor who made reeds for looms, received a patent for the flying shuttle, which increased the efficiency of the loom. For centuries weavers had had to throw the shuttle across the warp, requiring the exhausting extension of arms and hands. The flying shuttle made cloth production faster and more comfortable for the weaver. The lathe, to which the shuttle was connected, was lengthened, and strings were attached to a peg that was held in the weaver's hand. By using small, quick movements, the weaver could send the shuttle literally flying across the warp. Less fatigue quickly translated to greater production.[13]

The "spinning jenny," developed in 1764 by a weaver named James Hargreaves, combined rows of upright spindles with a movable carriage to increase the output of the hand-operated spinning wheel.

Richard Arkwright's water-powered spinning frame, first constructed and patented in 1769, used rollers arranged in a series, spinning faster and faster, to produce a tighter, thinner yarn. Weaver Samuel Crompton's spinning mule, invented in 1779, further improved spinning techniques by blending Arkwright's spinning rollers with Hargreaves's movable carriage to control tension and automate spinning even more. While yarn was produced in increasing quantities, most weaving was still performed on hand-operated looms with foot-operated treadles. Rev. Edmund Cartwright's steam-powered loom, made possible by James Watt's engine, pushed England further toward industrialization by requiring coal to operate the steam engines and better roads for moving goods from factories to ports.[14]

Arkwright, a barber by trade, quickly rose from inventor of the spinning frame to first-rank entrepreneur. With the financial backing of Jedediah Strutt, an inventor and businessman, Arkwright built the first textile factory in 1771 in Derbyshire. His machines were carved from wood, with some cast iron parts, and were powered by the water wheel. He employed three hundred workers, many of them children, and was so successful that by 1774 he received tariff protection from Parliament. Seven years later he had several mills, one thousand employees, and a knighthood. After his patents expired in 1785, making the design of the machinery open to anyone, Arkwright became very careful about who worked for him or visited the factories, and any of his workers who tried to slip out of the country were stopped by customs agents of the Royal Navy.

The introduction of new technology to the rapidly growing textile industry was accompanied by patent applications, infringements, and litigation. Hargreaves and Kay, for example, received patents that were supported by the courts, but both were victims of mob violence because their inventions threatened to eliminate jobs. Both men spent years in litigation over patent infringements; Crompton never filed for a patent at all. This concern for legalities would form a recurrent theme in the cotton industry.

Before the American Revolution, England had decreed that colonial cotton be sent to the mother country. The colonists were then expected to buy finished cloth from England. Early American attempts at textile manufacturing, primarily the spinning of yarn, were unsuccessful because of a lack of technology. Mechanized manufacturing, in large part due to the success of Richard Arkwright, was not allowed in the colonies. With American political independence came a shift in trade agreements between the United States and England, but Americans remained limited to what finished goods they could produce by hand. The silky Sea Island cotton (*Gossypium barbadense L.*), grown along the coastal areas of South Carolina, Georgia and Florida, had a ready market in England, but there was never enough, and coastal planters hoarded their seeds for future crops. Even had planters been more generous, the seeds would not have produced cotton in the interior because of differences in soil and climate. A few experimental attempts at hybridization failed. Inland planters had no choice but to raise the short-staple, green-seed "upland" cotton (*Gossypium hirsutum L.*). In 1784, eight bags of American cotton, each weighing between 150 and 250 pounds, were seized by English customs agents as contraband because they did not believe that so much cotton could be grown in America. England was still buying its cotton from India and the West Indies; clearly, American planters wanted their share of a semiclosed market.

Cotton yarn was produced in America, but because technology there was not competitive with that of England, finished textiles continued to be imported. In 1789, planters and mill owners began to demand an American cotton manufacturing industry. The United States government levied a duty of three cents per pound on West Indian and Brazilian cotton to encourage planters to increase cotton production, then about one million pounds, and, thus, to provide an export crop that would help stabilize the nation's economy. That same year, a twenty-two-year-old master craftsman, disguised as a farmer to elude English authorities, arrived in New York City with the plans of Arkwright's mills locked securely in his memory. His name was Samuel Slater.

At the age of fourteen, Slater had signed a contract of indenture with Jedediah Strutt, inventor of a spinning frame for ribbed stockings and a partner of Arkwright's. Slater served his term of indenture as a clerk, or bookkeeper, and when he completed his contract at the age of twenty-one, he remained at the mill as an overseer. He heard stories of the flailing efforts of American manufacturers to produce satisfactory cotton textiles and read of bounties to be paid to those who could make improvements to the current machinery, and he decided to immigrate to the United States. As a longtime employee, he was given permission by Arkwright to supervise the construction of a new factory in England, but he could not draw up plans or make any models; everything he had learned through the years had to be kept in his head.

When the factory was finished, he disguised himself as a farmer and fled to America. He arrived safely in New York and found a job in a yarn manufacturing mill that used old-fashioned machines. He might have remained there, but he learned from the captain of a coastal packet that Moses Brown of Providence, Rhode Island, was having difficulty producing cotton yarn strong enough for his weaving machines. Slater wrote to Brown, stating that he was familiar with the Arkwright-type machinery, known to have continuous rather than stop-and-start movement, and offered his services. An excited Brown invited Slater to Providence to try his hand at improving the equipment.[15] Slater proved equal to the task. In December, 1790, a year after his letter to Brown, Slater's water frame factory, which boasted seventy-two spindles, began producing high-quality cotton yarn.

Slater, Brown's son-in-law William Almy, and Obadiah Brown, a cousin, formed the company Almy, Brown & Slater, and within the first year of production turned out more yarn than they could sell and had to halt production temporarily. They found other markets and soon confronted the opposite problem: more demand than supply. In 1793, Slater settled in Pawtucket, Rhode Island, to construct the first large-scale textile mill. Five years later, he formed the new firm of Samuel Slater & Co. with other partners and built a second mill. In what was to become a pattern, Slater's millhands struck for higher wages and quickly took the opportunity to move to a nearby town and build their own mill. Cotton yarn mills spread throughout the area and the rest of the country. Slater tried to prevent others from copying his machines just as Arkwright had. He was not always successful, but he grew wealthy nevertheless, and when he died in 1835, his estate was valued at more than one million dollars.

News of Slater's success in building a yarn factory of the Arkwright design was carried deep into the South. At the same time, England was increasing its imports of cotton, from nine million pounds in 1790 to more than twenty-eight million pounds by 1793. Forward-thinking men such as Alexander Hamilton and Thomas Jefferson realized cotton's potential: An American textile industry would create tremendous demand for domestic cotton. Grown on a large scale, cotton would mean a continuing staple crop for southern farmers, provide northern yarn mills with raw goods for manufacturing, and supply shippers and merchants with yarn for export to European textile mills.

The demand for cotton was greater than the planters could satisfy. In 1790, about 3,000 bales of cotton were produced for both domestic and export purposes, and the following year 4,184 bales were sold for twenty-nine cents per pound. (A bale of cotton was not the well-known rectangular bale of 500 pounds. Cotton was packed by hand, tamped down by foot or with wooden pestles, and placed in sacks up to nine feet long. The filled sacks contained between 125 and 350 pounds of lint.)[16] It was clear that upland cotton could be grown in ever-increasing quantities, but its commercial success remained in doubt. In a single day a slave could manually separate only about a pound of the tenacious fibers from their troublesome but vital seeds.

Before fibers could be spun into thread and woven into cloth, they had to be separated from seeds, which, for countless centuries, had been removed by hand; however, at some time in antiquity, a simple technology was developed to make this laborious work faster and easier.

The earliest mechanical device was a foot-roller that separated the fibers from the seeds. Workers, seated on stools, turned the rollers between their feet and stones; at the same time, they pulled the fibers into piles behind the stones and pushed the seeds onto the ground in front. This method probably developed in India, where it was still used in remote areas as late as the 1940s.[17]

Eventually the foot-roller evolved into the churka gin. *Churka* is a Sanskrit word, sometimes spelled "jerka," and describes the jerking motion of the rollers when they are pulling the fibers away from the seeds; *gin* is an abbreviated form of the eighteenth-century term "cotton engine." The churka gin worked like a wringer washer. Two hardwood rollers less than a foot long, having diameters about the size of a dime and a nickel, were mounted on a wooden frame with the smaller roller placed above the larger one. Simple churkas had a crank or handle attached to each roller.

After 1770, churka gins were improved by means of a hand crank mounted on one end of the larger roller and a simple cogwheel on the other end. The smaller roller had no hand crank, but it did have a cogwheel on one end, enabling that roller to spin at about the same number of revolutions per minute as the larger one. Bearings allowed the rollers to be placed closely together so that the fibers could be tightly gripped and pinched free of the seeds. The seeds, trapped in grooves carved into the rollers, dropped out, and the cotton fibers passed between the rollers. The hand crank mechanism would have made the process more comfortable, since the oper-

Churka gins from India separated seeds from long-staple cotton. *Courtesy A. M. Pendleton*

ator would not have to bend over, and faster, since more seeds could be separated from their fibers in less time. But a churka gin could turn out only about five pounds of lint (fibers after seeds are removed) per day.[18]

As Sea Island, or black-seed, cotton began to be cultivated along the Atlantic seaboard in the 1700s, the only ginning device available was the churka. All of these handmade wooden gins came from the West Indies, and each cost about $10.00. Planters saw the need to process cotton in greater quantities, and they began to redesign the ancient gin.

As early as 1742, M. Debreill, a Louisiana planter, lengthened the rollers for greater ginning capacity, but no models or drawings remain. In 1772, a man named Krebs of Pascagoula, Mississippi, built a modified churka gin that would turn out seventy pounds of lint a day, as opposed to about thirty pounds produced by the older models. A British army officer, writing a history of Florida, stated that "the Krebs roller gin had foot treadles and two well polished, grooved iron spindles set into a frame approximately four feet high."[19]

Five years later, Kinsey Burden of Burden's Island, South Carolina, improved his roller gin by using old gun barrels for the rollers. This "gun barrel gin," which could clean about twenty pounds of seed cotton per day, was popular in the Carolinas, Georgia, and Florida.

In 1790, Dr. Joseph Eve, who had homes in Augusta, Georgia, and the Bahamas, made further improvements. The only written description of Eve's gin does not indicate whether it used a foot treadle or hand cranks, but does state that two pairs of rollers, each more than three feet long, were five-eighths of an inch in diameter and were made of stopper wood, a hard wood from the Bahamas. This gin could produce 250 to 300 pounds of clean cotton, was capable of 480 to 500 revolutions per minute, and was belt driven; several gins linked together could be powered by horses or mules. The Krebs gin, which could turn out 70 pounds of lint in a day, was operated as a single unit. Individually, the Eve and gun barrel gins produced less lint, but they were often linked in a series of five pairs and could produce 135 pounds of lint per day. Eve himself claimed that his gins would turn out between 250 and 300 pounds of lint per day, but that depended upon such variables as having good weather and the gin's being well maintained and attended during operation.

Roller ginning, however, had its disadvantages. The Eve gin had a feeding device that crimped the fibers, making the cotton unattractive to buyers and thus reducing its price. Alterations followed, including larger roller size (three-quarters of an inch) and faster speed (up to 600 revolutions per minute), but the continual shortage of Sea Island cotton, which could be grown only in limited areas, caused planters to concentrate on the short-staple, green-seed upland cotton for mass production.

Caught between the failure of early hybridization experiments between black-seed and green-seed cotton and the increasing demand for cotton from both Slater's yarn mill and British markets, planters began to seek more efficient ways of separating the green seeds from their fibers. Churka gins produced undesirable results. Besides crimping the fibers, the rollers had a tendency to break up the seeds and to scatter them through the fibers, or to pass the seeds through with the fibers which stained the lint. An unmodified churka gin, worked continuously by a slave, could turn out only about five pounds of clean upland cotton per day. Upland cotton's future seemed hazy, at best.

In 1793, a young Massachusetts schoolteacher found a faster and cleaner way to separate upland cotton from its seeds. Without intending to, Eli Whitney established cotton as the South's dominant cultural and economic force and the source of one of the nation's, and the world's, most vital industries.

CHAPTER TWO

Mr. Whitney's Cotton Engine

The year 1793 marked a quiet but important turning point in the nation's economic history. In Pawtucket, Rhode Island, Samuel Slater began constructing his first large textile mill, and on a plantation near Savannah, Georgia, Eli Whitney built a model for a machine that would separate upland cotton from its seeds. Those two independent events, taking place at opposite ends of the country, started an inevitable chain of events that would, in the next century, revolutionize the cotton industry.

Eli Whitney was born in Westborough, Massachusetts, on December 8, 1765. His father was a farmer and a justice of the peace. His mother came from a respectable family of independent farmers. Whitney was the eldest of four children; after their mother's death when he was twelve, he took over many of the responsibilities for looking after his younger brothers, Josiah and Benjamin. When Whitney was fourteen his father remarried, and his stepmother brought with her two daughters from a previous marriage. Whitney deeply felt the loss of his mother, but he was close to his sister, Elizabeth; he remained loyal and affectionate to his father throughout his life, and he always respected his stepmother, although she, according to Elizabeth, did not understand Whitney's statements that he could make things if only he had the tools.

Even as a young man, Elizabeth explained in letters to friends, Whitney seemed to have an understanding of "probable consequences."[1] He once pretended to be ill so that he could stay home from church and take apart his father's watch to find out how it worked. Unlike most curious children, however, he was able to put it back together so that it ran perfectly. By the time he was twelve, Whitney's mechanical ability was obvious. He had designed and made a playable violin, produced an exact replica of a table knife (except for the original craftsman's stamp), and made nails and replaced penknife blades for his neighbors.

Two years later, when the Revolutionary War caused shortages and inflated the price of nails, Whitney began to forge nails in quantity. He opened a small business, making a forty-mile journey to find an appropriate employee; he hired a man for one month and then retained him for three. After the war, when nails were dumped onto the market in large numbers, making them unprofitable, Whitney turned to the manufacture of hatpins and walking sticks. His familiarity with nails and spikes would play a prominent part in his invention of the cotton gin.

When he was nineteen, Whitney wanted to go to college but knew he was unprepared. Needing time to prepare academically and financially for college, Whitney responded to an advertisement for a teacher in nearby Grafton. He received the position and spent the next three years teaching school in the winter and attending Leicester Academy during the summer. In March, 1789, at the age of twenty-three, he left Westborough and traveled to New Haven, Connecticut, to enter Yale University.

Whitney graduated from Yale in 1792 and intended to return to study law. He had debts to pay, however, and Yale President Ezra Stiles, who had promised to find him a teaching post in New York, introduced another offer instead. A Major Dupont of South Carolina needed a private tutor for his children. Whitney was told the position paid one hundred guineas per year, an amount he could not afford to refuse.

Phineas Miller, a Yale graduate who was acting on behalf of Major Dupont, a neighbor, had asked Stiles to help him find a tutor and was pleased at Whitney's acceptance. Born and raised in Connecticut, Miller was manager of Mulberry Grove, a plantation belonging to Catherine Greene, the widow of Revolutionary War Quartermaster General Nathanael Greene. Miller, Mrs. Greene, and her children had spent the summer in Rhode Island and were returning to their home in Georgia. When Miller learned that Whitney, who at twenty-eight had not traveled much farther than New Haven, was reluctant to venture alone all the way to South Carolina, he asked Whitney to join him and Mrs. Greene, and Whitney accepted the invitation. Whitney was delayed by

Eli Whitney, engraving by King-Hinman. *Courtesy Yale University Archives, Manuscripts and Archives, Yale University Library*

a series of mishaps, including a mild case of small-pox, but in late September, Whitney, Miller, and Mrs. Greene sailed from New York City to Savannah, Georgia.

The voyage lasted a week, and after a night spent in Savannah, they journeyed the remaining twelve miles to Mulberry Grove. Whitney originally planned to rest for four or five days and then to cross the Savannah River and continue on to Major Dupont's plantation in South Carolina, but he became intrigued by the problem of ginning cotton. In a letter to his father written the following year, Whitney explained that in the few days before he was to leave for South Carolina, he had "heard much said of the extreme difficulty of ginning Cotton, that is, seperating it from its seeds. There were a number of very respectable Gentlemen at Mrs. Greene's who all agreed that if a machine could be invented which would clean the cotton with expedition, it would be a great thing both to the Country and to the inventor. Involuntarily happened to be thinking on the subject and struck out a plan of a Machine in my mind."[2]

Whitney had learned that the tutoring position would pay only fifty guineas, but he had not formally turned it down. He described an idea for the machine to Miller, who offered to bear the expense of materials for the model. If the machine failed to work,

Whitney would be out only his time and could still take the job as tutor; if it succeeded, he and Miller would share any profits. Within ten days Whitney made a model for a machine that would separate upland cotton from its seeds and for which he was offered one hundred guineas if he would give up the rights to it; he refused to sell. The model worked so well that he refused the position with Dupont, bought materials in Savannah, and began production of a full-sized "cotton engine."

From November, 1792, until April, 1793, Whitney worked secretly in a basement, not even communicating with his family. During that time, he designed and built a machine "which required the labor of one man to turn it," he explained in a letter to his father, "and with which one man will clean ten times as much cotton as he can in any other way before known and also cleanse it much better than in the usual mode. This machine may be turned by water or with a horse, with the greatest ease, and one man and a horse will do more than fifty men with the old machines. It makes the labor fifty times less, without throwing any class of People out of business."[3]

Whitney's spike gin patent specifications described the "new invented cotton gin, or machine for cleansing and separating cotton from its seeds."[4] The machine consisted of five parts: the frame, the cylinder, the breastwork, the clearer, and the hopper. The frame, "made of well seasoned timber, so that it may be firm and steady," was a square or a parallelogram and could be any size as long as it was in proper proportion to the other parts.

The cylinder was also made of wood, measured from six to nine inches in diameter and two to five feet long, and was placed horizontally across the frame. Whitney's own description stated, "After the cylinder with its axis is fitted and rounded with exactness, the circular part of its surface is filled with teeth set in annular rows. The spaces . . . between the rows of teeth must be so large as to admit a cotton seed to turn around freely in them every way, and ought not to be less than seven-sixteenths of one inch." (Whitney made the teeth of "common iron wire" cut into pieces four to five feet in length and straightened.) "Steel wire would perhaps be best if it were not too expensive." The wire was to be cut "with a machine, somewhat like that used for cutting nails," into pieces about one inch long. Whitney recommended flattening one end of each piece of wire so that "the flatted ends of the teeth are driven into the wood with more ease and exactness," and to prevent them from turning "after they are set." The other end of the wire was to be "cut

Model of an Eli Whitney gin, ca. 1800. Note hopper, spiked cylinder, and ribs. *Courtesy Smithsonian Institution*

smoothly and transversely off." At first, the teeth were inclined at an angle of fifty-five to sixty degrees; for later models Whitney would uniformly bend the end of each wire so that it would not tear the cotton fibers.

The breastwork, mounted above and parallel to the cylinder, "has transverse grooves or openings through which the rows of teeth pass as the cylender [Whitney varied his spelling] revolves: and its use is to obstruct the seeds while the cotton is carried forward through the grooves by the teeth. That side of the breastwork next the cylinder should be made of brass or iron, that it may be the more durable. The thickness of the breastwork . . . should be about 2½ or 3 inches, in proportion to the length of the cotton." The purpose was for the cotton caught on the teeth to be "disconnected" from cotton left in the hopper, "otherwise that which is carried partly through the breastwork will . . . become so collected and knotted . . . as to obstruct and bend the teeth." Whitney had already discovered the difficulty of ginning a matted seed roll.

Whitney presented two alternatives for the breastwork. The first, already mentioned, was of iron or brass and could be cast "in a solid piece and the openings for the passage of the teeth cut with a saw and files" or cut into pieces equalling the number of "spaces between the several rows of teeth in the cylender" and set, "by means of a shank or tenon, in a groove running lengthwise along the wooden part of the breastwork." The second was made entirely of wood. "Place a bar of wood one inch below the cylinder and parallel to it, then with straps or ribs of iron, brass or tin plate connect the breastwork of wood with the bar below." Ginning ribs, which have undergone many modifications over the past two hundred years, were an integral part of Whitney's earliest design.

The clearer, also parallel to the cylinder and having a length and diameter proportionate to the cylinder, had "two four [*sic*] or more Brushes or rows of Bristles fixed in the surface of the clearer in such a manner that the ends of the bristles will sweep the surface of the Cylinder. Its axis and boxes are similar to those of the Cylinder."[5] The brushes were made of hog bristles. The purpose of the clearer was "to brush the cotton from the teeth after it is forced through the grooves and separates from its seeds. It turns in a direction contrary from that of the cylender, and should so far outrun it, as completely to sweep its whole surface. The air put in motion by the clearer, and the centrifugal force of the cotton disengage it from the brushes. The clearer is put in motion by the cylinder, by means of a band and whirls," or a wooden pulley and a leather belt.

One side of the hopper, into which the seed cotton was placed, was "formed by the breastwork, the two ends by the frame and the other side is movable so that, as the quantity of cotton put in at one time decreases, it may slide up nearer the cylinder, and make the hopper narrower. This is necessary in order to give the seeds a rotary motion in the hopper, by bringing them repeatedly up to the cylinder till they are entirely stripped of the cotton." A grate or "crate [*sic*] of wire" was to be fixed to the frame or connected to the moving part of the hopper in order to allow sand and seeds to fall into a receptacle underneath.

"The cotton is put into the Hopper, carried thro' the Breastwork by the teeth, brushed off from the teeth by the Clearer and flies off from the Clearer with the assistance of the air, by its own centrifugal force."[6]

As will be seen, two difficulties with Whitney's design would lead to significant alterations. While the spiked teeth did not damage the fibers, they tended to work free from the cylinder and fly out, causing injuries to gin hands and requiring frequent repairs. In addition, the hopper would fill with seeds, and "the movable part drawn back, the hopper [would be] cleared of seeds and then supplied with cotton anew," making ginning slow and tedious. A competitor of Whitney's would solve both problems.

The gin, recorded Whitney, "requires no other attendance, than putting the cotton into the hopper with a basket or fork, narrowing the hopper when necessary and letting out the seeds after they are clean. One of its peculiar excellencies is, that it cleanses the kind called green seed cotton almost as fast as the black seed." The cotton engine, which could be powered by water or horses, was to be placed adjacent to a wall with a hole cut into it or over a hole cut into the floor of either a second-story room or a first-story room over a basement so that the cleaned cotton, known as lint, could be blown free of the machine and into a separate room where it would be stored until it was placed in sacks or baskets and carried to market.

It is curious to note several parallels between Whitney's machine and the roller gins being used in Georgia at the time, notably the advanced roller gin developed by Dr. Eve. Thomas Spalding, of Sapelo, Georgia, wrote the following description of the Eve roller gin. It is dated January 20, 1844, and was quoted in the *Cotton Planter's Manual* (J. A. Turner), in 1845:

> His gin consists of two pairs of rollers, more than three feet long, placed the one set over the other, upon a solid frame that stands upon the floor, inclined at an angle of about thirty degrees—so that the feeder may the more easily throw the cotton in the feed by the handful upon a wire grating that projects two inches in advance of the rollers, just below them; between these protecting wires, the feeding boards, with strong iron, or in preference brass teeth pass, lifting the cotton from the wire grating, and offering it to the revolving rollers. The feeders should make one revolution to every four revolutions of the rollers. The rollers are carried forward by wheels supported over the gin, and upon the axle or shaft of these rollers; at the center there is a crank similar to a saw-mill crank. . . . It is the crimping produced by the teeth and the wire grating, which has served as a cause for carping by the cotton buyers, and which has gradually led to the disuse of these gins, the only gin efficient for the cleaning of long cotton, which has ever been used in this or any other country.[7]

Whether used for cleaning black- or green-seed cotton, Whitney's machine speeded up the feeding process and incorporated the concept of carding the lint. He also employed the dual roller mechanism by using the doffing brush to cast off lint, his "clearer," which worked in opposition to the wooden cylinder just as the rollers worked in opposition to each other. Whitney's genius was to see that one cylinder with spikes was faster and more efficient than two cylinders with a spiked feeder.

In his letter to his father, Whitney referred to the "old machines" and to cleaning cotton in the "usual mode," indicating that he had either seen roller gins in use or had heard one of Eve's gins described. He apparently experimented with black- and green-seed cotton, the black seeds being more easily separated and falling more readily through the "crate" than green seeds whose "velvet coat" caused them to collect and remain in the hopper longer. Legend states that Whitney saw a cat clawing at a chicken through a slatted coop and thus determined to draw the fibers by means of teeth through a series of metal ribs. Considering how quickly he had to build a working model, it seems more likely that he worked from a combination of his own urgency, the planters' needs, and a basic understanding of the mechanical principles involved.

The cotton engine proved so successful that Phineas Miller and Eli Whitney entered into a tentative partnership agreement on May 27, 1793, which was formalized a year later when Whitney received his patent. In Miller, Whitney had found the perfect partner; they had much in common. A New Englander transplanted to the South, Miller had made a niche for himself by starting out as a tutor to the Greene children and becoming the plantation manager after their father's death. Miller was described by a historian as a "loyal friend, gentle, affectionate and high spirited" as well as "hard working, conscientious, and resolute. In later years, when Whitney gave way to despair, Miller maintained his faith in himself and refused to let Whitney's chidings spoil their relationship. Miller's graciousness and cultivation fitted him for a place in the world Georgia planters would create as cotton brought them wealth."[8]

The timing for Whitney's invention was also perfect. Alexander Hamilton's *Report on Manufactures,* published in 1791, had urged cotton growing on a large scale, especially since Slater's mill promised flourishing opportunities. The mill owners preferred the long-staple Sea Island cotton because dust tended to cling to the short-staple upland cotton, creating difficulties in the spinning process, but Sea Island cotton could not be grown in sufficient quantities to make high-volume textile manufacturing a reality. Upland cotton was still the answer, but of the 2 million pounds that had been harvested in 1792, much of the crop went unsold because very little of it could be cleaned. That same year only 138,000 pounds of long-staple cotton were exported to England. The spinning mills would have bought more had it been available, but the spinners' complaint was that American cotton, regardless of staple length, was not sufficiently clean.[9] Miller and Whitney knew that they possessed the means to make upland cotton a commercial success.

On June 1, 1793, Whitney left Georgia and sailed for New York; from there, he traveled overland to the capital at Philadelphia to apply for a patent to protect his invention. On June 20, he submitted both a letter describing his "cotton engine" and the thirty-dollar registration fee to Secretary of State Thomas Jefferson, assuring Jefferson that drawings, specifications, and a working model would soon follow.

Whitney then returned to New Haven where he began buying materials and outfitting a shop. Because he anticipated a large demand, he knew that the machines could not be built one at a time. In a day when screws had to be threaded by hand, Whitney understood the need for machine tools to repeatedly make identical parts. Whitney's difficulty was that first he had to invent the tools.

By autumn, after recovering from an attack of malaria, Whitney was ready to send detailed specifications and drawings to Jefferson. In his accompanying letter, he asked when he might present his model and receive his patent. While awaiting Jefferson's reply, Whitney wrote out a lengthy description of the machine and had it notarized by Alderman Elizur Goodrich, Jr., on October 28, 1793, in New Haven. This document is known as Whitney's "long description." Between 1795 and 1805, a total of twenty-four patent infringement suits were filed at the U.S. District Court in Savannah, Georgia. A copy of the long description, or specifications, and a sheet of drawings were filed with the court in the 1804 suit against Arthur Fort and John Powell, and the copy was certified by Secretary of State James Madison on April 27, 1804. The copy was to prove invaluable, particularly after the United States Patent Office burned in 1836, destroying all previous patent records. It was entered as a restored patent on May 1, 1841. The short description, quoted earlier, was written by the first commissioner of patents, Dr. William Thornton, in 1823 and was published in the *American Farmer* that year. It was summarized from Whitney's long description, which was still on file in the patent office at the time.

Jefferson responded to Whitney on November 16, 1793. Jefferson assured Whitney that he need only present his model in order to obtain a patent, but his letter indicated more than academic interest:

> As the State of Virginia, of which I am, carries on household manufacture of cotton to a great ex-

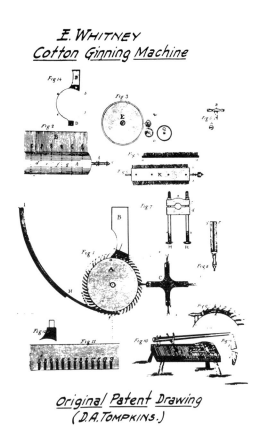

Duplicate set of Whitney patent drawings filed in Savannah. Drawings show grid (ribs), spiked cylinder, and "clearer" with four sets of bristles. *From C. A. Bennett,* Saw and Toothed Cotton Ginning Developments

tent, as I also do myself, and one of our great embarrassments is the cleaning the cotton of the seeds, I feel a considerable interest in the success of your invention for family use. Permit me, therefore to ask information from you on these points: Has the machine been thoroughly tried in the ginning of cotton, or, is it yet but a machine of theory? What quantity of cotton has it cleaned on an average of several days, and worked by hand, and by how many hands? What will be the cost of one of them to be worked by hand? Favorable answers to these questions would induce me to engage one of them to be forwarded to Richmond for me.[10]

Whitney was delighted at Jefferson's enthusiasm and responded with details on November 24. The machine he had completed in April in Georgia "cleaned fifteen hundred weight in about four weeks, which cotton was examined in N. York, the quality declared good and sold in the market at the highest price. . . . After the workmen are acquainted with the business, I should judge, the *real* expense of one, which will clean a hundred Wt. Pr. Day, would not exceed the price of ten of those in common use," (roughly one hundred dollars) referring to the roller gins.[11] Whitney clarified the gin's production by adding, "it is the stated task of one negro to clean 50 weight (I mean 50 pounds after it is separated from the seed), of the green seed cotton per day."[12] Since Whitney was obligated to place the first gins at Mulberry Grove, he explained, he would not have any for sale that winter. A machine, however, would take up only a couple of cubic feet of space, making it usable for individual homes and, with the addition of carding teeth, would make the cotton ready for spinning. He expected to take the model to Philadelphia in a few weeks' time, and Jefferson could see it work for himself.

Whitney's schedule was overly optimistic. He ran into unexpected difficulties in inserting the wires into the cylinder and had to design a machine that would cut the wires so that they would not split the wood when inserted parallel to the grain. That problem solved, he manufactured the model for the patent office and six large gins to be shipped to Georgia. In March, 1794, Whitney returned to Philadelphia with his model. Jefferson was no longer in office, but the new secretary of state, Edmund Randolph, showed the machine to several influential gentlemen in the city. On March 14, Whitney was formally issued his patent, retroactive to November, 1793. Elated by his accomplishment, Whitney prepared to return to Georgia to install the six gins. Afterward, he intended to sail from Savannah to England to apply for a patent there as well.

Miller, in the meantime, had urged area planters to increase their cotton acreage. In an advertisement in the *Georgia Gazette* on March 6, 1794, Miller stated that he would gin any amount of upland cotton, one pound cleaned for each five pounds of seed cotton, and boldly announced that gins would be set up in different parts of the country before the next harvest.[13] He decided not to sell the machines themselves, but to sell the services of the machines, with payment to be made in kind, two-fifths, or roughly 40 percent, of the crop. With hard cash in short supply, such payment was common. Flour millers and lumber mill owners had conducted business this way for centuries. Miller also realized that individual gin machines would cost too much at first for planters to buy (four hundred to five hundred dollars rather than Whitney's one hundred dollars) and that Whitney could not produce machines quickly enough to lease or to sell outright. Whether or not he intended it to do so, Miller's plan established a monopoly,

and his formal agreement with Whitney solidified that arrangement. Under Miller's plan the ginning fees would provide income until Whitney could produce gins in larger quantities. Because the patent protected the investors' exclusive privilege for fourteen years, the concept of monopoly was inherent. Had the ginning machine proved more difficult to construct or less beneficial to the planters' economy, perhaps Miller and Whitney's monopoly would not have created so many future problems for the partners.

Once the first six machines were operational, Miller and Whitney successfully processed some eight hundred thousand pounds of available cotton, and they expected to need enough machines to clean five to six thousand pounds per day. While at Mulberry Grove, Whitney made a bagging machine, and an optimistic Miller predicted that three slaves could gin and bag up to six hundred pounds of cotton per day.[14]

The new cotton engines worked so efficiently that Whitney decided to postpone his trip to England and return to New Haven to build more machines. In the meantime, Miller found farmers who were willing to expand their cotton acreage and whose land adjoined rivers or streams where gins could be efficiently powered and profitably run. Whitney devised a way to pack the parts for two gins into three crates, and Miller prepared to install the gins in pairs. By the spring of 1795, Miller had placed twenty gins at various sites in Georgia and South Carolina and acquired commitments for that many more.

During the winter of 1794–95, one misfortune after another struck the enterprise. Whitney suffered another attack of malaria, and shortly after he returned from an exhausting trip to New York to renegotiate a loan for his shop, the shop itself burned to the ground. Destroyed were Whitney's tools, some of them unique, and the parts and materials for twenty gins. Whitney had to begin all over again, building a new shop and remanufacturing tools. The loss was critical; during the autumn of 1795, Whitney shipped only twenty-six gins to Miller, whose advertisement had stimulated great interest among Georgia cotton growers. In addition, over Whitney's objections, Miller had speculated in real estate and, as a result, been involved in the Yazoo scandals. (Representatives of the four Yazoo companies had bribed Georgia legislators to sell to the few men comprising the companies over thirty-five million acres of virgin land for approximately one and one-half cents per acre, territory that included the future cotton lands of Mississippi. When the public discovered the fraudulent transaction, the Georgia governor and legislature were required to negate the sale. Miller lost money he had invested in the Yazoo companies' stock.) The backlash of public outrage indicted everyone involved. Even though Whitney himself had not invested money in the scheme, his name was tied to Miller's, and the partners could not borrow money from any source in the North or the South. Catherine Greene, however, kept her faith in both men and allowed Miller to use estate funds as collateral to maintain the partners' tenuous credit and fend off bankruptcy. In May, 1796, she and Miller were married, further obligating the plantation's resources to the venture.

Such financial reversals slowed Whitney's production, even while news of the gins' success traveled like wildfire throughout the South. Cotton production had increased from about three million pounds in 1792 to about eleven million pounds in 1797, and the price had climbed from thirty-six (1795) to forty cents (1797) per pound. Planters, however, complained that the ginning fees absorbed too much of their profits, and with increased cotton planting and the risk of another failed crop—in the face of an increasing market—they encouraged their own blacksmiths and carpenters to steal the idea of the Whitney gin and to build their own machines.

Miller learned that pirated gins were in operation in the vicinity around Mulberry Grove, and soon the patent-protected gins were idle. Added to that was a rumor that the spiked teeth damaged the fibers, and local planters had all the reasons they needed to ignore the Miller and Whitney machines and to make their own. Whitney was later able to establish that the rumor was started by envious entrepreneurs, but at this critical moment in the formation of the industry the rumor did as much damage as if it had been a fact.

Whitney's concern about the protection of his design and later of his patent began in the fall of 1793. On September 11, Whitney wrote to his father urging him to keep news of the gin limited to the immediate family, "*enjoining* it on them to keep the whole a *profound* secret."[15] The necessity for secrecy until Whitney could protect his invention was disquieting. Even before he left Georgia, the full-sized model had been stolen from a workroom at Mulberry Grove and the principles of its design made known. By the autumn cotton harvest, rough copies were already being built and used.

As early as the autumn of 1793, Edward "Ned" Lyons had attempted to learn about the workings of the gin. Colorful stories state that he was one of the group who broke into the basement to steal the model or that he disguised himself as a woman in

order to enter the building and examine the gin (for a time, only women were allowed inside). According to Miller, however, Lyons made inquiries from Savannah to Augusta and eventually found a man who had been a visitor to Mulberry Grove in 1794 and who ignored Miller's directions to friends to keep the design of the gin a secret. Soon after, Ned Lyons and his partners, Jesse Bull and Charles Lin, began to construct and sell gins in large numbers, claiming that they were improvements over the Whitney gins. The first of more than sixty lawsuits for patent infringement began against Lyons in 1795. Miller and Whitney's lawsuit against Lyons was settled in favor of Lyons by a biased jury, and a new trial was denied on the basis of a technicality in the patent law. In a letter written to Robert Fulton years afterward, Whitney stated that he had been unable to prove that his gin was in use in the state of Georgia—even when the rattling of three different machines, only fifty yards distant, could be heard from the courthouse steps.

The earliest gins were housed in single-story buildings with the hand-cranked gins placed on the main floor, above or adjacent to the lint blow room (which had access to the outside), and the basement used for packing the cotton into sacks. Much of Whitney's problem in proving the illegal use of his machines stemmed from their being placed where they could not be seen and where slaves, who were not allowed to testify, were the only people besides their owners who knew of their existence.

A more formidable opponent than Lyons was Henry Ogden, usually referred to as "H. Ogden" or "Hodgen," Holmes of South Carolina. He was a gifted mechanic employed by Captain James Kinkaid, a cotton planter and ship owner who had homes in New York and Charleston. Holmes worked for Kinkaid at his gristmill and plantation in Craven (now Fairfield) County. With Kinkaid's assistance, Holmes applied for and received a caveat of invention for a saw-toothed cotton gin on March 14, 1789. Before the formation of the United States Patent Office in 1787, the War Office issued caveats of invention, which granted the inventors five years' privilege.

There were important differences in Holmes's and Whitney's gins. Instead of wires or spikes mounted on a cylinder, Holmes's design used saw teeth cut into the edges of six- or eight-inch diameter circular disks (or portions of circles if complete disks were not available). The saws were mounted on a shaft that was no more than forty-eight inches long. (Whitney's cylinder was about twenty-six inches long.) Saws were spaced approximately one inch apart with wooden

Hand-cranked rather than an animal-powered Whitney farm gin. *From* Harper's Weekly, *December 18, 1869; courtesy Institute of Texan Cultures*

discs in between to keep the saws separated. Holmes's gin featured flat, reversible ribs with slots through which the saw teeth passed. (Whitney's design used either a metal grate or ribs and rib rail placed directly above the rows of teeth.) And while Whitney's gin required that the seed hopper be emptied regularly, temporarily halting the ginning process, Holmes's design permitted the seeds to be cast off as fast as they could be separated from the fibers, resulting in continuous action.

Holmes's caveat expired on the same date Whitney's patent was granted, and Holmes refiled and received a patent on May 12, 1796. Because of the rumor that Whitney's spiked or wire teeth damaged cotton, the ginning fees required by the Miller and Whitney gin plants, and the ease with which a Holmes gin could be constructed, cotton growers tended to favor Holmes's saw tooth design. Whitney's last cotton gins, built in 1823, incorporated circular saws.[16]

By 1797, Whitney was so frustrated and discouraged that he was ready to drop the enterprise and began to explore the possibility of obtaining a federal weapons contract. Miller persevered, however, sending a son-in-law to Tennessee, Kentucky, and parts of Virginia to find locations for the installation of Miller and Whitney gin plants, but that search was unsuccessful.

With the help of Yale classmate and friend Russell Goodrich, Miller devised a new plan. Beginning in 1799, Miller and Whitney would sell the cotton gins as units as well as the rights to both manufacture and lease the gins; licenses for the rights were priced as low as two hundred dollars. Almost immediately, their fortunes began to improve. Planters bought sev-

eral machines, and favorable comments from English manufacturers regarding the quality of Miller and Whitney ginned cotton offset the earlier rumor.

The number of lawsuits continued to escalate, however, and in 1800, Miller was forced to sell Mulberry Grove at auction. He received only fifteen thousand dollars for the plantation, and he and Catherine moved to a smaller property nearby.

In April of 1800, federal law was changed to better protect inventors' patent privileges. After all the previous losses, Whitney was vindicated in December, 1806, when the court awarded him a perpetual injunction against the earlier mentioned Arthur Fort and John Powell. One at a time, other lawsuits began to be settled in the inventor's favor. Tennessee purchased rights to use the gin, and the states of North and South Carolina honored earlier royalty agreements. Altogether, Whitney received about ninety thousand dollars, but it was hardly enough to make up for legal fees, travel expenses, and manufacturing costs. Miller's and Whitney's good names were restored, but the victory came too late for Miller to enjoy; that loyal partner and friend had died in 1803 at the age of thirty-nine. In South Carolina, Hodgen Holmes filed a countersuit against Miller and Whitney but lost his claim and had to pay the licensing fee. Whitney was officially honored as the inventor of the cotton gin, but Holmes's principles of saw teeth passing through flat ribs and continuous, rather than intermittent, action are used in cotton ginning today.

In 1798, with the threat of a new war looming between the United States and France, Whitney signed a contract with the federal government to manufacture muskets. He established an armory at Mill Rock, Connecticut, around which grew one of the nation's first factory towns, and he invented several machine tools to make possible the mass production of arms. Such was his success that his contracts were consistently renewed, and while he never grew wealthy, he was able to settle his debts and to live comfortably. In 1817, at the age of fifty-two, he married thirty-one-year-old Henrietta Edwards, daughter of his friend Pierpont Edwards and granddaughter of New England minister Jonathan Edwards. They had four children: Frances, Elizabeth, Eli, and Susan, who died as a baby.

In 1820, two years after the final settlement of Miller's estate and after a lifetime of stress and overwork, Whitney's health began to steadily decline. In past years he had suffered from malaria, influenza, and possibly stomach ulcers; his final illness was most likely enlargement of the prostate gland. True to his nature, he invented a catheter-like device, which provided a measure of relief and added at least two years to his life, but he passed away quietly on January 8, 1825.

Despite Whitney's personal disappointments regarding the invention of the cotton gin, its long-term success is undisputed. In 1793, only sixty-three thousand bales were sent to market; three years later, two hundred thousand bales were produced. Cotton plantations began to spread out across the South. By 1819, the year of the Missouri Compromise, the practice of slavery, which had faced extinction twenty years before, was more deeply entrenched than ever. Alexander Hamilton's vision of a successful cotton industry was becoming a reality. Samuel Slater's mills for spinning yarn were no longer dependent upon export markets. In 1813, Francis Cabot Lowell reproduced a power loom from memory for spinning and weaving, and in 1823, he established a full-scale textile factory.

Two years later, young Leonard Groce, son of Colonel Jared Ellison Groce, who had been one of Stephen F. Austin's original three hundred colonists, finished his education in Georgia and returned to his father's plantation on the Brazos River. He took with him one of the first cotton gins used in Texas and, thus, innocently initiated cotton's climb to cultural and economic power in Texas.

CHAPTER THREE

Gin Irons and Buzzard Wings

When Jared Groce arrived in Texas in 1822, he must have felt as though he were stepping backward in time. A plantation and timber owner, the forty-year-old widower was accustomed to the luxuries of the settled South. In contrast, Texas, on the very edge of civilization, was primitive. He would have to adapt established southern agrarian and cultural practices to the raw frontier.

Groce was born in Virginia in 1782. At the age of twenty he moved to South Carolina, where he bought land, and he married Mary Ann Waller there in 1804. The couple moved to Georgia, bought a plantation, and grew cotton. Four children were born to them: Leonard, Edwin (who died in his youth), Sarah (who eventually married William H. Wharton), and Jared, Jr. Mary Groce died in South Carolina in 1813 while visiting relatives. The following year Groce married Annis Waller, his sister-in-law, and they moved to Alabama, where he invested in thousands of acres of timber and earned a respectable fortune in lumber. The couple had two children, Edwin and Waller William, but Annis died in 1818. While on business in New Orleans in 1821, Jared Groce heard about a proposed Texas colony in the rich cotton growing area between the Brazos and Colorado rivers. Rather than sell his landholdings, he gave them to a niece of his wife, then spent weeks organizing the journey.[1]

Groce was enticed by the Mexican government's offer of vast tracts of land to farmers and ranchers at extremely low prices and by the knowledge that cotton was becoming an increasingly profitable commodity. He reasoned that large-scale cotton growing could provide him and his children with secure, if not luxurious, futures. The temptation was too great for Groce, with his vision, to ignore or reject. With planning equal to that of a Spanish expeditionary force, or *entrada*, Groce gathered his family, slaves, tools, household goods, and treasured belongings and led the second *entrada* into Texas.

Three hundred years earlier, Spanish explorers, part of the first *entrada*, had found native peoples throughout the Southwest wearing cotton clothing. The Hopi were known to trade kilts, sashes, and robes, and the Zuñi wore cotton blankets tied or knotted over their left shoulders. The Tiguex, who lived along the Rio Grande, had a custom that required a young man who wished to marry to first make arrangements with the tribal elders, then to spin cotton into thread, weave a blanket, and present it to his beloved as an offer of marriage. If the young woman chose to wear the blanket, she accepted his offer and soon became his wife.

When the Spanish missions were established in San Antonio de Béxar in the 1720s, the Franciscan friars found the native Coahuiltecans growing, spinning, and weaving cotton. Theirs was a simple, corn-based culture, and cotton was grown for clothing rather than for trade. The missions were self-sufficient communities that included, among the granaries and smithies, special workrooms for storing and weaving wool and raw cotton to make cloth.

Texas remained a buffer between Mexico and French-held Louisiana until the United States purchased the Louisiana Territory in 1803, but the rich interior prairie was unpopulated due to the frequency of Indian attacks. Since Spanish colonial citizens refused to move inland, the government began to welcome the idea of a few Anglo colonists inhabiting the broad stretch of open prairie. Agents, or *empresarios*, were commissioned to advertise and to draw selected colonists into the area with titles to large amounts of land in exchange for Spanish citizenship.

Stephen F. Austin, taking over his father's empresarial commission upon Moses Austin's death, chose as his colonial territory the rich, rolling hill country between the Brazos and Colorado rivers. Austin was keenly aware that timber and game were plentiful, that the soil and the rainfall were suitable for growing cotton, and that the rivers drained into the Gulf of Mexico. Ships sailed the Gulf waters bound for the American ports of New Orleans and Mobile, which were rapidly becoming known as cotton trade centers. Austin hardly had time to advertise before

Jared Ellison Groce II in 1822, just before he arrived in Texas. *Courtesy Barker Texas History Center, University of Texas*

settlers began to enter his colony, some coming from nearby East Texas and some, like Jared Groce, coming from as far away as Alabama.

Groce set out in the fall of 1821 with a caravan of fifty wagons, taking everything required for homesteading in the wilderness, from farm tools and seeds to spinning wheels and looms. Horses, mules, sheep, hogs, and cows were included, and overseer Alfred Gee kept up with over ninety Negro slaves. The wagon train reached New Orleans in December, 1821, reprovisioned, and continued westward, reaching Austin's Colony in January, 1822.

The Spanish and later the Mexican governments were more than generous in their land policies, selling land for the price of a *medio* (one-half silver *real* or $0.125) per acre. In addition, the government charged a small flat title fee, deferred customs duties for seven years, and postponed general taxes for ten years. Families who intended to farm were entitled to one *labor* (177 acres), and family heads who intended to raise stock could purchase one *sitio* or *legua*

(4,428 acres). Since most plantation owners included stock raising as part of their livelihood, they could claim more land.[2] Slaveholders were offered an additional incentive of 80 acres per slave. In all, Groce bought ten *sitios* (over 44,000 acres), including parts of what are now Waller, Grimes, and Brazoria counties.

Groce picked out one league on a high point above the Brazos near the present town of Hempstead in Waller County. He built a log cabin there, named his surrounding plantation "Bernardo," and planted corn and cotton. A drought destroyed his first corn crop, forcing Groce, his family, and slaves to live for months on wild game and mustang jerky with neither bread nor salt. But the same drought that was so destructive to corn ripened cotton into fat bolls and produced a more abundant crop than Groce and his family had dreamed possible.

After the cotton had been picked that autumn, the lint was squeezed into bales of seventy-five to eighty pounds each; the bales were loaded in pairs onto pack mules for transport to market in what is now northern Mexico. Groce himself led the mule train, traveling along Indian trails and covering about twenty miles per day. Earlier experience with the Bidais Indians who lived near his plantation had taught Groce well. The Indians refused to pick cotton in exchange for food because they were afraid of the Negroes. Expecting the same reaction from other Indians, Groce took with him black trail drivers and Edom, his personal servant, on the long trip to Mexico. The Anglos traveled well armed but encountered no difficulties with Indians. In northern Mexico they traded the cotton for clothing and for food items, including coffee and tea, and then safely returned home.[3]

The journey overland to Mexico had proved so lengthy and so rigorous that Groce decided to build a ferry landing on the Brazos so that he could move his cotton by flatboat down the river to the port of Velasco. The cotton would then be transferred to a schooner and shipped to New Orleans, where an agent, or factor, would sell his cotton to American or English mills. In time, planters who lived upstream would also make use of Groce's Ferry, and the landing would prove important in Texas's campaign for independence in 1836.

In addition to the need for his ferry landing, Groce also recognized the need to speed up the long growing, harvesting, and marketing cycle. He sent his son Leonard back to Georgia to finish his education, and when the young man returned home in 1825, he brought with him a cotton gin for use on the plantation. The small but powerful machine made it possible to increase the plantation's production of marketable cotton, the only cash crop grown by colonists like the Groces.

Jared Groce chose to have Leonard bring a single ginning machine from Georgia in 1825, but deep in the piney woods of East Texas, gin manufacturing had already become an infant industry. Stephen F. Austin, keenly aware of the need for gins in his cotton-based colony, offered additional parcels of land as incentives to those who wished to come to Texas to build ginning machinery. Mississippi blacksmith George Huff came to Texas in 1825 and later that year sold a gin to one of Austin's relatives for $450.[4]

Cotton production began in East Texas in 1825, and a number of gins were set up near San Augustine. The first gin to be built in Texas, in 1825, may be credited to John Cartwright, a carpenter and blacksmith; other sources claim that John Sprowl set up a gin near San Augustine as early as 1824. As predicted by Austin, cotton plantations in the lower Colorado River bottom succeeded as well as those along the Brazos. In that area, a Colonel Robert Williams is believed to have built the first cotton gin at Caney in 1827, although one may have been erected in Matagorda as early as 1825. Groce's gin was the first erected in Austin's Colony. Community gins were unknown because settlers lived so far apart; each planter had his own gin and an outdoor, or yard, press that could process a maximum of about two hundred bales per season.[5]

By 1828, Austin's Colony could boast five plantation gins, and there were a few more than that in East Texas. The talents of early gin manufacturers, spread out as they were, made each individual highly important and no doubt inspired him to be as creative as possible.

In 1827, at the age of nineteen, North Carolina–born Noah Smithwick immigrated to Sterling Robertson's colony deep in Central Texas. He traveled from Kentucky to Dimmitt's Landing near Matagorda, where he contracted malaria. When he was feeling better he continued inland but was forced to stop often, and his memoirs of the hospitality of the people with whom he stayed show them to be honest and generous. One of those early Texans was Josiah Bell, a respected friend of Stephen F. Austin and owner of a plantation on the Brazos River near Columbia, where Smithwick recorded that "Johnny McNeal, out on the gulf prairie, was in need of a blacksmith. There were quite a family of the McNeals. They had raised a crop of cotton and were building a gin. They had a shop and tools, and so I went out

Planting cotton in the spring. *From* Harper's Weekly, *April 24, 1875; courtesy Institute of Texan Cultures*

and in the intervals between relapses of the fever I made the gin irons." Since iron was scarce, Smithwick scavenged. He and McNeal "found an ample supply in the wreck of an old vessel that lay high and dry in a belt of timber at least five miles back from the gulf." The vessel was little more than a rotting shell, and all that remained of the masts were the "knotted hearts of two pine trees," but there was enough iron, though it was rusted, for Smithwick to make the saws and ribs for the gin stand.[6]

The process of planting, tending, harvesting, ginning, and marketing cotton took a full year to complete. Beginning in late February or early March, planters along the Brazos and Colorado rivers directed their slaves to plow the cleared fields into furrows; East Texas planters began in late March. Because of the uncertainty of the weather, no more than half the crop was planted early in the spring; the remainder was planted a few weeks later.

On plantations, one team of slaves used plows to open the furrows, a second team planted seeds by hand, and a third team covered the seeds with earth. On smaller farms, one laborer used a hoe to open the furrow, another placed the seeds in the ground, and a third covered the seeds. English-made drills for planting seeds were available to Americans during the late eighteenth century but were used infrequently. By the 1840s, drills that could drop the seeds in regular amounts were widely available and became commonplace as they were improved in design and manufacture. Cotton-planters made of hollow drums with holes became available during the 1840s but did not provide careful measurement of seeds until they were redesigned after the Civil War. Hoes or plows continued to be used for covering the seeds.

Maturing bolls are bright green. Locks of exposed fibers contain hidden seeds. *Courtesy National Cotton Council*

As soon as the new cotton plants reached a few inches in height, slaves used hoes to chop out grass and weeds that could smother the young plants. Once the seedlings gained several inches in height, the plants themselves were chopped, or thinned, leaving clusters of two or three plants that were separated by about six inches. This clustering of plants helped keep young plants warm in the event of a late frost; the spacing restricted cutworm movement and contributed to better drainage in the event of a heavy rain. A few weeks later the plants would be thinned again, leaving them about two feet apart.

In May, buds, or *squares,* would appear on the cotton that had been planted earliest, and within two weeks the plants would begin to bloom. The pale yellow flowers opened in the morning, and on the following day they would turn pink, purple, or blue and begin to fall off. As the flowers dropped, small bolls appeared on the branches. While the bolls matured, turning from shiny, bright green to dull brown, the slaves might rest briefly, but the planters kept a close watch on the crop to make sure it was

not injured by weather or insects. If all went well, the plants would be fully mature in six to eight weeks, or about 150 days after planting (usually in September). If weather or insects damaged this crop, the fields planted later would be ready to harvest in October.[7]

At the end of July or the beginning of August, the bolls split open from the top, exposing the white fibers. The fibers divided into four or five locks, with each lock containing between five and nine seeds with an average of seven. As the sun dried the fibers, it also dried the boll, now termed a burr, and the burr began to shrivel, thus exposing the fibers even more. The cotton was then ready to be picked.

Slaves were set to work in the fields, picking the cotton from the bolls and stuffing it into willow baskets or into long bags, the tops of which formed loops or straps and were slung over their shoulders. The bottoms of the heavy bags dragged along the ground behind the workers. Harvesting forty to fifty pounds of cotton per day was average when the season began, but as more plants burst open in the late summer sun, each slave was driven to pick between two and three hundred pounds per day. A slave who could pick five hundred pounds per day was newsworthy. Slaves were urged to work faster by either punishment or reward, depending upon the inclination of the planter.

When the slave's basket or bag was full, it was weighed on a field scale, the weight recorded, and the cotton dumped into a wagon. The slave then returned to the field with the empty basket or bag. Wagons full of seed cotton were taken to the gin houses or to the slave quarters for further cleaning. Roughly fifteen hundred pounds of seed cotton filled each wagon, and a wagon load usually equaled one bale. At that time, normal cotton production was defined as one bale per acre.[8]

Before the cotton could be ginned, it had to be free of extraneous sticks, burrs, leaves, and other trash. The early gin stands were designed to separate the seeds from the fibers, not to clean the cotton; that had to be done manually, usually at night after the worker had spent a long tedious day in the field. Ginning began to have its own terminology. "Gin plant" or "gin house" referred to the building, "gin stand," to the machine, and "ginning," to both the separation of the seeds from the fibers and the entire process of turning out a finished bale.

Whether in Texas or the Deep South, the gin buildings and yard presses were constructed alike. The earliest gin buildings were one story plus a basement. Seed cotton was stored on cabin porches or in family-

Harvesting cotton in the fall. *From Edward King* The Great South, *1875; courtesy Institute of Texan Cultures*

assigned bins inside the building or was emptied directly from wagons and was then hand-fed into the single gin stand. Ginned lint was blown, dropped, or carried in baskets to the basement where a pit roughly thirty-six to forty-two inches square had been dug into the earth. A wooden frame was constructed at the perimeter of the pit; bags or sacks were suspended into the pit from hooks mounted on the frame. Lint was packed into each bag and tamped down with wooden pestles or by foot. The filled bags were then lifted from the pit and placed on a worktable where they were "tied out" in long sacks or in small dense rolls. Both long- and short-staple cotton were packed into bags or rolls weighing between 125 and 350 pounds.[9]

By the time that Jared Groce ventured into the Texas wilderness, two- and three-story frame buildings were in use, each expansion having depended upon the amount of cotton grown and stored before ginning. In two-story buildings, which had very limited storage space, the gin stand was placed on the second, or ginning, floor, and the animal-powered gears and sweeps necessary to operate the gin stand were at ground level. Slaves unloaded baskets of seed cotton, fresh from the field, or cleaned cotton that had been stored on porches or in separate buildings onto a second-floor platform (loading dock) at one end of the gin house. Workers then carried the cotton inside where it was stored in a stall or bin until ready for ginning.

Next, the cotton was removed from its stall or bin and placed on a shelf or tray level with the gin stand. A slave would pull or rake the cotton from the tray into the open gin stand.

Three-story buildings allowed room for seed cotton storage inside the gin building on a floor in the area above the gin stand. Cotton was hand-fed down a shelf that tilted from an upper-story window to the gin stand below.

The gin stands were still very much a combination of the Holmes/Whitney design. Circular saws passing between ribs had replaced the spiked cylinder and slotted bar, while stiff brushes, made of hog bristles and attached to wooden bars that were mounted on drums, revolved and cast off (doffed) the lint from the saw teeth. The brushes acted as a fan to blow the cotton out of the gin stand. The seeds could not pass through the small openings between the ribs and fell to the floor, where they were periodically swept away. The lint was carried in baskets, blown by centrifugal force, or allowed to fall into a "lint room" that was either behind or below the gin stand. The lint room had outside access so that the lint could be carried to the yard press and baled.

The ginning process had changed little from the time of Whitney's invention. The belt-driven gin stand was powered by draft animals as Whitney had originally intended. Two teams of horses, mules, or a yoke of oxen were hitched to two levers, called sweeps, that were attached to a horizontal drive wheel at ground level. For this reason, the ground level of the gin building was open on three sides; the fourth side was the wall of the lint room. As the animals trudged in a circle to turn the wheel, usually about ten feet in diameter, the drive wheel exchanged power by means of a bevel gear to a vertical wheel that was about seven and one-half feet in diameter.[10]

A leather belt transferred power from the vertical wheel to the gin stand. Depending upon the construction, the belt passed through a slit cut into the flooring, or the vertical wheel itself passed through an opening in the flooring. In either case, the long belt was attached to a pulley connected to the shaft of the gin saws.

Other types of power came from tread wheels set at an angle and worked by horses or oxen. Water wheels were also used in some areas. After 1854, Texas gin owners began to experiment with steam power, which gradually permitted an increase in the number of saws from fifty to eighty, but until the last quarter of the nineteenth century, horses or oxen were the most common power source.[11]

While Whitney's design for the gin stand and the two- or three-story gin house arrangement remained common throughout the South, one important addition—the screw press—became popular by the early 1830s. Since more cotton was being cleaned and shipped to market than ever before, the packaging of that cotton became vitally important. Nine-foot-

Plantation gin showing feeding tray. Cotton was emptied from baskets onto the tray and raked by hand into the gin. Restored Westville Gin, Lumpkin, Georgia. *Courtesy Pete Daniel, Smithsonian Institution*

long bags could be easily loaded onto flatboats, but they were awkward to carry overland by oxcart or on muleback. Even the smaller seventy- to eighty-pound bales taken on muleback to Mexico or by schooner and barge to the United States meant a slow return for the planter's investment. The invention of the screw press made it possible to ship cotton in fairly uniform bales. Thus, it simplified the shipment of cotton to market.

Outdoor wood and iron screw presses had been tried as early as 1799. The same Ned Lyons sued by Whitney for patent infringements opened a public saw gin in 1795; he and his two partners purchased iron screws in Philadelphia for the public gins they continued to build, and Lyons later built a gin with an iron screw press in Wilkes County, Georgia. A Sir William Dunbar ordered an iron screw press cast in Philadelphia in 1801 at a cost of one thousand dollars, and when it did not prove commercially successful, he tried using it as a cottonseed crusher.[12] Iron screw presses were not popular, however, and after 1810 wooden screw presses were consistently used throughout the South.

The screw press was a separate structure built near the lint room of the gin house. The ginned cotton was taken by basket loads to the press. The bale box was often made of pine, but the hand-chiseled screw was made of sturdier oak. While the screw with an attached plunger, or pressing block, was raised to its highest point, the lint was dumped into the bale box, which was lined with bagging. Horses or mules were harnessed to two beams, called "buzzard wings," that were attached at a steep angle above the screw. The apex of the beams was sometimes covered by a hip roof that turned with the screw. The horses or mules walked in a circular path, lowering the screw until the pressing block had compacted the cotton in the bale box.[13]

When the bale box was full, the screw was released and top bagging was slipped into place. The screw was turned several more times in order to achieve the desired density. Finally, gin hands used a windlass to tighten the six or eight ropes that were commonly used to secure bales before iron hoops or straps became available after 1840. Some early presses had pits where the bales were tied out, but more often bales

Mule harnessed to drive wheel; driver beats stick on the sweep to keep mule walking. Vertical pulley extends through ceiling to ginning floor. Restored Westville Gin, Lumpkin, Georgia. *Courtesy Pete Daniel, Smithsonian Institution*

were finished either on the platform around the screw and cotton box or on the ground. The bales, weighing between four and five hundred pounds, were dropped to the ground or rolled out from under the press and placed in oxcarts for transport to market.[14]

Large plantations employed as many as ten slaves inside the gin house. At least four lifted seed cotton from the wagons onto the loading dock and carried it to the storage rooms, moved it again from storage to the shelf above the gin stand, collected and removed the seeds from the floor, and assisted the worker turning the crank to the saw shaft (if belts were not used) and/or feeding the gin stand. Two more workers were needed to oversee the teams of horses or oxen that kept the drive wheel turning, and four or five might be required to handle the horses or mules harnessed to the beams of the screw press. Fewer gin hands were needed on smaller plantations, where four or five might work in the gin house until the lint room was filled, and then they would all stop work and move to the press.[15]

In many areas, farmers did not own ginning ma-chinery and took their cotton to a neighboring planter who would gin and bale the farmer's cotton for one-eighth or one-tenth of the crop. Public or cooperative ginning facilities did not become customary until late in the nineteenth century.

Because ginning and baling were slow, planters often required an entire winter, when their slaves were not occupied in the fields, to finish ginning the crop. One season's crop might not be finished until the following February or March, just as the new year's crop was being planted; thus, cotton processing, including planting and harvesting, "scrapping" the fields for leftover cotton to use in bedding, and the spinning and weaving needed to make clothing, required year-round effort.

Cotton traveled to market all year long as well. At first, with few inland merchants to help the planters sell their crops, growers like Jared Groce took their cotton to market in small bales loaded on mules. Oxcarts and wagons, which could carry ten to twelve bales, were commonly used to haul the cotton to towns such as San Augustine, Nacogdoches, and Jefferson in East Texas. Planters along the Brazos used

Drive wheel and bevel gear. Restored Westville Gin, Lumpkin, Georgia. *Courtesy Pete Daniel, Smithsonian Institution*

both rafts and wagons to reach the ports of Velasco and Quintana. Harrisburg and Houston (after 1837) became important gathering points for the sale and movement of cotton, by steamship or barge, to Galveston for shipment to the United States. Wagon trains, each driven by slaves or hired teamsters, traveled between ten and fifteen laborious miles per day. Oxen were used to pull the wagons since their hooves were better suited to the soggy prairie and muddy roads, and wagons were loaded according to the number of available oxen. For example, a load of six bales required six yoke of oxen.[16] These trips to market towns or ports could take several weeks, depending upon the weather and the road conditions, and the return trips were equally slow because the wagons were laden with food, clothing, and farm implements. Because of the distances to markets over poor roads, as early as the 1840s planters and merchants began discussing the need for a railroad. Many planters lived near rivers, and it was common practice for bales of cotton to be loaded onto log rafts and floated downstream to market. Raftloads ranged from thirty to two hundred bales. When the rafts reached port,

the bales were put into wagons or onto ships, and the rafts were broken apart and their logs sold for lumber.

Flatboats were only slightly more sophisticated than log rafts, having crude roofs to protect the bales. Neither rafts nor flatboats had rudders, and slaves used poles to navigate the rivers. Keelboats were constructed with bows and sterns and enjoyed both the steering advantage of rudders and the stability of cargo holds; with galleys and bunks on deck, they were more comfortable than rafts or flatboats. Unlike rafts or flatboats, however, keelboats could return home. They were either poled upriver by a crew or tied by ropes to oxen that trudged along towpaths on the banks and pulled the boats upstream. Like the wagon trains, the keelboats also carried supplies to the plantations on the return trip.

Steamboats, such as the *Yellow Stone*, the *Laura*, the *Washington*, and the *Brazos*, had begun operating on Texas rivers in the 1830s, and both sternwheelers and sidewheelers transported passengers, carried imported goods to coastal merchants and inland planters, and delivered bales of cotton to mar-

Typical plantation gin with yard press. *From* Frank Leslie's Illustrated Newspaper, *October 7, 1871; courtesy Library of Congress*

ket. Sternwheelers drew less water, and the paddle wheel was more protected from sandbars and debris, but sidewheelers had greater maneuverability. Like the log rafts and flatboats, steamboats were susceptible to driftwood tangles blocking the rivers and could not be navigated in times of high or low water; moreover, steamboats were subject to the additional dangers of exploding boilers and cargo fires started by sparks from smokestacks. Plenty of water for the boiler was available from the rivers, but wood to fire the boiler had to be provided along the way. At each landing, the steamboats took on between fifty and one hundred cords of wood, and planters were paid three dollars per cord. Jared Groce's share of fifty cords was required for the *Yellow Stone* to reach its next landing downstream at San Felipe.[17]

In Texas's struggle for independence from the new nation of Mexico during the spring of 1836, Groce's landing served as crossing point for Sam Houston's army, which was safely ferried across the Brazos by the steamboat *Yellow Stone* that had been loaded with cotton bales to protect the boiler, engine, and pilot house. Bales were stacked so high that only the pilot house and smoke stacks could be seen, and the cotton-armored steamer was successfully protected from Mexican rifle fire and grape shot in an engagement with Mexican troops near Thompson's Ferry on the lower Brazos.

Cotton had been one of the chief reasons for the settlement of Texas—with its vast amount of cheap land and a climate suited to cotton production—and it would continue to play an influential role during Texas's decade of independence: Increased cotton production would require factors such as William Marsh Rice and bankers like Samuel May Williams. Seaports would flourish. And in the years of growth to follow that decade, changes in both cotton production and ginning would lead to an emphasis on worldwide marketing and justify the belief that "white gold" could direct the destinies of nations.

CHAPTER FOUR

To Market, to Market

Jared Groce's long trek to interior Mexico taught him a great deal about the difficulty of marketing his only cash crop. The following year (1826), he contracted with John Harris to sell the crop for him, and when the cotton was harvested that fall, Groce delivered around one hundred bales, by ox-drawn wagons instead of mule train, to the Harrisburg founder in his village on Buffalo Bayou.[1] Harris, in his role as factor, then shipped the consigned crop to New Orleans to be sold.

When Jared Groce settled in Texas in 1822, the factorage system was already well established in the South as a natural outgrowth of the tobacco trade. During the colonial period, coastal planters had often acted as merchants for inland farmers, supplying manufactured items to the farmers on credit during the year. In the autumn, farmers shipped hogsheads filled with tobacco downstream to the planters. They could either take their shares of the farmers' crops in payment for those earlier purchases and ship the rest to commission merchants in coastal cities, or they could buy all of the tobacco and add it to their own for sale to English markets.

During the Revolutionary War, British representatives, or agents, of English mercantile houses were replaced by colonial agents. After the war, these "resident merchants," who had become known as factors, remained in place, their ties to the southern planters and northern capitalists stronger than ever. With increasing demands for cotton by northern and European textile mills, and the growing supply made possible by Whitney's gin, planters reduced their tobacco acreage in favor of cotton or moved further into the interior where land was cheap and fertile and concentrated on growing cotton instead of tobacco. Whether or not farmers owned slaves and had to cope with the attendant problems of slave labor, they continually grappled with the dual problems of isolation and the forces of nature. They had no choice but to rely on customary business practices. For isolated farmers, agents or commission merchants provided a connection to American and European cotton markets that they would not have had otherwise. These commission merchants, who subtracted the fee for their services from the sale of consigned crops, established themselves in seaport cities, and the interior farmers and coastal planters began to depend on them to handle the details of selling their crops and purchasing manufactured goods with proceeds from the sales.[2] While the term *factor* originally applied to any type of commission merchant, many of these merchants began to specialize in selling cotton, and by the 1820s, "factor" had become synonymous with cotton.

In the earliest years of the nineteenth century, before inland planters had established ties with coastal factorage firms, planters had acted as their own factors, taking their cotton to Charleston or Savannah and selling it directly to cotton buyers or trading with merchants for the manufactured goods they needed. The merchants then sold the cotton to shipping company agents or speculators.

In the Mississippi River valley, farmers and planters took their cotton by oxcart to the marketplace in town, usually near a river, where they could sell it to a local merchant in exchange for credit for manufactured goods. They could also barter with the merchant for manufactured goods in his store. Hard cash was rarely seen and the credit/barter system based on cotton remained in common usage for many years.

The local storekeeper then loaded all of the cotton onto a flatboat. The storekeeper traveled downstream to New Orleans with the cotton and sold it to the agent of a shipping company, a speculator, or a factor. It was not unusual for merchants along the Mississippi River to stop a flatboat headed downstream and to buy such goods as bacon, flour, or cornmeal, and the boat itself. Merchants then advertised for planters to haul their cotton to the store and to trade for the new stock of supplies. When the supplies were gone, merchants took the cotton by flatboat downstream to New Orleans and returned with cash and goods for their stores. Merchants could, if they chose, accompany the cotton by ship all the way to New York, purchase goods for their stores, and return overland by wagon.

Whether the planters took their cotton to a seaport for sale or to the local storekeeper, this tedious means of conducting business placed the planters at a disadvantage. They had to accompany their crops, locate buyers or bargain with merchants, and sell or trade their crops immediately instead of storing them and waiting for a better price. The system was slow, inefficient, and not at all conducive to the planters' getting the best price.[3]

During the early nineteenth century, as the price of cotton wobbled as much as five cents per pound, southern planters—who were moving farther into the country's interior—began to rely less on local storekeepers and more on firms of commission merchants (factors). These firms sent their agents inland from the coastal cities to take charge of shipping the cotton downriver to the ports and on to New York, Philadelphia, or Liverpool. Whereas farmers had bargained with local merchants who subsequently dealt with agents in the ports, the farmers (and the local merchants) began to employ factoring firms themselves. Factors sampled, classed, and graded the cotton in each bale in order to establish its value; a single crop might contain several grades and each would be sold in separate lots, or the entire crop might be sold at one time with a price structure that was averaged. Factors charged a commission of 2.5 percent of the gross price of the crop for their basic services, and they offered the additional services, at varying fees, of warehouse storage, movement of the cotton to the wharves for shipping, and general labor. If the bales were damaged, they had to be repaired. If the crop were to be shipped to Europe, there were additional fees for compressing the bales to a smaller size, insurance against fire and water damage enroute, and import duties. The factor paid for these costs and charged them to the planter's account and was reimbursed after the cotton was sold.[4]

During the period of the Republic, as steamboats made transportation to Texas coastal cities more reliable, more Texans turned to cotton for a cash crop. As the cities themselves grew in importance, entrepreneurial factors such as Thomas W. House, William Marsh Rice, and Samuel M. Williams saw opportunities to become as wealthy and respectable as their counterparts in New Orleans and Charleston. House, an Englishman, had come to Houston, temporary capital of the Republic, in 1838. He began as a baker, became a merchant, and was a moneylender by 1840. He soon became a factor, shipping cotton to Liverpool and purchasing manufactured goods

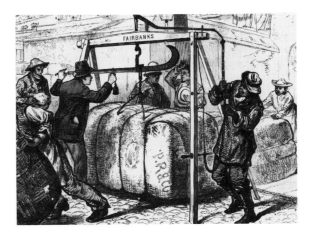

Weighing in bales of cotton before exporting. *From* Frank Leslie's Illustrated Newspaper, *November 16, 1878; courtesy Institute of Texan Cultures*

from American port cities for sale in Houston and beyond. As a merchant/factor, he accepted bales of cotton as payment for purchases of food, liquor, cloth, gunpowder, and lead or percussion caps. His trading network encompassed the distant towns of Crockett, Bastrop, Caldwell, Cameron, Springfield (near Mexia), and Columbus. During the Civil War he tried to smuggle cotton to England through the port of Matamoros on British ships.[5] After the war, he once again sold cotton to Liverpool, served as mayor of Houston, and invested in banks, railroads, and public utilities. When House died in 1880, his estate was valued at one million dollars.

His counterpart William Marsh Rice came to Houston in 1839, tended bar for a while, opened a general store, and eventually became a highly successful cotton factor. He sold cotton through Mexico during the Civil War and became a millionaire. He left Houston in 1863 but later established the funding for what is now Rice University.

Samuel May Williams had acted as Stephen F. Austin's assistant and secretary during the colony's early years, and in 1834, Williams formed a partnership with Thomas F. McKinney, a Nacogdoches merchant. They moved their mercantile enterprise from Quintana on the Brazos to Galveston in 1837, before town lots had even been sold, and rebuilt their warehouse and store when they were destroyed by a storm. Williams and McKinney included banking with their factoring services, and for many years controlled the sale, storage, and shipping of much of the cotton that passed through Galveston.[6]

As factors, House, Rice, and Williams all had to establish intricate and personal relationships with the planters whom they represented. The close working relationships of farmers/planters with their factors and the factors' willingness to advance money or credit gradually created a fragile and yet deeply embedded financial arrangement. Factors were expected to advise the planters of the best prices available and to act upon the planters' instructions about the crops' sale, or to use their best judgment if the planters so wished. Factors purchased goods and shipped them to the planters, and factors served as bankers, with the planters' cotton the basis of a credit system that allowed for advances against crops that had not yet been sold.

It was a short step from factors loaning money or extending credit for crops not yet sold to doing so for crops not yet grown, and planters could find themselves in debt for months or even years at a time. They had to trust their factors to be knowledgeable about fluctuating prices of cotton and to know when to store the crop so as to sell it at the best possible time to achieve the highest profit. The factors kept the planters' accounts straight from year to year, sending statements at the end of each year (if they had not been requested earlier) so that the planters could assess the state of their affairs. If sales did not repay advances, the factors would be required to extend more funds even before previous loans had been paid off, normally charging 8 percent interest, with as-yet unharvested, or even unplanted, crops as collateral.

Planters had four acknowledged problems: uncertain crop yields due to unpredictable weather and insect damage; land was still cheap, but using slave labor meant long-term expenses; planters were dependent upon middlemen to sell their crops; and their income was subject to the ebb and flow of prices, often determined by speculators, over which neither planters nor factors had control. Nevertheless, after the fees and charges were paid, loans retired, and goods purchased, there was usually enough profit, and assurances of increasing profit in the future, in an ever-expanding marketplace, to keep the planters enslaved to cotton.

James Montgomery, a Scottish visitor to the United States for several years beginning in 1836, wrote a detailed comparison of English and American textile manufacturing that was published in 1840. For example, in 1827 fifteen cotton factories in Paterson, New Jersey, had used 6,000 bales of cotton and produced over three million yards of cotton cloth. And more factories along New England rivers were being constructed. Montgomery presented statistics for 1839, "compiled from authentic sources," that showed that the twenty-nine factories in Lowell,

Massachusetts used 890 bales (or 347,000 pounds) of cotton on a weekly basis and turned out 255,000 yards of dyed and printed materials per week. Montgomery also noted that cotton factories were being built in Virginia and North Carolina and that mill owners were experimenting with the use of slave labor.[7] By 1840, cotton was beginning to intensify its influence over northern manufacturing and southern agriculture.

It had already become the primary export crop of Texas. Some cotton was grown in East Texas and near San Antonio, but most cotton was produced along the Brazos River in what had been Austin's Colony. Some five hundred bales had been exported from that area in 1828, and twice that amount, the following year. In 1835, Ira Ingram, a surveyor and Matagorda's first mayor, wrote to his uncle who lived in Michigan that the previous year's crop was selling at fourteen and one-half cents per pound. A friend who owned ten slaves had sold his crop for forty-five hundred dollars, and land that had originally sold for a dollar an acre was then selling for three to four dollars per acre. Ingram stated, "Once a planter had 20, 50 or 100 slaves paid for, all he had to worry about were boll worms and getting the money to the bank."[8]

But if expectations were high, setbacks were frequent. In 1842 and 1843, periods of drought were followed by heavy rains that flooded the Brazos watershed and produced an infestation of army worms. The resulting decimation of the cotton crops led to a temporary revival of the barter system.

Early customhouse records show that 29,000 bales cleared the ports during the fiscal year ending October 31, 1845, a figure that did not include cotton smuggled from East Texas into the United States to avoid duties. Customhouse records for 1844 reported the value of cotton exports at more than $580,000, while hides, the second most valuable export, were worth about $17,000.[9]

Cotton production continued to be measured in terms of the number of bales harvested per slave, with between eight and ten bales per harvest considered average per capita production. Many farmers did not have their own gins and paid plantation gin owners either one-eighth or one-tenth of their crop as a ginning fee, plus about $2.50 per bale for hemp bagging and rope ties.[10] Whether farmers hired teamsters to haul their cotton to market, which was expensive, or drove it themselves when their draft animals were not needed in the fields, the condition in which the cotton arrived often affected its price. Texas cotton was highly desired because of its fine staple but was frequently undervalued because of the way it was baled. Planters used old clothing when bagging was not available, and varieties of cotton were sometimes mixed within the bale; both practices lowered the price of the cotton.[11]

Prizes were sometimes offered by members of the early equivalents of chambers of commerce for the first bales of the season to be delivered to market. In 1842, Houston merchants awarded Leonard Groce a silver cup for delivering the first five bales of the season to Houston on July 29. A week later he received a gold cup, or second prize, for delivering the first twenty bales thereafter.

In December, 1845, Texas joined the United States but remained on the frontier of the Cotton Kingdom. Land was still cheap, a network of railroads was being planned, Houston and Galveston were competing for the shipping of imported and exported goods, and more cotton than ever before was being produced. According to the *Texas and Telegraph Register*, some 14,000 bales of cotton had reached Houston in 1844, as opposed to 1,000 bales five years before, and in 1854 almost 39,000 bales were recorded. Cotton shipments climbed steadily until 1860, when more than 115,000 bales were shipped out of Houston and Galveston, but in the first year of the Civil War, only 70,000 were shipped.[12]

A screw-pressed bale, which was four feet eight inches long and twenty-two inches thick, weighed between 475 and 500 pounds.[13] Round-bale presses, available after 1844, created bales that had an average density of 25 pounds per cubic foot and weighed about 250 pounds each. Because cotton was shipped by sea, and the price of transport was based upon volume instead of weight, cotton was re-pressed, or "compressed," to create uniform bale size and weight. The compressed bale was about half its original size. The earliest cotton compress in Houston was built by N. T. Davis in 1844 and could re-press a bale of cotton in fifteen minutes.[14] This was probably a screw-powered compress; hydraulic compresses were not available until after 1845.

The volume of cotton being produced required more gin stands with greater capacities, which led to both technological advances and the rise of gin manufacturing companies. As stated earlier, gin manufacturing was largely the work of blacksmiths and carpenters. Austin had encouraged settlers such as George Huff, John Cartwright, and John Sprowl to come to Texas to build gins, but not until the 1840s did gin manufacturing become an industry in its own right. An iron foundry was opened in Galveston in 1845 and, among other products, cast parts for gins. A gin manufacturing shop was established in Clarks-

ville to handle Red River cotton in 1847, and a Matagorda County manufacturer advertised a "Sliding Breasted Gin Stand" with fifty saws that could process seven thousand pounds of seed cotton a day. German immigrant L. Vollbracht owned a small gin manufacturing plant in Victoria County; he started the company with only $100 in capital and a single employee, and reported a total worth of $500 in the 1850 census. A San Augustine manufacturer with one employee turned out ten gin stands worth $150 each in 1850.[15]

In 1850, J. S. Alexander of Marshall owned the largest gin manufacturing plant in Texas. Alexander invested $2,500 and hired three employees, each of whom earned $50 per month. His gin stands were made with between fifty and fifty-six saws and were reportedly able to process three or four bales in a day. The 1850 census did not indicate the number of gins produced by this company or their value, but the 1860 census reported twenty gins worth $3,500.[16] A Smith County gin manufacturer reported production of fifty gins, with a total value of $7,500 in the 1860 census. Four gin manufacturers were in business in Texas in 1860 with a total of nineteen employees and gins worth more than $28,000.[17] But by far the most popular gins in the South, including Texas, were those made by Daniel Pratt—in Alabama. In contrast to the small gin manufacturing companies in Texas, the Daniel Pratt Gin Company was one of the largest in the nation.

Pratt, born in Temple, New Hampshire, on July 20, 1799, was educated in local schools with their strong Puritan philosophies and was apprenticed to a carpenter named Putnam when he was sixteen years old. Putnam, a master carpenter, had provided financial security for a friend and when the debt came due and the friend defaulted, Putnam mortgaged his home to fulfill his obligation. Three years later Pratt, recognizing the financial burden his apprenticeship was causing, asked Putnam to release him from the contract, to which Putnam agreed. Taking a tool kit, saw, hammer, and level, Pratt worked his way to Boston in 1819. He approached the captain of a ship and asked for passage to Savannah, Georgia. Pratt made such a good impression that the captain gave him free passage and loaned him twenty-five dollars when he disembarked.

Pratt went to Milledgeville, Georgia, where he worked as a carpenter. In 1827, with his fortunes much improved, he returned to New Hampshire. He found Putnam and gave him sufficient funds to pay off the mortgage on his home. He also married Esther Ticknor. On the return trip, Pratt and his wife happened

Daniel Pratt. *From* DeBow's Review, *ca. 1850; courtesy Continental Eagle Corporation*

to be sailing with the captain who had first given Pratt passage south, and he not only paid for the earlier passage but repaid the loan, with interest.

In 1831, Pratt and his wife moved to Clinton, Georgia. Pratt managed a gin manufacturing plant owned by Samuel Griswold, and a year later the two men formed a partnership to manufacture cotton gins. Pratt was a talented architect, and during his years in Georgia, he designed and built a number of very fine homes, several of which stood well into the twentieth century. He later turned this talent to the construction of a cotton gin manufacturing plant, cotton mills, and his own home in 1842.

Lack of water power limited the plant's production, and in 1833, Pratt moved to Autauga County, Alabama. He asked Griswold to join him, but the latter, fearing Indian attacks, turned down the offer. Pratt began conservatively, manufacturing a few cotton gins on the plantation of a General Elmore. Soon after, he moved to McNeill's mill on Autauga Creek, leased the use of water power for a small amount of money, and began to produce gins in quantity. In 1838, only five years after his arrival, Pratt bought one thousand acres further up Autauga Creek, built a gin factory, and established the town of Prattville.

The decade of the 1840s saw a steady expansion of Pratt's business interests. His nephew Merrill Pratt left New Hampshire and joined the Daniel Pratt Gin Company in 1841. His only child, Ellen, was born the following year. In 1846, Pratt built a cotton mill,

followed by a grist and flour mill, and he built a woolen mill for treating wool and weaving it into fabric. The cotton mill was severely damaged during the Civil War but was rebuilt; the woolen mill was eventually used as an experimental laboratory for cotton gins.

While Texas planters experienced difficulties getting their wagon loads of cotton to market, Pratt faced problems shipping his gins from Prattville. The gin stands had to be transported by steamboat, and the road from the plant to the ferry passed along the main street of Prattville, which had several saloons. To keep his drivers' minds upon their business, Pratt built a four-mile-long plank road, at a cost of fourteen thousand dollars, from the plant to Washington Landing on the Alabama River.[18]

The Civil War struck hard at all manufacturing enterprises, and Pratt was as hard hit as any. Cotton gin sales declined, and the mills suffered much damage. Pratt, however, was ready for his next venture. He had bought several thousand acres of land in northern Alabama, land that was rich in coal and iron, and he built the Oxmoor furnaces near Birmingham. His daughter, Ellen, married Henry F. DeBardeleben in 1862, and Pratt turned over much of the mining enterprise to his son-in-law. The Red Mountain Iron and Coal Company at Oxmoor was the first to use ore to make pig iron during the war, although the furnaces were soon destroyed by Wilson's Raiders. After the war, Pratt and DeBardeleben recouped their losses and reorganized the Red Mountain Iron and Coal Company as the Eureka Mining Company. The furnaces were rebuilt and the company was reopened only a short time before Pratt's death on May 13, 1873.

Daniel Pratt is considered the South's first industrialist. He established a New England–type mill town in Alabama, providing homes, schools, and security for employees. He began the large-scale manufacturing of gins after Whitney's patent had expired, and he moved manufacturing into the South, which had been generally considered unsuitable for industry, in order to gain both cheap power and closeness to the planters who would buy the gins. By 1860, the Prattville plant was producing fifteen hundred gin stands per year.[19] After Pratt's death, his nephew Merrill Pratt continued to run the company that became the foundation of Continental Gin Company, created in 1899, and the predecessor of today's Continental Eagle Corporation.

Gin manufacturing, of course, had not been limited to the South. Eleazer Carver journeyed from Massachusetts to Natchez, Mississippi, in the fall of

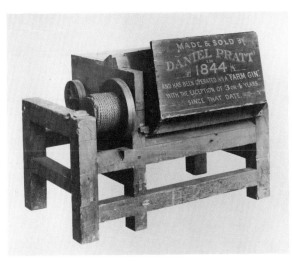

Daniel Pratt farm gin, ca. 1844; many were purchased by Texas planters. *Courtesy Continental Eagle Corporation*

1806, where he met a Major Miner of Natchez who had seen a saw gin and hired Carver to make one like it for his plantation. Miner provided materials and labor, and Carver made a gin that was somewhat primitive in construction but superior to others then in use. They formalized their enterprise and produced gin stands for six years. When the War of 1812 broke out, Carver returned East, traveling by horseback through the Choctaw country of Alabama. As an apprentice, he had helped to build an iron works at Franconia, New Hampshire, and he recognized the rich iron deposits in the area of present-day Birmingham, where Daniel Pratt would later build his furnaces. When the war was over, Carver returned to Natchez, but he left behind instructions with Seth and Abram Washburn, who owned a forge on South Brook Street in Bridgewater, Massachusetts, to make saws and ribs according to his patterns. In Natchez, Carver's friend Miner provided financial backing, and they built a shop for the gin stands for which the Washburns provided the gin irons, primarily saws and ribs (or Whitney's grates). Fun-loving Natchez offered too many distractions to Carver's employees, and he returned to Bridgewater to begin a new company. The Bridgewater Cotton Gin Company, usually referred to as Carver, Washburn & Company, was incorporated in 1816 and remained in business until a fire destroyed the plant in 1852.

Of interest is the simplicity of Carver's gin manufacturing plant. Power machinery consisted of one lathe, one circular saw, one emery wheel, and two grindstones, all driven by a single water wheel. The four machines were placed on three floors of the building, and a rope to control the flow of water through a gate was placed near each machine. Raising or lowering the gate regulated the flow of water and controlled the speed of the machinery. The lathe had only one speed, and when iron was to be worked, the lathe operator alone had control of the gate to keep the wheel turning very slowly. The circular saw was used only in winter or spring when there was plenty of water and only at night, so that other work could be carried out during the day. The saw was used to make cylinder coverings and grates. The gin frames were made from hand-cut lumber that had been sawed to exact dimensions in Maine, shipped to Weymouth, and then transported overland to Bridgewater. Pulleys and cylinders, shaped by axe and plane, were made of hornbeam.

Wooden pins were used to hold the gin stands together; iron did not come into common usage until much later. A saw was made by welding a bar of steel between two bars of iron and hammering them into shape, after which the saw was trimmed, ground, polished, and the teeth cut. The steel acted as a support for the iron which wore down quickly and had to be refiled. Screws, which were imported, were used to construct the grate and saw cylinder and to attach various small parts. Hand-wrought nails were used to attach the brushes. Brushes were made with horsehair that was imported in bales from South America. The hair was straightened and cut into three-inch lengths, spread out to form the brush wing, and put together with glue and nails.

Pairs of workers, known as stand makers, labored from twelve to fourteen hours per day, beginning as early as three or four o'clock in the morning, and not having breakfast until about seven o'clock. Unless there was a special need, work did not continue after dark; lights and fires were not permitted. Subjected to these primitive conditions, stand makers produced only two sixty-saw gins per week.

Worker productivity was also affected by alcohol. Beginning about 1830, Carver ordered that no rum be brought into the shop. Before that, small amounts of rum had been issued for the birth of a child, the arrival of a new employee, or even the birth of a calf. A gallon of rum was brought in, and each worker drank from a small blue mug that was characterized by its broken handle. Apparently, on the day that this order was issued, all hands quit the shop and left at eleven o'clock in the morning. This may have been one of the nation's first industrial strikes.

Carver made a number of improvements to the gin stand and received patents for his inventions. He developed the flat moting bar which was placed be-

Hand-made 40-saw gin stand ca. 1840. First located in Greenwood County, S.C., it was donated to Clemson University, which in turn gave it to the Division of Textiles, Smithsonian Institution. *Courtesy Smithsonian Institution*

tween each gin rib and in front of the brush cylinder to deflect trash from the ginned lint. His gins incorporated the use of seedboards, first designed by Hodgen Holmes, which were made of three-inch planks, cut the width of the roll box, shaped by hand tools to three-fourths of an inch thick, and then curved to a twelve-inch radius. The seedboard was lifted out, or propped open with locks of seed cotton, to allow seeds to fall out of the roll box. (Holmes' seedboard was placed at the lower edge of the roll box; Carver's was dropped in from the top.) Each saw had a single reversed tooth to keep cotton from catching in the grates, or ribs, and choking its passage. Mote boards, used by both Whitney and Holmes, were covered with tin and bent to catch the immature seeds for removal. A belt (sometimes termed a "band") extended from the vertical wheel, which projected two or three feet through the floor to the saw shaft, and powered the gin stand. Carver gins later used straight seedboards and cast-iron grates, sheet-steel saws, hog bristles instead of horsehair, and varnished frames.[20]

Carver turned over the business to Albert Washburn in 1836 and concentrated on his inventions. Carver formed his own company, E. Carver Company of East Bridgewater, Massachusetts, in 1842. Carver, Washburn & Company did little business after 1845 and was dissolved about 1853. Other gin manufacturing companies began to form. Bates, Hyde & Company, also of Bridgewater, Massachusetts, was created in 1833 with nine partners, four of whom had worked for Carver, Washburn, & Company. The company's manufacturing plant had once been a wheelwright's shop. It used a small steam engine for power instead of a water wheel.

The railroad from Boston came to Bridgewater in 1846, and two years later Bates, Hyde & Company moved from the center of town to a location on the rail line, expanding into a bigger factory and warehouse. A fire destroyed the factory on April 1, 1850, and the old Carver, Washburn, & Company factory was offered for use in exchange for Bates, Hyde & Company's agreement to manufacture gins which Carver, Washburn, & Company had on order but could not produce. The factory was rebuilt during the fall of 1850, and it remained in use for many years.

Partners in Bates, Hyde & Company had relatives and friends in Boston's shipping trade who helped the company establish a large export trade in hand-powered gin stands. During the Civil War, foreign demand for the gin stands outstripped the company's ability to supply them, even though the factory was enlarged twice. In March, 1866, Bates, Hyde & Company shipped 654 gin stands out of the country, most of them hand-operated. Gins were hauled to Boston by ox team and wagon, with local farmers as teamsters; there the gins were placed on ships bound for New Orleans, Mobile, or Galveston. Traveling salesmen and agents in the cities of New Orleans, Natchez, Vicksburg, and Memphis sold many of the gins to planters who lived along the major rivers. The gins were especially popular with planters in the Natchez and Vicksburg areas. The opening of rail lines made shipment west easier. Joseph Hyde served as the company's treasurer from its beginning, and in 1852 he bought out the interests of cofounders George W. Bates and Samuel W. Bates. Samuel P. Gates, who joined the company in 1857 as Joseph Hyde's assistant, became treasurer after Hyde's death in September, 1877, and bought out Hyde's stock. In October, the company was reorganized as the Eagle Cotton Gin Company, with Gates remaining as its treasurer. Eagle became part of Continental Gin Company in 1899.[21]

Joseph Carver, Eleazer Carver's son, succeeded his father in the manufacturing of gins. He later worked for Eagle from 1878 until 1890.

Gin manufacturing was a steadily growing industry in the south as well as the north. A few entrepreneurs were daring enough to compete with Pratt. One was Benjamin David Gullett, who began manufacturing saw gins in 1849 at Aberdeen, Mississippi. He made gin stands during the winter, then loaded one or two at a time onto a wagon and traveled about the countryside selling his winter's production. In time, he delivered gins as far away as Texas by means

Interior of 40-saw cotton gin showing brush cylinder. *Courtesy A. M. Pendleton*

of a train of ox-drawn wagons. He made a number of improvements to the gin stands, and in 1869, moved his factory to what is now Amite, Louisiana. Gullett gins were popular well into the twentieth century, and the company was bought by Continental Gin Company.[22]

While gin manufacturing struggled to keep pace with cotton production, ginning itself changed little. There were signs, however, of the technological advances to come. A gin frame made of cast iron was patented by a Mr. Lester in 1831, and Alex Jones patented a double-cylinder gin in 1834. Descriptions of his duplex gin and feeder indicate that the gin worked like Whitney's, but the frame held two saw cylinders, space blocks, and continuous flat ginning ribs found on two sides of the frame, with independent hoppers for supplying cotton to the saws. This

Gin breast and ribs raised to show saws. *Courtesy A. M. Pendleton*

is the first indication of a mechanical feeder. This gin also pulled the cotton through the ribs and over a screen for precleaning.[23] The J. Perkins adjustable seedboard, patented in 1837, was placed at an angle to the roll box. It could be slid in and out of the roll box and wedged into different positions to regulate the amount of seed cotton pulled in by the saws. The seedboard prevented cotton from falling through to the seed box below without being ginned.[24] This seedboard was incorporated into many gin designs for over fifty years.

As more cotton was planted and harvested, it became increasingly difficult for the slaves to pick the cotton from the stalks as cleanly as before. Additional leaves, stems, and dirt lowered the price of the cotton because it did not spin as well at the mills. Tired field hands, precleaning the cotton by firelight at night, could not clean enough cotton fast enough, and some form of mechanical assistance was needed. A horizontal whipping device, patented in 1830, was composed of paddles mounted on a shaft and placed over slats that extended the length of the machine. The paddles beat or whipped the cotton against the slats, pushing out trash and some seeds, and acted as an auger to force the cotton to an outlet so that it could be collected and placed in baskets. Cotton whippers were used with both upland and Sea Island cotton.[25] A wooden, steam-driven cleaner was invented by a slave on the Blakely Plantation near Vicksburg, Mississippi, in 1840, but it remained in limited use.[26]

Other inventions included a brush gin with an overhead box to allow cotton to be hand fed, and this 1844 gin included the Perkins adjustable seedboard. Theodorick James, a Mississippi inventor, placed a stripping brush above the saws and behind the ribs so that the fibers could be combed as they were held in place by the saw teeth. This straightened the fibers and removed small bits of trash. Other improvements included Abram Washburn's repairable ribs (1841), and Carver's guard and mote bar assembly set between gin saws and the brush cylinder (1844).[27]

Some improvements were quite elaborate. An inventor named D. Phillips was issued a patent in 1841 for a railroad cotton gin. The gin stand was placed on a circular track approximately fifty feet in diameter. The gin was belted or geared to the wheels, and cotton was ginned as a horse pulled the stand around the track. Cotton was fed into the gin stand's hopper through a hole in a floor or platform above the track each time the gin passed underneath the opening. It is not known how the lint was disposed of.[28]

Whipping, or cleaning, seed cotton. *From* Frank Leslie's Illustrated Newspaper, *October 7, 1871; courtesy Library of Congress*

Other modifications included the use of iron strap bale ties (beginning about 1840), a hydraulic press (1841), and a hydraulic compress (1845).

An unusual device was the gin spinner invented in 1805 by J. McBride of Nashville, Tennessee. The gin spinner, often mistaken for a Whitney gin, had between fifteen and twenty saws eight inches in diameter, reversible ribs, brushes, a condenser box, and carding cylinders. This machine was designed to separate the seeds from the fibers, card the lint, and spin the lint into the yarn or thread used to weave the coarse fabric from which winter clothing for slaves and utility bagging were made. Usually termed a "Spinster," this machine, which sold for $130, could spin enough cotton yarn on a daily basis to make seven to ten yards of cloth one yard wide. A later model, patented by William Bryant of Nashville in 1823, was used across the South from Louisiana to the Carolinas, was sold under the name Spinning Jenny, and cost about $100. J. & T. Pearce of Cincinnati, Ohio, began selling the Columbian Spinster in the 1840s. Twenty years later, at the outbreak of the Civil War, three thousand of these machines were in use on Southern plantations. The destruction of

the plantation system, however, also marked the end of a need for the "Spinster."[29]

While saw ginning was undergoing small but steady advances during the 1840s, improvements were also being made in roller ginning. The long-staple Sea Island cotton was preferred by the mills and often brought higher prices than upland cotton, and those planters whose soil was conducive to Sea Island cotton increased production just as the upland cotton planters did. Houstonian Ashbel Smith, a philosopher, physician, and secretary of state under Texas President Anson Jones, experimented with Sea Island cotton on his Gulf Coast plantation.

Still in use, prior to 1840, were a few of Kinsey Burden's old-fashioned gunbarrel roller gins; and Dr. Joseph Eve's gin that had two rollers, three feet long, set in a wooden frame, were available, although the wires in the feeding boards damaged the cotton. Because these gins turned out only about 30 pounds of lint per day, as many as five pairs of rollers were linked together to increase production. About 135 pounds of ginned lint per day resulted, but this could not compare with the 600 to 900 pounds of lint ginned per day with a Whitney saw gin. In the 1820s,

Gin-Spinner ("Columbian Spinster") made by J. and T. Pearce, Cincinnati, Ohio. *Courtesy Smithsonian Institution*

treadle gins with large flywheels on the roller shafts were imported from the West Indies and cost about ten dollars each, but while the worker may have turned out more lint due to the comfort and speed of the treadle, the difference would have amounted to only a few pounds per day. Clearly, simple mechanical improvements to the old churka gin were not enough.

In 1838, Eleazer Carver turned his inventive mind to roller ginning. He placed spiralled rollers in pairs that virtually became gears; cotton was fed to several pairs of rollers, mounted on a flat plane, and seeds were conveyed to the ends of the rollers. The lint then fell onto a moving belt. Such construction would have been very difficult for blacksmith or machine shops of the day to achieve, and Carver's design may never have been implemented.[30]

On July 3, 1840, the first of many patents was issued to Fones McCarthy of Demopolis, Alabama, for revolutionary changes to the roller gin. McCarthy mounted a fixed blade ("doctor knife") to the top of the frame (pointing downward) and positioned it to fit snugly against the gin roller. A moving knife with fine teeth ("hacker blade") was mounted on a

crank leg (or connecting rods) at the bottom of the frame (pointing upward). According to Charles A. Bennett, ginning specialist for the United States Department of Agriculture and expert in the history of ginning, the moving knife "hacked at the seed which were held between the ginning roller and the fixed knife or doctor blade. The single McCarthy ginning roller was much greater in diameter than churka type rollers and hence had greater capacity from the start. Its porcupine-like surface seized the fibers and drew them between roller and fixed blade so that there was a constant pull against the seed in order to make a clean separation. McCarthy's first moving knife, which he called "the saw," had fine teeth on its working edge. The McCarthy roller was made up of coarse leather, grooved to permit motes and other unyielding matter to pass the knife without injuring it."[31]

The first rollers were approximately four inches in diameter and three feet long, but by 1850 the rollers were enlarged to seven inches in diameter and stretched to forty, sixty and seventy-two inches long. Forty-inch lengths were standard on single roller gins until the 1940s. Double roller gins were also developed, and their rollers varied between 60 and 72 inches in length. American manufacturers such as Foss, Continental, and Murray produced roller gins, but the British Middleton roller gin was popular in Middle and Far Eastern countries where long staple cotton was produced in abundance. Bennett succinctly clarified the advantages and disadvantages of roller and saw ginning. Roller gins "have usually been lower in cost than saw gins and have been more readily operated by unskilled labor, and on all varieties and staple lengths of cottons, regardless of whether the cottons have smooth or fuzzy seeds. Saw gins, on the other hand, are not universally adaptable to all cottons. They have not served well in ginning sea-island [*sic*] or American-Egyptian long staple cottons, and their ginned lint has met with objections from the cotton mills. They blend the cotton fibers much better, however, than do roller gins."[32] The saw gins had five to seven times greater capacity than roller gins, and long staple cotton had limited areas of cultivation.

In 1840, Fones McCarthy, who would receive patents until long past the Civil War, could not have imagined that his double knife cleaning system would last for more than a century and have worldwide use. But he could see, in his own lifetime, the expansion, near-demise, and revival of the Cotton Kingdom.

CHAPTER FIVE

"Personally Interested Labor"

When Jared Groce arrived in Texas in 1822, one of his first duties was to build a rough cabin to shelter his family. His primary residence, constructed later that year, was far more elaborate. "Bernardo" may have resembled other early plantation homes in its "dogtrot" or "dog run" style (two rooms connected by an open corridor), but it was considerably more comfortable. Built of cottonwood logs hewn until they were smooth, the house was one and one-half stories high and had a central hallway fifteen feet wide with two large rooms on either side. A front gallery fifty-five feet long was supported by six columns, and a rear gallery linked the house to a separate kitchen. Outbuildings included a home for overseer Alfred Gee, an office, a small infirmary, slave quarters, a nursery for slave children, and a community kitchen and dining room. Groce's original cabin served as a "bachelor's hall" for young men. Groce later built another home in Grimes County, which he called the "Retreat," to escape the mosquitoes and malaria of the Lower Brazos, and he died there on November 20, 1836.[1]

Leonard Groce and his family continued to live at Bernardo, maintaining the plantation's reputation for lively entertainment and generous hospitality. Leonard Groce was well prepared to take his father's place in the community. He received a law degree in 1840, continued to grow cotton, and expanded his landholdings in 1841 by buying part of a Mexican land grant that had once been owned by Justo Liendo. He purchased the remaining portion of the original grant in 1849, and in 1853 he built a plantation mansion, which he named "Liendo," six miles northeast of Bernardo. Liendo was designed in the traditional Greek Revival style with brick walls and broad verandas, rooms with high ceilings for greater coolness in summer, and broad hallways for ease of movement and better ventilation, and the interior was furnished with fine drapes, upholstered furniture, and other luxuries. Deed records show that Leonard owned more than sixty-seven thousand acres spread over five counties.

Like his counterparts in what was becoming known as the Cotton Kingdom, Leonard Groce's livelihood depended upon slave labor. In the early years of slavery, many individuals were assigned specialized tasks, whether carpenter or cook, weaver or personal servant, but as more acres were planted in cotton, more slaves were sent to the fields; specialization was reduced to a few essential skills such as blacksmithing or cooking. Articles suggesting management techniques were published in agricultural magazines and in newspapers, and while rewards were generally favored over punishments as a psychology for getting more work out of slaves, each planter's own system developed according to his temperament, education, and expectations.

Economics aside, the demands of the crop entrenched and regulated slavery. In the field, a distinct social structuring took place. The master's overseer was unquestionably in charge, but he was often required to inspect various parts of the estate, and foremen and slave drivers of the hoeing and plowing gangs took over in his absence. Because the foremen and drivers were not required to perform field work, they received privileged status within the internal order and maintained that status in the slave quarters after work. On plantations where these positions were rotated, there tended to be less resentment and greater productivity.

Beginning in June, when weeds had to be chopped out of the rows of emerging plants, the grueling, monotonous work of growing cotton continued through the summer until the cotton was ready to be picked in late August or early September. Awakened by a bell, the laborers dressed quickly and hurried to the fields just before daylight to begin picking cotton as soon as they could see well enough to distinguish the bolls from the shadows. On some plantations, a breakfast of cornbread and syrup was brought to them in the fields. On others, slaves carried both their breakfasts and lunches to the fields with them. After a short rest for a midday meal, the slaves continued working until nightfall, pausing only to drink water.

Women with babies were allowed to leave the fields four times a day to nurse their children and were not expected to produce as much as the other men and women; however, each slave was required to meet a daily individual quota.

Each worker was issued two bags made of coarse cotton which had straps, so that they could be suspended from the shoulders, and a large willow or reed basket. The slaves would leave the baskets at the ends of the rows and take the two bags with them. When one bag was full, it was left on the ground and the worker would continue along the row until the second bag was filled. When both bags were full, the slaves carried them to the baskets and tramped down by foot as much cotton as possible, a process that was repeated throughout the day. At the end of the day, slaves carried the full baskets on their shoulders or their heads to the wagon where all the cotton was collected. Each basket was weighed on a field scale and a careful record made of the slave's productivity for the day. In some cases, the cotton might be carried directly to the gin yard, weighed, and then stored in the building. Rewards or punishments were then dispensed, depending upon whether quotas had been met or missed.[2]

In addition to manually cleaning cotton at night, slaves worked in the fields on Saturdays. Some plantations worked slaves during the early morning hours, others required half days on Saturdays, but most plantations allowed the slaves to rest on Sundays. Problems with weather or insects could vary the schedule. Slaves were expected to keep their own gardens and in many cases were allowed to have their own cotton patches, to sell their produce, and to keep the money they made for their own use.[3]

Scrap cotton was collected for use in mattresses and quilts, and a certain amount of cotton was retained to be spun, dyed, and woven into cloth. The remainder was baled and carried to market. Since ginning was a slow process, oftentimes the last bales were being loaded onto ox-drawn wagons just as the new crop was being planted in the spring.

In contrast to the East Texas and Gulf Coast plantation owners with their strong ties to the Deep South, the German immigrants who moved into the Hill Country of Central Texas during the 1840s and 1850s absolutely refused to own slaves. The first German immigrants reached Galveston in December, 1844, but they continued on to the port of Carlshafen (Indianola), which had been established by Prince Carl of Solms-Braunfels for the immigration society known as the *Adelsverein*. In the spring of 1845, Prince Solms led the first group of settlers inland to

"The Oldtimer," a catalogue illustration of an antebellum gin house and yard press. *Courtesy Continental Eagle Corporation*

a site on the Comal River where they built the town of New Braunfels, bought land, and began to grow cotton.

Later that year, under the leadership of Baron Von Meusebach, German settlers moved into the Comanche territory northwest of New Braunfels, and they founded Fredericksburg early in 1846. Meusebach signed a peace treaty with the Indians, and the settlers began to physically occupy and culturally dominate the Hill Country. The Germans had raised cotton in the areas around New Braunfels and Castroville before 1850, and the New Braunfels newspaper (*Neu-Braunfelser Zeitung*) announced a fall crop of nine bales in its April 1, 1853, edition.[4]

Because they were so far from cotton towns such as Galveston and Houston and too far from Indianola to ship directly to New Orleans or other ports, the Germans transported their cotton to northern Mexico and its textile mills just as Jared Groce had. In November, 1861, fourteen wagons of twenty bales each began the three-week journey from New Braunfels to Saltillo. That trade continued until the arrival of the railroad in the 1870s.[5]

An admiring description of those hardy German farmers was provided by Frederick Law Olmsted who traveled through Texas with his brother in 1854. A Staten Island farmer with Utopian ideals and no use at all for slavery, Olmsted wrote a series of articles for the *New York Daily Times* which detailed his adventures in Texas. Olmsted was a respected journalist, and his abiding interest in agriculture eventually led him to become the nation's first landscape architect.

Olmsted described the average German home as a small log cabin surrounded by about ten acres of land. The entire family worked in the garden or the fields. Somewhat more prosperous families had homes with boards over the logs and even plaster or brick improvements, but all German farmers were similar in their attention to the cleanliness and variety of crops. Regarding one large farm, Olmsted noted that "the picking had been entirely completed, and that with care and exactness, so that none of the cotton, which the labor of cultivation had produced, had been left to waste. The cotton-stalks stood rather more closely, and were of less extraordinary size, but much more even or regular in their growth than on the plantations."[6] German farm wives worked alongside their husbands and were reputed to clean dirt off bolls of cotton with their lips.[7]

Olmsted went to great lengths to point out the superior quality of free-labor cotton versus slave-produced cotton. Eight hundred bales, the combined produce from small plots in New Braunfels and from the neighboring farms, were sent as a single crop to Galveston where it "brought from one to two cents a pound more than that produced by slaves, owing to the more careful handling of white and personally interested labor; but the expense of hauling cotton to the coast prevents any large profits at this distance." Olmsted suggested that either the building of a local textile mill or the arrival of railroad service would provide the impetus for greater cotton cultivation. "With water-power and hands upon the spot, it certainly seems an unnatural waste of labor to carry the staple to Massachusetts to be spun, but such, for want of local capital, is now the course of trade." As for that eight-hundred-bale crop, it "goes in one body to market, entirely separate from the great mass exported, and from their [the Germans] peculiar style of settlement, it may be even considered as the product of one large plantation, worked by white hands, and divided into well-marked annual tasks."[8]

Olmsted devised cost estimates comparing small and large plantations on the Upper Guadalupe. Land was sold in tracts ranging from six hundred to two thousand acres, and his estimate was based on a cost of $2.50 per acre for an average farm of one thousand acres. His estimate for a gin, mules for the press, tools, and harness was $800. He also estimated the weight of a bale at 450 pounds, with between three and five

bales produced annually per slave, valued at between six to eight cents per pound. With the initial cost of a small plantation at $9,000, Olmsted estimated that the farmer would have a loss of $40 per year. Olmsted stated that he knew of a single county in Mississippi where five landowners produced five thousand bales each, but a southern plantation of two thousand acres and costing about $120,000 would show a profit of only $6,800 because of the expense of slavery.[9]

If Olmsted's admired German farmers were growing corn and cotton and experimenting with sheep raising, East Texas and Gulf Coast cotton growers, unable or unwilling to find substitutes for the evils of slavery, were responding to improvements in ginning. In 1854, Benjamin Gullett substituted brushes for Eleazer Carver's flat moting bars and added a revolving stripper brush beneath each saw. Four years later Gullett received a patent for a design that included a stripping brush, a lower carding brush, and a doffing cylinder of steel blades that acted as a fan.

An 1857 patent was issued to Daniel Pratt for a hinged roll box that could be lifted to release the seeds or the roll of seed cotton. (The roll box was a rounded enlargement of the gin breast. Seed cotton fell into the roll box and collected on top of the saws in a mat, or seed roll. The roll box held the revolving mat in place as saws caught the fibers and pulled them through the ribs.) The patent described the spiralling motion of the roll, which kept the seeds agitated and offered more cotton to the saws.

In 1858, A. Q. Withers, of Tunica, Mississippi, received a patent for a design that permitted the cleaning of cotton within the gin stand by using a series of four cylinders placed horizontally. The first was a saw ginning cylinder that turned at about 350 rpm. The second cylinder, made of brushes rather than saws, carried the lint downward over a concave screen to release bits of trash. The third cylinder, composed of saws rotating at 700 rpm, doffed the fibers from the second cylinder, thus re-ginning the fibers, and carried lint across another screen for additional cleaning. The fourth was a brush cylinder that cleared the cotton from saw cylinder number two and expelled the lint. Withers claimed to receive as much as four cents per pound more than was paid for cotton ginned by the usual, single saw-cylinder gins.[10]

George W. Payne received a patent in 1858 for a gin stand with huller ribs. He modified the smooth, curved ribs, which were intended to protect the saw blades from wearing down, by adding a small projection, or "knuckle," to each rib that would keep hulls from entering the roll box. He also set a small

Cotton wagon with round bales. *From* Harper's Weekly, *May 12, 1866; courtesy Institute of Texan Cultures*

picker roller in the bottom of the roll box to feed the seed cotton through the huller ribs. In November, 1859, Benjamin G. Beadle was issued a patent for a single-rib huller gin that had a "knee" cast onto the metal ginning rib. Saw teeth pulled cotton fibers past this "knee" and deflected the hulls. Unfortunately, seeds and hulls were discharged at the same place; this was undesirable since seeds and trash were then mixed together. The single rib huller was, nevertheless, an improvement and was manufactured consistently until modifications to the design were introduced by Ellis in the 1880s.

D. G. Olmstead, a Washington County, Mississippi, inventor and manufacturer of the Eureka Gin, received a patent in January, 1858, for a gin that incorporated several improvements. The outer breast and roll box were oval rather than concave in shape with a rotating cylinder placed in the center of the roll box. This solid cylinder, with pins and/or spirals cut into the core, acted as an auger to carry the seed cotton and ginned seed to either end of the roll box; a different construction using a solid core with an external grid allowed the discharge of seeds at the side of the roll box without losing cotton. This bottom-fed gin stand had a roller in the lower part of the breast that acted as a picker roller, although it was made

more like a revolving screen, to pull seed cotton deeper into the roll box.[11] (Later, the picker roller would extract coarse trash by a carding action rather than by pulling the fibers across a grid or screen.) The Eureka Gin was so successful that Daniel Pratt bought the rights to manufacture the gin in March, 1867, shortly after Olmstead's death, and agreed to pay a 5 percent annual royalty to the probate court of Washington County, Mississippi, to be used by Olmstead's survivors. By 1859, Daniel Pratt was manufacturing sixty-saw gin stands.

Improvements were also made in the baling process. Round bales were being used in some areas, but most bales were still rectangular, wrapped in burlap bagging, and tied with rope. Iron straps had been tried as early as 1840, but even with the bale buckle, patented by D. McComb of Memphis, Tennessee, in 1856, rope was commonly used until the turn of the century.[12]

M. L. Parry invented and manufactured an indoor baling press in Galveston, and an 1857 advertising circular illustrated this iron screw press, which cost $400, in detail. The Star Cotton Press was not shipped as a complete unit; only the mechanical parts were supplied by M. L. Parry's Star Foundry, but directions for assembly, which any mechanic could follow, were also provided. Plans for the frame would be included with the working parts, and any carpenter could build the frame. Timbers were to be no larger than ten inches square and twenty-two feet long: the press would occupy four by ten feet of floor space and would require a roof height of twenty feet.

The circular listed several important selling points for the press. It was intended to be run by the same power source and belt that drove the gin stand. The screw could be started and stopped or raised and lowered without reversing or stopping the power source. The press was to be used inside the gin house, for both convenience and freedom from cold, wet, or windy weather. Women and children could operate it safely. The unit was believed to be so durable that only a sledgehammer could break it. Capable of packing up to forty bales per day, the Star Cotton Press was billed as the most advanced of the time, and advertisements claimed that the cotton it baled would bring the highest prices.[13]

Hand- and screw-powered compresses were most commonly used, but after 1845 a hydraulic compress was available. For cotton to be shipped economically, the standard 450- to 500-pound bale had to be compressed to about half of its original size. Compresses were located in southern port cities where factoring, warehousing, and shipping facilities were available. In 1854, the Galveston Shipper's Cotton Press took up an entire city block and could store up to fifty-five hundred bales at one time. For better fire protection, the building that housed the press was made of brick and had a tin roof. An 1854 advertisement for the Shipper's Cotton Press announced machinery designed by Tyler (inventor of the hydraulic press), which included a forty-eight inch cylinder, and assured cotton shippers that the press frame was the best built. Only employees experienced in sampling and weighing would handle consigned cotton, and a night watchman would be on duty at the warehouse "to guard against fires and other casualties."[14]

One of the "casualties" of the Civil War was gin manufacturing, which was severely limited due to the shortage of iron. Cotton continued to be grown during the war years, however, and patents were issued for improvements to the gin stand. Israel F. Brown received a patent in 1861 for a design that featured a set of two saw cylinders with differently sized saws that were placed horizontally in the roll box so that one brush cylinder could doff lint from both saw cylinders. Thomas C. Craven obtained a patent in 1864 for a gin with wire teeth that clawed into the roll box to catch the fibers and then thrust the fibers into a suction air stream for doffing. This gin also

Men operating a cotton compress. *From* Harper's Weekly, *1879; courtesy Institute of Texan Cultures*

included an internal condenser with suction fan, and a brush to pull the batt of lint from the drum of the condenser.[15] Craven's gin may never have been manufactured, but its fan and condenser foreshadowed future developments: fans would be used throughout the ginning process to supply air for cleaning and moving cotton, and individual condensing units, wooden boxes placed behind the gin stand and attached to it by a flue, would make the movement of cotton to the press faster, easier, and cleaner. In the meantime, cotton expelled from the gin stand continued to be dropped into lint blow rooms where it was collected to be taken to the press.

Only a few modifications were made to the roller gins still in use. James F. Furguson, of Miconopy, Florida, was awarded a patent in 1861 for improving the action of the rollers by means of spiral windings. His more adjustable fixed knife and vibrating moving knife (with alternating long and short teeth) resulted in better ginning. Significant changes in roller ginning would not gather momentum until long after the Civil War.

At the beginning of the war, cotton had still been shipped regularly to Europe, and most of the enormous crop of 1860 had been sold before the Union blockade took effect in July, 1861. The Confederacy's official position was to refuse to allow cotton to be shipped to England and France, intending to create such a shortage that those countries would come to the South's financial and military aid, even to the extent of breaking the blockade. Until that happened, the Confederate government passed into law a bill known as the Produce Loan (May, 1861) to induce planters to turn over money earned from the sale of agricultural products to the government in exchange for bonds. The law was later changed to permit planters to turn over the produce itself. Cotton was to be used as collateral for loans from Europe since Northern banking facilities were unavailable. Many patriotic planters complied with the law, and the Confederacy did indeed collect numerous bales of cotton; however, many planters, advised by their factors to be cautious, kept their cotton at home.[16]

Because of the overextended credit system, many factoring houses closed during the war. Northerners came south to open new firms, and the few older houses that continued to operate charged planters the usual fees, retired their debts, sent them cash, and sold their cotton to the Confederacy or to European markets as they were able to. They also provided as many of the planters' requested goods as were available.

When Confederate paper money dropped in value, farmers and planters returned to the barter system, and cotton again became the medium of exchange. Village storekeepers continued to act as agents, buying, selling, and holding cotton for planters as well as for factors in the port cities who were willing to buy the cotton but had no market for it. To minimize potential losses, planters stockpiled their cotton in sheds that contained only twenty-five to fifty bales each. Planters, merchants, and factors alike predicted a "cotton boom" as soon as the war was over.[17]

New Orleans was captured by a Union force in April, 1862, and its port reopened, allowing limited shipping. The success of the Confederate government's plan to create a shortage of cotton became apparent as cotton prices rose steadily. A New York price of 13¢ per pound from 1860 through 1861 became 31¢ in 1862, 67¢ in 1863, $1.50 in 1864, and dropped to 83¢ per pound in 1865. Liverpool prices rose and fell accordingly in pence per pound. The risks of blockade running were well worth taking, and many speculators and blockade runners made fortunes. By 1863,

however, Union forces began to defeat Southern armies, and Europe remained neutral.[18]

In reality, Europe had no need to become involved. In spite of the Confederacy's economic pressure and the Union blockade, American cotton continued to reach English and French textile mills. As soon as the blockade became effective in the summer of 1861, Texas planters along the Brazos and Colorado rivers began hauling cotton to Matamoros. European ships gathered off the coast and prevented Union ships from reaching Mexico. At that time, each pound of cotton was valued at one dollar in gold. Virulent objections arose because Texas cotton was bid for and bought by agents of Northern textile mills, and because this spot market was controlled by individual merchants who were as likely to bring back silk ball gowns as medicines and gunpowder to their stores in the interior of the state. In November, 1862, Texas military commander General Paul O. Hébert ordered that cotton could be exported only by the government, but he had no means of carrying out that directive. The following year General John Bankhead Magruder, who replaced Hébert, rescinded that plan and tried others, but there was no way to prevent or control the exportation of cotton through Mexico. In all, some two million dollars' worth of cotton slipped through Mexico and on to Europe.[19]

Matamoros, with its long tradition of smuggling, was the logical escape route for Texas cotton. After the border hostilities of the Mexican War had ended, townships had been built on the east, or the Texas, side of the Rio Grande. Cotton growers were lured to the area with the guarantee of dependable steamboat service for much of the year due to the navigability of the river far into the interior. Mifflin Kenedy, a Pennsylvania Quaker and a steamship captain, established Roma to compete with Charles Stillman's Rio Grande City for movement of goods along the river. Because Mexico had rigid protective tariffs on raw materials as well as on manufactured items, and many Texas or United States goods could not be imported, smuggling thrived. Commodities such as the Mexican peso (prized for the quality of its silver), gold and silver bullion, lead, animal skins, and salt reached American markets. Cotton had long been sold to the textile mills in Monterrey and Saltillo. Brownsville, on the Texas side of the river opposite Matamoros, commanded an excellent harbor and became the staging area for goods awaiting shipment into Mexico.[20]

While the Union blockade was in place, merchants, agents, and even foreign dignitaries crowded into Matamoros to buy cotton and to sell both luxuries and war materiel. European trading vessels dropped anchor in international waters, and goods were transported from ship to wharf and back by lighters. On the Texas side, steamboat captain-turned-rancher Richard King could watch long wagon train loads of cotton traversing his own open rangeland. He sold horses and camp supplies to the wagon train bosses and directed them toward the more honest cotton agents. King did not grow cotton, but he contracted to haul hundreds of bales and acted as his own agent to speculate in the market.[21]

The blockade was strengthened even more in 1863, and the Confederate government established the Cotton Bureau in Shreveport, Louisiana, to seize cotton, take it to Matamoros, and sell it for war supplies. Planters were to be paid in Confederate certificates for half the cotton (the certificates were only promises to pay), and the rest of the crop was to be confiscated and sold. Texas planters were also supposed to yield half their crops to the Confederacy, but Texas governor Pendleton Murrah devised a plan that authorized the state to buy half the planters' cotton with bonds. The plan also authorized the Texas Military Board, the state's procurement agency for war materiel, to transport all of a planter's cotton to Matamoros. Planters could sell their half for gold or goods. Planters, factors, and speculators made fortunes with absolutely no risk at all. The Cotton Bureau disintegrated. In 1864, the Confederacy forbade the exportation of all cotton unless authorized by Jefferson Davis.[22]

Plantation owners kept their slaves busy by continuing to grow and store cotton, while farmers turned to food crops, such as corn, and grew cotton on a limited scale. Cotton was expected to be the grower's cash crop as soon as the war ended.

This rationale was not unreasonable. Cotton exports had been about two billion pounds in 1860, followed by three hundred million in 1861. A mere five million pounds had been exported in 1862, with increases to eleven million in 1863 and almost twelve million in 1864. By 1865, exports had leveled off at approximately nine million pounds.[23] The logical assumption was that as soon as the war ended the cotton business would return to normal.

As hostilities drew to a close, cotton was selling for as much as $1.80 per pound. Northern armies were urged not to destroy cotton because it was needed by the textile mills, and it was the only medium of exchange available for Southerners to pay their debts to Northern bankers and merchants. Roughly two million bales were thought to be stored in remote areas, with another million to be harvested in the autumn of 1865. Unfortunately, privately owned cotton was often declared Confederate and was confiscated by unscrupulous government agents who altered the ownership identification on the bales, then sold them through independent "consignees" as privately owned, and everyone but the planter profited from the fraud.[24]

Once the war ended, planters and farmers who had saved their cotton hurried to sell it, and a few made fortunes overnight, but most planters and farmers were not so lucky. Their money was nonexistent or worthless, and the soil was either worn out from overproduction or thinned by erosion. Factors as well as farmers lost their cotton to confiscation for Confederate and state taxes, to theft, or to fires. Both groups suffered from the system of extended credit that had been in practice for more than a generation. Those factors or commission merchants who had dealt in goods besides cotton and kept their Northern business ties survived, but many declared bankruptcy, and the overall economic toll was severe.

Small farmers who owned their land and had no slaves recovered first. Their cotton was grown to pay taxes; although they had nothing left over with which to purchase material goods, they were able to feed their families and any remaining livestock. Plantation owners did not fare as well. Leonard Groce attempted to sell Liendo in 1866, planning to go to Brazil and start over. When the new owners could not make the plantation self-supporting, Groce took it back and declared bankruptcy in 1868. He began selling off parcels of land and died at Liendo in 1873.

The former slaves had gained their freedom, but they had no money, few skills with which to compete in a shattered marketplace, and no experience in self-determination. Without money for housing, food, clothes, tools, and seeds, the blacks had no way to provide for themselves. Few blacks applied for the land offered them by the federal government's 1866 Homestead Act because the land was undesirable for farming and because of white opposition to black land ownership.

Plantation owners in the Deep South tried to hire their former slaves but had no money with which to pay them. This lack of money, the rancor left over from the war, and the high price of cotton caused many landowners to offer the freedmen unacceptably rigid contracts. Wages were better "out West" where the war had not torn up the land and large farms were in need of labor, and many blacks moved to Arkansas or to Texas to begin their new lives. As cotton slowly regained its economic ascendancy, the labor supply had to be stabilized. Eventually the dual system of sharecropping and tenant farming evolved, but the laborer, whether black or white, often fared worse than the former slaves had.

Sharecropping involved an agreement between a landowner and a laborer, including the laborer's family, to work a twenty- to forty-acre farm, about all one family could physically manage. The landowner furnished everything the family needed: a house, tools, seed, and a mule; the family provided labor. They received a share of the crop as payment, usually half. Without money to buy food or clothing, however, they were forced to borrow money, usually six to ten dollars per month, or the equivalent in supplies. The landowner, whether a long-time resident or a recently arrived northerner buying up old plantation lands, provided a store from which the sharecroppers purchased goods, and he kept the account records. When the cotton crop was harvested, the sharecropper was obligated to relinquish his crop to the landowner who would sell it for him and settle the account at the store. If the crop did not make enough money to repay the advances, the sharecropper remained in bondage as inescapable as if he were a slave.

Land tenancy offered only slightly more flexibility. Farmers who had survived the war with a small amount of money, draft animals, and/or tools and equipment were able to rent their farms from a landowner for a prearranged amount of cotton. If the tenant supplied most of his needs, his share of the crop was two-thirds and that of the landowner one-third. The tenant who paid the landowner for his use of the land might, with diligence and luck, gain a measure of economic independence.[25]

Both labor systems, however, were designed to keep blacks and poor whites tied to the land. Because manufactured consumer goods rose in price as the value of cotton fluctuated, and because there were few manufacturing centers in the South to attract a large labor force, the overabundance of labor and the limited number of farms led to a debt/labor intensive system that did not begin to break down until World War II. In many ways Texas suffered the ravages of the Civil War equally with her sister states, but in one particular regard Texas enjoyed a distinct advantage. There was enough unexplored, unsettled territory left to attract even the weariest visionary. Fresh soil. Fresh seed. Fresh hope.

One by one, the river valleys between the Trinity and the Navasota and between the Brazos and the Colorado began to fill with a flood tide of immigrants who discovered that, contrary to what they had been told, the Blackland Prairie would support all the cotton they cared to plant.

CHAPTER SIX

Rebirth of an Industry

The formal end of political "reconstruction" in 1874, the year after Leonard Groce's death, marked the return of Texas to its own brand of self-government and the reentrenchment of cotton as Texas' dominant cultural and economic enterprise. Texas might have been spared military hostilities, but the breakup of the plantations and the destruction of a way of life that had been a goal to many farmers, added to the tension of restructuring the labor system and a shortage of spending capital, created as many economic wounds and emotional scars for Texans as the war did for farmers and planters in the older southern states.

In out-of-the-way places, however, pride and independence remained as intact as ever. Cotton had been grown in northeast Texas for decades due to the navigability of the Red River. Jefferson, on the Texas-Louisiana border, was a marketing and transportation center. After the war, deep East Texas, with its antebellum roots, remained a microcosm of a lost way of life.

Samuel A. Goodman, Jr., was an attorney who moved with his family from South Carolina to Tyler, Texas, in 1857. He practiced law, dutifully served throughout the war, and returned to Tyler when it ended. His health was ruined in the war, and he was unable to revive his legal practice. In 1873, he bought several hundred acres outside of Tyler, and he built a cotton gin about six miles northwest of the city between 1874 and 1875. Goodman hired as gin hands former slaves who had come to Texas with the Goodmans and remained with the family after the war.

Like others of the time, the Goodman gin building was two stories with a cotton receiving platform that opened through a door onto the second, or ginning, floor. Seed cotton, handpicked and generally free of sticks, burrs, and trash, was unloaded from the wagons and carried in baskets to storage bins on the second floor. Mules furnished power to the gin stand by means of drive wheels, pulleys, and leather belts.

The division of labor was much like it had been in earlier times. Four men were needed to carry seed cotton by basketloads from the storage bins to the gin stand and to shovel or sweep piles of seeds from the floor in front of the stand. One man oversaw the gin stand to keep it running properly. A separate baling crew carried cotton from the lint room to the indoor wooden screw press, tamped it into the box by foot, worked the mule-powered press, and tied out the finished bales. One or two mule drivers, who kept the teams moving and changed them at midday to allow them to rest, earned about twenty-five cents per day. The other men made a little more. At the end of each long, exhausting day, only six bales had been wrapped and tied for shipment to market.

The building measured sixty-four feet long by thirty-four feet wide, and except for a metal roof that was added later, had been constructed entirely of hand-hewn timbers joined by large pegs. Many of those timbers were eleven inches square, and joists thirty-six feet long supported the ginning floor.

Two teams of mules trod a path 24 feet in circumference and were harnessed to two, 12-foot-long tongues, or levers, that extended from a horizontal drive pulley, also termed a bull wheel or bull gear. This 122-inch wheel was raised 56 inches from the ground. According to Alfred M. Pendleton, cotton ginning specialist for the USDA extension service in Dallas who examined the gin in 1954, "Transfer of power to an 89-inch vertical pulley, along with increased pulley speed, was obtained by use of a cog track around the circumference of the horizontal pulley driving a 13-inch beveled [pinion] gear located on the same shaft with the 89-inch vertical pulley."[1] The vertical pulley passed through an opening in the ginning floor, and power was provided by a leather belt that connected the vertical pulley to the 8-inch diameter pulley on the saw shaft of the gin stand.

The gin stand itself did not bear a manufacturer's label, but it had 48 ten-inch saws, metal ginning ribs, and a 15-inch diameter brush. Interior breast dimensions were 38½ inches, and exterior dimensions were 41 inches. Neither overhead feeder nor condenser, available after 1868 and 1878, respectively, were used. Cotton blew into the lint room where it was collected and carried by armloads to the press.

The press, built indoors to permit baling in wet weather, was unique in design. Instead of a two-mule team, harnessed to "buzzard wings" and turning the wooden screw inside a stationary box, at this gin plant the mule team turned the press box itself around an 8-inch diameter wooden screw that remained in place. A cross member was attached to the top of the screw, and it, stated Pendleton in a 1954 article, "worked up and down in two vertical guides to keep the screw properly aligned as the two mules turned the entire press assembly around the screw." The press was down-packing, and the bale was finished out at ground level.[2] Apparently the gin stand, pulleys, and gears were manufactured, but the screw and press box were locally made and were of rougher construction. The press box door slid aside to allow access to the bale.

Used until about 1890, this plantation gin was never converted to steam power, as many nineteenth century gins were, but because of the durability of its construction the gin survived many years of neglect. Sallie Goodman Callaway, Samuel Goodman's daughter, had a sheet iron roof added to protect the interior of the building. The gin drew attention in 1954 because of its remarkable state of preservation. Pendleton, Edward H. Bush, then executive vice-president of the Texas Cotton Ginners' Association in Dallas, and Beverly G. Reeves, ginning specialist for the Texas A&M Extension Service at College Station gathered support for the relocation of the gin. In 1961, the building and its entire contents were moved by truck to the Texas Tech University campus in Lubbock, and they remain part of the University's museum system today.[3]

With hard work and good business sense, the Goodmans survived the post–Civil War years, but most Texans and Southerners could not achieve the same economic independence. Cotton that had sold for eighty-three cents per pound dropped steadily: a pound sold for thirty cents in 1866, seventeen cents in 1870, and thirteen cents in 1875. Land became worthless, and while bartering sufficed for most economic transactions, taxes had to be paid in cash. Plantation owners lost their property and their cultural identity.[4] The surviving small farmers did not fare much better; with cotton as their only cash crop, they had no choice but to keep planting and praying that their factors would find a better price and extend a little more credit.

Those factoring firms that had survived the war returned to normal, and a few new firms opened for business. They sold cotton, bought goods, loaned cash, retired debts, and made investments, but now their primary objective was to help the farmers regain their credit.

One such factor was Harris Kempner, a Polish immigrant who had arrived in New York City in 1854 at the age of seventeen, worked as a bricklayer's assistant during the day, and studied English at night. He tried working as a brick subcontractor, but a slump in the housing market put an end to that. In 1856, he traveled to Texas and settled in Cold Springs (now Coldspring) in San Jacinto County. He opened a general merchandise store in Cold Springs. Then, leaving a young man in charge of the store, he traveled about East Texas as an itinerant peddler. At first he sold only what he could carry on his back, but he soon expanded his sales territory by means of horse and wagon. In his travels he wore a black suit, white cravat, and beaver hat, and he made a very favorable impression. In a short amount of time, he became quite successful, even hiring a young man to travel to Houston or Galveston to buy goods for the store when he could not make the journey himself. Like many other rural merchants, he made loans and extended credit, took payment in the form of notes against future cotton crops, accepted payments for debts in cotton, and bought and sold cotton for area farmers. He fought for the Confederacy during the war, and when he returned to East Texas afterward, he was able to reestablish his business.

Although successful, he believed his future was limited in East Texas, and in 1871, he moved to Galveston. The following year he formed a partnership with Marx Marx, an established wholesale grocer, to sell wholesale groceries, tobacco, coffee, and sugar, and to import liquor. According to Kempner's biographer, from this solid base of diversified interests, Marx and Kempner

> adapted their business practices to the fact that their inland customers could pay bills only seasonally, after selling harvests, and then often in kind. Crop-sharing and crop liens were becoming increasingly common adaptations to these situations, but Marx and Kempner did not find these devices attractive. . . . Losses resulted when the promised crops did not come in. Aware of the risks, Marx and Kempner extended credit to retail merchants inland and to farmers, their security being their interest as agents in the sale of future crops. The partners had to find purchasers for the commodities pledged to them as payments for debts and, if cotton was the security, also to adjust selling prices to cover the costs of

grading, compressing, bagging, and warehousing the commodities."

Marx and Kempner sent their traveling agents inland to the new railhead towns as well as to older communities. The salesmen, or drummers, offered credit to local merchants. "Some of the more adventurous grocers and a few favored cotton farmers became local bankers by re-extending to growers in need of foodstuffs, seed, labor, and tools, the credit granted to them by Marx and Kempner, and, later, by Kempner alone. Growers consigned future crops to the local lenders, who would sell them for a fee or percentage to apply against loans. Some number of these inland banker-cotton agents then committed these assets to Marx and Kempner as agents for either the grower or businessman, or both."[5] This was basically a continuation of the old factoring system, but with the addition of salesmen traveling inland to acquire the business in place of the factor/planter one-on-one relationship. The element of risk remained the same. Kempner's wisdom in keeping his cash assets during the war and in moving to one of the nation's most active port cities made him a millionaire before his death in 1894.

By 1870, in other parts of the country, the golden age of independent factoring was drawing to a close. The New Orleans Cotton Exchange, organized that year, regulated the futures market and established cotton prices. Transatlantic cablegrams and telegrams made pricing changes from around the world immediately accessible. English buyers and even steamship captains participated in the "spot" market, referring to cotton immediately available ("on the spot"), and transactions had to be made more quickly than the factors' time-honored methods allowed.

English buyers examining samples of cotton in a broker's office. *From* Frank Leslie's Illustrated Newspaper, *November 16, 1878; courtesy Institute of Texan Cultures*

Nor did a factor's knowledge of where to find the cotton remain his special field. Agents of brokers and of textile mills traveled inland from the ports, and either farmers or merchants handling the farmers' cotton on consignment could make their own arrangements. As rail lines were rebuilt and expanded throughout the South, farmers and merchants began to deal directly with northern and foreign textile mill buyers.

Other improvements also reduced the factor's role. Compresses were still in use in the ports, but many were being set up in the interior growing areas so that more and smaller bales could be shipped at accordingly lower freight rates. Another advantage was the newly invented through bill of lading by which a farmer or merchant could ship cotton by rail to ports on the Atlantic and then by steamship on to Europe. Contractors made arrangements for sampling, classing, and compressing the cotton but did not perform the personal services of the factors. On the other hand, the farmer or village merchant could establish a price quickly, then sell, and transport the cotton straight to the buyer. Some factoring firms diversified to other commodities, some joined the larger brokerage firms, and some closed their doors forever.[6]

With or without the factor, King Cotton began to regain control over the South and to spread his domain westward. Worn-out soil in the Deep South and a Texas law that protected up to two hundred acres of a farmer's homestead from foreclosure for debt led to a tide of immigration into Texas that began in 1872. Over one hundred thousand people arrived that year alone. Texas's population jumped from about eight hundred thousand in 1870 to over two million in 1890. Cotton production rose from approximately one-half million bales in 1874 to one and one-half million in 1886.[7]

The German communities, which had not relied on slave labor, were among the first to recover from the war. Cotton cultivation expanded westward into Gillespie, Medina, and Bandera Counties. Gins were built at Fredericksburg and Pipe Creek, Comfort and Castroville. New Braunfels became a cotton center with buyers from Saltillo, Mexico, contracting for Hill Country cotton. As Frederick Law Olmsted had advised, a textile mill was built on the Comal River. The water-powered mill, known as the Comal Manufacturing Company, opened in March, 1863, with 900 spindles and 21 looms. It turned out common yarn and such fabrics as domestic (a general-purpose cloth used for sheets and clothing) and Osnaburg (a strong, heavy-to-medium-weight fabric that used all white or waste cotton and from which sacks, upholstery,

Shipping cotton from Charleston, S.C. *From* Frank Leslie's Illustrated Newspaper, *November 16, 1878. Courtesy Institute of Texan Cultures*

or curtains were made). The mill employed forty workers, mostly women and children, and had a payroll of ten thousand dollars per year. Clean local cotton was bought for ten cents per pound and inferior, or "spotted," cotton for four cents per pound. The mill ceased operation when a tornado ripped through the mill's third floor in September, 1869.

F. B. Hoffman, who had built a horse-powered gin in New Braunfels in 1857, converted from animal to steam power in 1870, signaling the coming shift in technology. That same year rail lines reached San Antonio, opening land to immigrants and new markets to established cotton growers.

Many historians equate the westward expansion of the railroads with the need of ranchers to get cattle to midwestern markets, but since cattle were still driven overland twenty years after the war, the equally powerful need of farmers to get their cotton to interior cities, to ports, and to the northern textile mills cannot be minimized. The postwar years became synonymous with the rapid development of the railroads and the more dependable movement of goods.

Because of the tiresomely muddy conditions of the few available roads and the long distances to American markets, Texas had begun planning a railroad system during the days of the Republic. Between 1836 and 1841, four railroad companies were chartered by the legislature to provide service to Houston, Harrisburg, and Galveston, but all four failed due to lack of funding. Between 1850 and 1851, Sidney Sherman, backed by Eastern investors, started construction of the Buffalo Bayou, Brazos & Colorado Railway in the Harrisburg area. Houston tapped into that line in 1856 and diverted a significant amount of commerce from Harrisburg. Two years later, the tap line was

sold by Houston to Brazoria County planters who pushed the line southward into their sugar cane district, and the "Sugar Road" brought sugar and syrup into Houston in 1859.[8]

Paul Bremond's Houston & Texas Central Railroad, established in 1853, reached Cypress Creek in 1856 and Hempstead, fifty miles west of Houston, in 1858. Even while under construction, the rail line had begun earning back its investment by hauling passengers and cotton in early 1857. A causeway built by the Galveston, Houston and Henderson Railroad connected Galveston and Houston in 1860. A passenger ticket cost $2.50 and cotton sent by train reached Galveston's wharves in less than three hours instead of the twenty hours the overland trip took.[9]

Merchants like Kempner influenced the type and amount of business that flowed through port cities such as Galveston. Exports rather than imports dominated trade, both before and after the war. Goods came overland to Houston and were transferred by barges and steamers to Galveston where they were placed on deep-draught ships. In 1854, the year Harris Kempner had arrived in New York City, Galveston exported 82,000 bales; by 1900, a few years after his death, 2,278,000 bales were shipped from Galveston.[10] Galveston might not have been as progressive as Norfolk, Virginia, where trains backed cars onto the wharves so that cotton could be loaded directly into cargo holds. But there was no question that the railroads were reorganizing the market patterns of the Cotton Kingdom.[11]

Local railroads began to merge with the great national lines: International and Great Northern (1873), Missouri-Kansas-Texas (1873), and Southern Pacific (1881). No longer were barges and ox-teams the only ways to transport cotton to market. If the price of cotton per pound was low, land was also plentiful and cheap. The arrival of the railroads made immigrating worth the gamble that the price of cotton would rise. Farmers, many of them Czech and German immigrants, bypassed heavily timbered East Texas and the crowded bottomlands of the Trinity and Brazos rivers, and they moved onto the open plains. The Blackland Prairie not only supported cotton, but turned out enormous crops.

In 1870, 8,829 bales were produced in McLennan County (compared with 2,320 bales in 1860, which were taken by wagon train to Houston for sale), and the arrival of the Santa Fe, Missouri-Kansas-Texas (M-K-T or "Katy"), Cotton Belt, and International & Great Northern (I & GN) railroads made Waco, with its strategic position on the Brazos and in the heart of the newly opened blacklands, the new commercial hub of Texas. Twenty years later, Waco businesses included cotton mills, compresses, cottonseed oil mills, and a textile mill. A cotton picking machine was being developed, and a cotton chopper was being manufactured and sold by an inventor in nearby McGregor.

As the gins moved westward into the Blackland Prairie, so also did the compress companies. No longer confined to the ports, the compresses were erected in strategically situated towns to take advantage of large crops and expanding railroad facilities. For example, the prairie and the river bottoms produced large crops that had to be hauled overland to market by wagons until the Cotton Belt Railroad reached Gatesville, Coryell County, in 1882. Shortly thereafter, the Southwestern Compress Company of Tyler, Texas, established a compress facility alongside the Cotton Belt tracks and near the depot. The compress consisted of a long, open, wooden platform with an office at one end, the compress machinery in the center, and the boiler room at the other end. Steam was used to provide power for a hydraulic ram that squeezed a five-hundred-pound bale of cotton to about half its original size, making it possible to store or ship two bales in what had been the space taken up by one. Baled cotton was brought into town in wagons and was first taken to the cotton yards for storage, then moved to the platform in dray wagons. After the bales were compressed, owners' names were stencilled on the bales, which were then placed in box cars or on flat cars for shipment.

The Tyler company sent Earl Fain, an experienced superintendent, to Gatesville to manage the facility, six black men who were skilled press men and truckers (a "truck" was a four-wheeled, hand-pulled cart), and John Bohopolo to take charge of the steam engine. Bohopolo was a Greek who came from Goose Creek in Harris County and was known to earn his living by fishing and smuggling in the Gulf of Mexico when not occupied as chief engineer at the compress from October through December. An impressive man weighing two hundred pounds, he was known for his strength. He wore a suit of black broadcloth and a white shirt with no tie instead of the usual blue overalls, and he wore gloves when he operated the pressure levers. He had a dark complexion and a waxed handlebar mustache, drank whiskey as if it were water, and yelled deep-sea curses to keep everyone "stepping lively."[12]

Cotton was such a powerful force in the livelihood and culture of Central Texas that Wacoans built the Texas Cotton Palace in 1894 to celebrate the previous year's sales of 120,000 bales. Governor James S. Hogg opened the festivities, complete with horse- or ox-drawn floats, and a large crowd attended the exhibits and a carnival with games and rides. Elaborate balls, with the crowning of a cotton queen, took place inside the Cotton Palace coliseum. The wooden structure burned to the ground six weeks after it opened, but the Cotton Palace was rebuilt and was reopened in 1910 with a large carnival midway and rides for children and adults. The gateposts and archway at the main entrance were filled with cotton bales, and the entire pavilion was brilliantly lit at night. This more successful Cotton Palace lasted until 1930.

After a long hard spring and summer of backbreaking work and heartbreaking worry about insect and weather damage, farmers had yet one more concern before they could buy essential supplies and head home. No longer dependent upon or advised by factors, they found that selling their cotton could be as risky as growing it. For example, cotton buyers occupied many offices lining Waco's courthouse square, and McLennan County farmers brought wagon loads of cotton to the square to be sold to markets in Europe, South America, and India. The buyers cut samples from the farmers' cotton in the morning and then waited until the end of the day, when the farmers were eager to start home, to set a price that was often below its true value. Since the farmers were in a hurry and had no idea what their cotton was worth, they were at the mercy of the buyers. To combat this system, newsman Ephraim S. Fentress, who was later owner and publisher of the *Waco News-Tribune,* traveled by train to College Station to make arrangements for a cotton classer to come to Waco to establish fair prices. The local buyers protested until Fentress threatened to publish their names. The cotton classer from Texas A&M University set fair prices, and area farmers benefited by more than one-half million dollars.[13]

Farmers also benefited from the discovery that cottonseed, always considered a waste product, had surprisingly valuable properties. Crushed cottonseed hulls were useful as fertilizer and cattle feed, and the oil was quite good for cooking. Either local ginners acted as buyers for the seed and sold it to the cottonseed mills, or farmers collected their seed from the storage houses adjoining the gin plants and sold what they did not need for the next year's crop to the mills in Waco.

The arrival of the railroads established many small towns and gins in the Waco area. As soon as the depot was built, the usual collection of saloons and hotels, mercantile businesses and cotton gins immediately followed. The Katy railroad reached Elm Mott

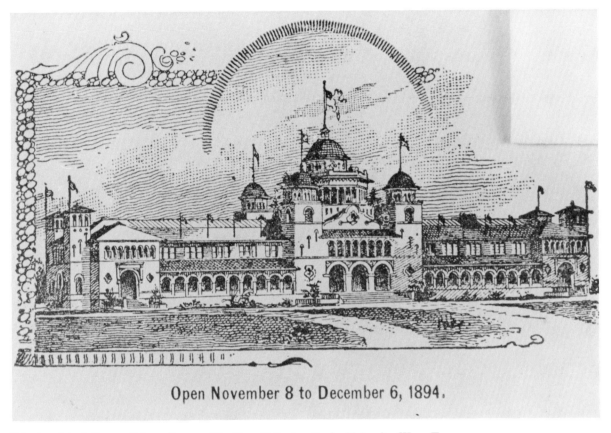

Open November 8 to December 6, 1894.

Waco's original Cotton Palace. *Courtesy The Texas Collection, Baylor University, Waco, Texas*

in 1881, and the town's first gin was established the same year. McGregor's first gin was built in 1882. As the railroad advanced, gins were set up in Crawford (1885), West (1890), and Lorena, where five gins were operating by 1900. The town of Riesel was named for William H. Riesel, who remodeled and improved an older gin in 1890. The Bosqueville gin was known to run twenty-four hours a day during the season.[14]

The importance of these small community gins cannot be minimized. The day of the single plantation gin, except in a few isolated places, was gone. The gin plant, as much as the general store, the school, and the church, was the purpose for the town's existence. It was more than a place for commercial enterprise, for storytelling by old-timers, and for education in the mysterious ways of cotton. It was more than a laboratory for creative genius to keep old machinery running and to modify or invent for the sake of speed and dependability. The gin was the gathering place for hopes and dreams—based upon the price of cotton—to flourish, to adapt, or to die. No greater symbol for the all-pervasive importance of the gin to the community can be found than in that of the pond behind the gin at Cego (near Bruce-

ville-Eddy), which was often used for community baptism.

The gin was the center of the community's activity, and much of the success of that activity depended upon the gin plant's technology.

Newer gin plants did not use mules at all but burned wood, coal, or gin trash to fire the steam engines that powered the pulleys. A turn-of-the-century photograph of the "modern" gin at Elm Mott shows walls constructed of sheet metal, a large, covered drive-through area for the wagons, a smokestack, and a yard full of uniform rectangular bales wrapped with jute or burlap, tied with steel straps, and secured with buckles. Cotton continued to be handpicked and taken to the gin in wagons where it was unloaded into baskets and placed in storage stalls or bins until ready to be ginned.

Hand-feeding cotton into the gin stands, with its inherent danger, was made faster and safer by the addition of a feeder box placed directly over the gin stand. A patent for a mechanical feeder was issued to Alex Jones as early as 1834, but the first feeder with a flat, slatted apron that moved inside the box was patented in 1872. Its purpose was to move, rather

Cotton buyer classing a farmer's crop in McGregor. *Courtesy* The McGregor Mirror

than to clean, the seed cotton dumped into it from baskets.

A better design was that of J. W. Thorn of Courtland, Alabama, whose 1868 patent for a feeder included a "cotton picker," a spiked cylinder that cleaned some trash from the cotton and served to discharge cotton into the roll box. According to inventor and historian Charles A. Bennett, the Thorn "cotton picker" had two beater cylinders with "concave screens and ratchet feeding devices to regulate the flow of the cotton."[15] This cleaning feeder would become an integral part of the gin stand.

Condensers, vertical wooden boxes placed directly behind the gin stands and linked by flues, became commonplace after 1878. The movement of air forced the cleaned cotton out of the stand and through the condenser where an internal drum of fine wire formed batts. These batts were carried to the iron or steel screw press, which was placed directly behind the condenser. Moving the press into the gin building made the entire process of ginning and baling faster.

The press remained limited to a single box manually operated by lever and rope winch or by a wooden screw press operated by horses. The first up-pressing, single-box steam press appeared in 1870. Up-packing presses with iron or steel (either double or single) screws were available, and by 1878 screw presses had

Main Street, McGregor, where market day was every third Monday. *Courtesy* The McGregor Mirror

The gin plant at Sparta. *Courtesy The Texas Collection, Baylor University, Waco, Texas*

Community baptism at a pond behind a gin plant at Cego (near Bruceville-Eddy). *Courtesy Ken and Jane Gates, Moody, Texas*

steam plungers that were driven by the same engines that powered the gin stands. The operator raked cotton from the lint slide into the press box and controlled the steam piston tramper by means of a valve. Only one bale at a time could be formed, compressed, wrapped, and tied. A public or "custom" gin plant might consist of two gin stands and a single press. As mule power was replaced by the steam engine, commercial ginning began to be profitable.

Cotton was still cleaned by manual sorting or whipping, and by the feeders above and moting bars inside the stand, but some trash always entered the

Modern gin at Elm Mott. *Courtesy The Texas Collection, Baylor University, Waco, Texas*

gin stand with the seed cotton. One particular improvement in the gin stand during this period was the double-rib huller. Because of damp weather resulting from early frosts, bolls would rot on the stalks and pull off with the cotton when it was picked. Bolls

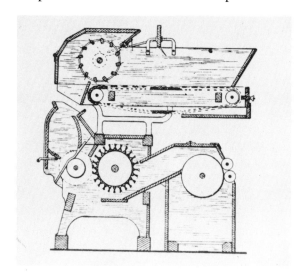

Feeder, gin stand, and condenser in 1891. *From C. A. Bennett,* Cotton Ginning Systems in the United States and Auxiliary Developments

fed into the gin damaged the lint. The single-rib huller with its "knuckle" or "knee" attached to the straight ginning rib, as designed by Holmes and modified by Beadle, knocked out hulls, leaves, sticks, and stems. However, it permitted hulls and seeds to mix, which was undesirable.

On November 22, 1881, Washington L. Ellis, who was employed by the Daniel Pratt Gin Company, received a patent for a two-piece, or split-rib huller, which Pratt began manufacturing in 1883. The split-rib, or double-rib, huller was a device with two "fingers" through which the saw passed and which deflected hulls or trash. The two-piece huller proved unsatisfactory, however, because of the way one piece was attached to the roll box cover and the other piece was attached to the bottom of the breast. On August 27, 1889, Ellis received a patent for a solid, or one-piece, split-rib huller. This curved rib kept the "knuckle" or "knee" used on straight ribs. The single-rib plain gin, without hullers on the ribs, was used as late as 1920, and double-rib huller gins, which successfully separated hulls from seeds, were manufactured into the 1950s.[16]

Gin manufacturing companies were limited to gin stands, feeders, and condensers. The presses were

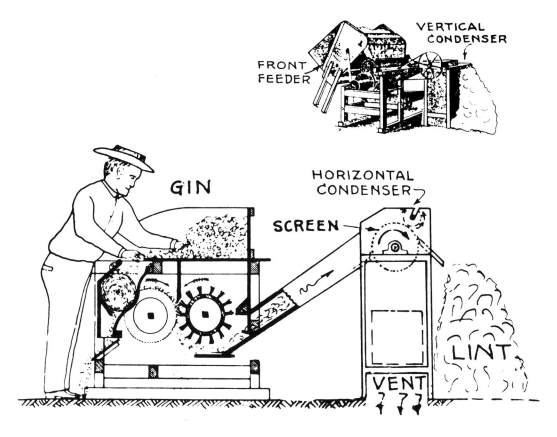

Feeder and gin stand with detail of condenser. *From C. A. Bennett,* Cotton Ginning Systems in the United States and Auxiliary Developments

made by other companies. Both were sold through agents until 1886, when they began to be sold directly to their customers. Carpenters and blacksmiths may have made a few gins, but most were bought in pieces and assembled by carpenters and blacksmiths or were bought as complete units through hardware or general merchandise stores. The Goodman gin was a combination of purchased and handmade parts. M. L. Parry's Star Foundry shipped the iron portions of presses and included plans for building the frame. Once a carpenter had built the frame, any mechanic could assemble the iron parts and complete the press. Manufacturers such as Pratt, Eagle, Gullett, and Lummus began to provide complete gin and press units after 1886.

There were fourteen gin manufacturing companies in 1886, including the Chatham Machine Company in Bryan, and seven press manufacturers, none of which were in Texas.[17] The R. K. Chatham Machine Company of Bryan was the only gin manufacturing company in Texas in the late nineteenth century and served ginners for thirty years.

Roland Kinchen Chatham was born in Perry County, Alabama, in 1834. His father, George K. Chatham, had worked for Daniel Pratt and met William R. Rhodes, an engineer who also worked for Pratt. Rhodes married George Chatham's sister Elizabeth. George Chatham, who had fought in the War of 1812 and fathered twelve children, gave up manufacturing Pratt gins and became a cotton planter. The Chatham and Rhodes families immigrated to Leon County, Texas, which reminded them of home, where they settled in 1851. They bought large tracts of land and manufactured furniture and cotton gins. Several years later they moved to Huntsville, in Walker County, where they continued to make furniture and cotton gins.

Young Roland Chatham fought with Terry's Rangers at the battle of Shiloh in 1862, sustained a head wound at a later battle in Pennsylvania, and was sent to a doctor's home in Louisville, Kentucky, to recuperate. There he met T. M. Nagle of Akron, Ohio, whose family owned a company that manufactured, among other things, boilers for steam engines. The

Hand-operated bale press. *From C. A. Bennett,* Cotton Ginning Systems in the United States and Auxiliary Developments

two men agreed that if they survived the war, they would form a partnership. As soon as Chatham was better, he made his way farther south to stay with a cousin. When the war ended, he walked back to Texas, where his family had been forced to declare bankruptcy and sell the factory. The last mule was sold for $1.25. The family moved to Bryan in 1866 and opened a gin manufacturing plant in 1869. Roland was the salesman, Rhodes the engineer, and Nagle furnished steel for the plant's machinery and for raw materials for the gin stands.

The plant site, located near railroad tracks, consisted of a small office, a smithy, two warehouses, a lumber kiln, a water tank, the manufacturing plant, and a paint department. The Chatham home was about five hundred feet from the paint building. The gin plant was an L-shaped building. The shorter section housed an iron lathe room downstairs, and the upstairs was used for woodworking, warehousing, and had a mill rock room for the grist mills that the company also made. The longer section was dedicated to saw sharpening and to finishing condensers and feeders. A cistern and well provided water to the boiler for steam power. Fire prevention was a concern since the building was wooden, and barrels of

water were placed on top of the building; a triangular gong was used to announce fire drills. Sixty to seventy-five people were employed there.

According to a catalogue dated February 21, 1876, the company manufactured gins of 40, 45, 50, 60, 65, 70, and 80 saws, and the gins were priced at $4.00 per saw. Feeders, condensers, and indoor presses were also made, and the company acted as manufacturers' agents for engines, boilers, shafts, belts, pulleys, and other types of presses, and it later added elevators to its list of gin equipment.

Many gin plants were still animal-powered and used "common ginhouse gearing." A sixty-saw gin could turn out four bales per day and one thousand bales per season. Fifty-saw gins could produce ninety bales per season, or with four horses, four bales per day. Steam plants, however, produced considerably more: seven bales per day for a fifty-saw plant and one bale per hour or ten bales per day for an eighty-saw plant. In the 1880s the Chatham Gin Machine Company advertised its gins by displaying complete units (gin stand, feeder, and condenser) in New Orleans and at an exposition in Atlanta. Roland Chatham sold the company to two nephews (A. M. and H. G. Rhodes) in 1897. The factory burned in 1899, the year of Chatham's death, and the company ceased to exist.[18]

By 1880, the rich Brazos bottomlands and the Blackland Prairie were producing more cotton than the gins could handle, and the entire process, from unloading cotton from the wagons to tying out the bales, took too long. Farmers needed the money from the sale of their cotton to make purchases and settle debts, and they were not prepared to wait weeks or months for their cotton to be ginned, baled, and sold. If forced to wait, they could lose stored cotton to fires, and there was always the risk that cotton prices would drop. The few remaining plantation gins and the growing number of custom gins could not keep up. A revolution in the ginning process was inevitable.

Between 1883 and 1885, Robert S. Munger would devise system ginning, the concept and technology still in use today. Born in Fayette County in July, 1854, Munger had been educated locally, but attended Trinity University, then at Tehuacana in Limestone County. His father, a sawmill owner, moved to Mexia, a few miles from Tehuacana, and built a gin which he turned over to the young man to operate.

Frustrated by the long lines of wagons, impatient farmers, and an inability to fill available rail cars, Robert Munger completely reorganized the hundreders formerly attached to each gin stand. The condenser contained a screen drum which separated the cotton from the air flow, creating a batt, and provided another cleaning phase. Dust and fine particles were blown out through chimney stacks that passed through the roof.

According to John Streun, chief engineer for Hardwicke-Etter in Sherman, Texas, who knew Munger, the inventor had originally designed his lint flue with a belt in the bottom to run horizontally along the flue and then incline upward to the condenser. Soon after putting this into operation, he discovered that the belts were not running, and yet cotton was spilling out of the condenser as it was supposed to. He was told that the belt had not operated for several days. What must have been Munger's relief to find that brushes inside the gin stands provided enough air to blow the cotton all the way to the condenser.

Robert S. Munger, inventor of system ginning. *Courtesy Continental Eagle Corporation*

year-old tradition of plantation ginning. His concept was to automate the process, eliminating as much of the hand labor as possible, by using fans to create a pneumatic system. Seed cotton was drawn out of wagons by "telescope" suction pipes in the wagon drive-through. The seed cotton was conveyed by air stream to a separator, mounted above the gin stands, that was also known as a "vacuum box," a "blow box," or a "cotton dropper." Inside the separator was an elongated section of screen. A suction fan was placed at the back of the screen, and a pipe was placed in front of the screen. The separator was attached to the distributor, a wooden trough or conduit with a moving, spiked belt ("drag belt"). When the fan was turned on, cotton was drawn from the wagon into and through the separator, and was dropped through the pipe into the wooden conduit. The cotton was then distributed by means of the moving belt to Thorn feeders above each stand. In this way a series, or battery, of gin stands could be linked together, resulting in a continuous flow of cotton to the stands.

All gins were connected to a common lint flue that was placed behind the gin stands. The lint was then blown through this long wooden flue to a single large condenser that replaced the small unit condens-

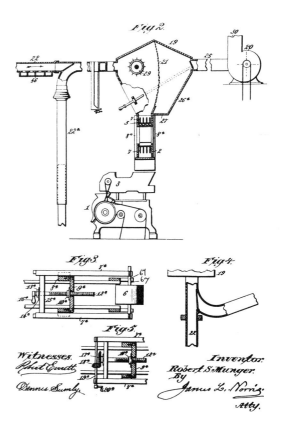

Robert Munger patent drawings (July 12, 1892). Note telescope, fan, separator, "dropper," feeder, and gin stand. *Courtesy Continental Eagle Corporation*

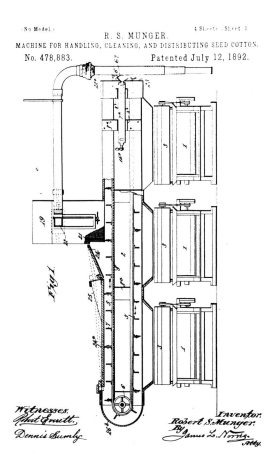

Artist's drawings of Robert Munger's system gin at Mexia in 1883 and of its 1898 expansion. *From C. A. Bennett,* Cotton Ginning Systems in the United States and Auxiliary Developments

Robert Munger patent drawings (July 12, 1892). Note battery of gin stands connected by belt distributor. *Courtesy Continental Eagle Corporation*

To handle the increased amount of cotton coming from the condenser, Munger invented the double-box press. Each box, attached to a wooden center post, was sized to contain one bale. Even though the press relied on a screw for compression, the first presses had required foot power to tamp cotton into the box. Still, the presses were an improvement because lint was no longer carried by hand from individual condensers or from the old-fashioned lint room. The lint now flowed along a slanting chute or slide from the condenser to the press box. As one box was being filled with lint, the other was being pressed, wrapped, tied, and rolled out onto the floor to be weighed, making baling as continuous as ginning.[19]

One component of Munger's design elevated and moved cotton to the feeders, but a man was needed to cut off the suction to the feeders when they became full. There was no way to discharge excess cotton because the distributor was closed. Since Mun-

ger's goal was to create a constantly moving stream of cotton, this stop-and-start action defeated his purpose. Munger opened one end of the distributor to allow excess cotton to fall out. This overflow was signaled by a bell or horn. The fan creating the suction would then be shut off. The excess cotton was fed by hand into a hole in a floor or wall until it could be picked up by a separate telescope and returned to the system. Eventually a "circulation loop" allowed cotton to return to the wagon to be picked up again by the telescope.[20] Munger's system used fan-driven air to move seed cotton through rectangular pipes into storage houses in the gin yard to await ginning, and the same pipes were used to convey seed to storage bins where they could be retrieved by the farmer. Ten years later (1895–96), the Mexia gin plant was the largest in the country. It consisted of three batteries of five, seventy-saw gin stands.

In the intervening years, Munger's radical new system had been so successful that he built a manufacturing plant in Dallas. He incorporated the Munger Improved Cotton Machine Manufacturing Company in 1887, selling stock to acquire needed funds. To fill orders for ginning systems from east of the Mississippi River, Munger realized he needed to be closer to that market. He traveled to Birmingham and formed a partnership with W. T. Northington (an attorney) and Daniel Pratt (nephew of the founder) to create the Munger-Northington-Pratt Company. Supported by the foundation of the Dan-iel Pratt Gin Company, this new alliance would form the framework of the Continental Gin Company. Robert Munger's system ginning led to a technological explosion that paralleled the invention of the gin in importance—and opened vast stretches of the far West to the cotton farmer.

White Gold and the Gin Rush

In 1888, while Robert Munger was expanding his company in Dallas and enlarging his gin in Mexia, German immigrant Hermann Focke was building his own gin plant only a few miles from Mexia, between the ghost town of Springfield and the Navasota River bottomlands (near the site of the 1836 Comanche Indian raid on Fort Parker).

Although steam engines were being used more often then, Focke's was a mule-powered gin. The single gin stand was a sixty-saw unit with a feeder and a condenser. When a batt of lint had passed through the condenser, it was hand carried to an up-packing press that stood on the ginning floor only a few steps from the condenser. The slotted horizontal feeder, gin stand, vertical condenser, and baling press were manufactured by the Carver Cotton Gin Company of East Bridgewater, Massachusetts.

Most of the second, or ginning, floor was made up of fourteen bins or stalls, indicating that Hermann Focke was ginning his neighbors' cotton as well as his own. Seed cotton was carried in baskets or sacks from the loading platform and stored in the stalls until ginned. After the lint was baled, cottonseed was placed in an assigned stall until it was retrieved by the farmer to whom it belonged.

The gin plant bore characteristics that made it unique. Hand-lettered signs painted around a second-floor window and on the steps leading inside read, "No Smooking [*sic*], No Credit, No Matches." A copper stencil used for labeling the bales was designed with M-F Focke, a star, and GALV. "M-F" meant Mary Focke, the ginner's wife; the star represented Texas; and GALV was the abbreviation for Galveston, the cotton's destination. Focke's plantation gin was outdated even when it was new, and Focke closed his gin in 1900. The building was cared for by Focke's son and grandson until it burned in the late 1960s.[1] Individuals such as Hermann Focke may have ginned their neighbors' cotton, but by the turn of the century, Robert Munger's system ginning made their traditional gin plants obsolete.

System ginning, which depended upon less hu-

man labor and yet produced an increased number of bales at a faster rate, made cotton ginning more profitable than ever. Cotton growing expanded west toward Lubbock and south into the Rio Grande Valley. San Diego in Duval County, west of Corpus Christi, had two system gin plants in place by 1890. Only four years previously, cotton had been ginned in San Diego by a mule-powered, thirty-saw gin manufactured by the Brown Cotton Gin Co. of New London, Connecticut, which could turn out two or three bales per day. The baled cotton was taken by wagon trains to Corpus Christi for shipment. At the time (1886), Corpus Christi itself had no gin. That thirty-saw gin remained in the possession of the owners as they modernized but was later sold, and it changed hands several times after that. The gin stand was donated to the Texas Tech Museum in 1968.[2]

Cotton was grown in limited amounts on the South Plains; only twenty-six bales were produced in 1901, and they were ginned in Colorado City, one hundred miles southeast of Lubbock. In 1904, a group of Lubbock County farmers formed a cooperative to build a gin, and the "Cap" gin (named for the nearby Caprock Escarpment) was completed in December, 1904, at a cost of four thousand dollars. The gin turned out seven hundred bales during the 1905 season.

The gin was first built of wood but was covered with corrugated tin in 1906. The cotton was brought to the gin in wagons, which were emptied by means of a "sucker pipe." The plant was powered by a steam engine that burned cotton trash such as sticks and burrs for fuel. The bales were shifted from a dock onto flatbed wagons or were stored on the site. West Texas cotton went to textile mills along the Mississippi River and in Mexico.[3] Steam power and technological improvements made commercial ginning profitable, and gin plants established by their owners for public use became known as "custom" gins.

Early photographs indicate the turn-of-the-century transition from plantation to commercial gin-

Hermann Focke family in front of their new gin a few miles from Mexia, 1888. *Courtesy A. M. Pendleton*

ning. A two-story, 1910 gin plant built at Coleman, 230 miles southeast of Lubbock, had corrugated metal siding, a seed hopper so that the farmer could collect his own seed for the next year's crop, and a screw conveyor to carry extra seed to an auxiliary seed house. Steam furnished power to the gin stands and to a pump for the indoor press. A tower supplied water for the boiler, and a smokestack rose high above the roofline so that wind could carry away any sparks. The bales were rolled down boards from the ginning floor onto the loading dock and weighed on a platform scale. The farmer's initials or cattle brand and a bale number were painted on the bagging with a short-bristled brush and india ink. Jute bagging and metal straps were used consistently, and bale size was

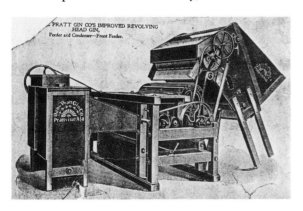

Pratt gin stand with feeder and condenser, 1890. *Courtesy Continental Eagle Corporation*

uniform. In contrast to the neatness of the bales, the photograph shows gears from an indoor screw press thrown carelessly about the yard.

Steam engines had been available since the early nineteenth century, but they remained in limited use due to manufacturing irregularities, the constant danger of fire, and the cost of an engine (about two thousand dollars). Steam power for cotton gins was tried in the 1850s but was not generally accepted until after the Civil War. As improvements in manufacturing made the engines safer and increased production made them more plentiful, the price of an engine dropped to about one thousand dollars. Individual gin owners like Samuel Goodman and Hermann Focke might not have the capital for a steam engine, but an association of farmers could combine resources to build a custom gin plant. By the 1890s this practice, foreshadowed by the arrival of the railroad, had become commonplace.

Steam plants, as they were known, were all designed similarly. Water was pumped into a tower, still a prominent feature of many old gins. The flow was controlled by valves, and the water was forced by gravity into pipes connected to either a steam injector or a feedwater pump to maintain a safe, correct water level in the boiler. Wood, coal, and even gin trash were used to fuel the fire in the boiler, which converted the water to steam. Kept under pressure and regulated by safety valves, the steam forced a piston to move back and forth inside a cylinder. A

Gin at Coleman, on the South Plains, in 1910. *Courtesy Donald Baird*

connecting rod attached to the piston was linked to a crankshaft on which a large, heavy flywheel was mounted.

A governor regulated the flow of steam to the cylinder to maintain the number of revolutions per minute needed to drive the machinery. When the engine reached the desired speed, a lever controlling a clutch was engaged, and power was transmitted by means of a pulley to a line shaft, underneath the ginning floor, that extended the length of the building. Large pulleys on the line shaft were connected to smaller pulleys by flat belts, and once proper speed was achieved, each component began to rotate: fans (for suction), belt distributors, saws and brushes inside gin stands, and seed conveyors. The gradual buildup of power kept belts from being thrown and allowed machinery to begin working simultaneously. An individual belt shifter acting as a clutch controlled power to the tramper and to the hydraulic pump that furnished power to the bale press. This allowed the press to be stopped and turned as one bale was tied out and another begun. (With the diesel engines that soon followed, the same buildup of power was required to "pull" the gin, but the diesel required more revolutions per minute to begin than did the steam engine.) As demands were placed on the line shaft, stored energy in the flywheel, with the governor sensing the load, enabled the engine to maintain a constant velocity and bring the gin to life.

Since steam was used to power gin plants well into the 1950s, the experiences of contemporary ginners reflect the practices of almost a century.

L. V. "Tiny" Risinger stood well over six feet tall and at one time had weighed more than three hundred pounds. By the time we met in Lubbock in 1989, he was considerably thinner. He had a deep rumbling voice and, when he spoke at all, his words carried the rhythm and tone of the steam engines he had worked on for over half a century.

He had become a machinist, he said

like you learn everything else, by doing. In the first place, after you become a machinist, what you machine is immaterial. Whether the problem with your machine is a crosshead or the rails or piston or cylinder or whether it's a boiler feed pump, it's all the same as far as the machine is concerned. I think the thing to me that was the most appealing about steam is that the power was more visible on a steam engine than anything else. You could hear the steam entering the cylinder. You could hear when the governor took over. You could listen to the steam engine and it would sing a song to you if you knew what you were listening for. You could tell exactly what was happening to it. And with that big belt coming off the flywheel, you stood there and could witness steam coming out of the boiler, going into this machine, producing the power to go through the gin and gin that cotton.

Ginning season began in late summer and continued into the winter until all the cotton had been ginned, baled, and shipped out. Machinery was overhauled in the summer. "But," Risinger added, "you could never predict or guess what would burn up or cause trouble during ginning season. The secret to making any steam engine work is cleanliness. If an engine burned up, you had to ream it out and put it back together. All of that machining and putting back together was more or less routine. The proof of the pudding was turning that throttle valve, opening it up, and seeing that connecting rod start moving. You'd get it running, listen to that governor, go out and watch that exhaust puff off those doughnuts. That was music."[4]

One reason for the longevity of steam in the South Plains was the care taken to maintain the ginning equipment. Ginner Charlie Hunter described the routine at his two gin plants. "The first thing we did every morning was shut the gin down if it had been running during the night. We'd clean up. We'd check all of our flat belts to see that the lacing was good and that each belt was tight enough. If it wasn't, we'd cut that belt to make it shorter, relace it, and get it ready for the day's work." At the same time, the engineer would inspect his steam engine and boiler, "make it cough up a lot of water and blow it out. Then we'd start the engine. If we did four or five bales an hour we had a big day's run."[5]

The need for cleanliness occasionally called for improvisation. According to Hunter, the boilers "had this great tall stack that the smoke came out of. Up at the top we had a four foot screen around the stack to keep sparks from flying out. It would get stopped up sometimes and sparks would come out of there and light on our wagons of cotton and set them afire. We would take a rifle and shoot that screen or one of the braces, and jar that stack and shake the ash loose."

Another reason for the longevity of steam use in the South Plains region was a cheap and abundant fuel source. "We used cotton burrs to fire the boiler," Hunter explained. "The farmer brought his own fuel. I had two gins, and I'd use about a car load of coal per season. The only thing I used it for was to fire the boiler, up to a certain point, when I washed the boiler out every week." Using burrs for fuel required constant attention to cleanliness. "We'd usually shut down on Saturday night and wash the boiler out Sunday morning, fire it back Sunday afternoon and start ginning that night."

The steam engine was the heartbeat of the gin plant and controlled the gin's output. Engines became entities, virtually personalities, in their own rights. An engine could become as familiar as a family member. "It was always warm in the engine room," said O. R. Carey of the United States Department of Agriculture ginning laboratory in Lubbock. "The head on those old steam engines was just right that you could cook on it. It'd take a while to cook, but there'd be a pot of coffee and you'd go back about eleven o'clock and it smelled like a cafeteria. Everybody was cooking something. I was at a steam gin out there in New Mexico, and I smelled something cooking there one night, and they'd run a little old cottontail rabbit down in the gin yard and dressed that thing, and they were barbecuing it back there on that old engine."[6]

Steam engines could also be dangerous. "Charlie Hunter had a Skinner steam engine," stated L. V. Risinger. "They had a back door and a water faucet turned upside down right by the door for a drinking fountain. There was a fella stooped over to get him a drink one night, and the governor weights in the flywheel broke and part of it flew over there and hit right where the wall came down to the floor, right by that drinking fountain when he was stooped over drinking. He just jumped out that back door and they haven't seen him since." The flying chunk of cast iron that bounced off the wall near the man's head would have weighed about 150 pounds.

Whether it was a new installation or a combination of old and new machines, each gin plant had its own personality. That personality reflected the climate and type of cotton grown, weather conditions, insects, financial ability of the owner or group of owners to maintain the machinery, and finally the natures of the men who kept the machinery running.

Donald Baird grew up in Coleman County, southeast of Lubbock, where his father had owned and operated a gin. A well-preserved photograph shows a gin house, rather isolated and lonely on the flat prairie, with a few wagons lined up nearby. Two men are sitting on horseback, Baird's father and his business partner. Baird pointed out that they were both wearing revolvers in their holsters. The Indians were gone; it was the wrong place for cattle rustlers, and only snakes posed a threat requiring firearms. Asked why they wore them, Baird said with a mischievous twinkle, "Why? To keep each other honest, that's why!"[7]

Early South Plains gin at Trickham, Coleman County, ca. 1890. There was no pneumatic system; cotton was unloaded by hand. Ginners, on horseback, are wearing pistols. *Courtesy Donald Baird*

Baird is now a retired ginner who worked part of the year in Lubbock and part of the year in Harlingen because of the different ginning seasons in the South Plains and Rio Grande Valley areas. To Donald Baird can be attributed tales of the legendary Frank Smoot.

Old Smoot was one of the most interesting characters I've ever met. In 1940, I went to Harlingen to run the Producer's Gin for the co-op there, and he was to fire the boiler for the steam engine to pull the gin. Smoot was a Dane. He must've been six feet six inches tall and just as slick baldheaded as he could be. He didn't have but about three or four teeth, and they didn't match. His elbows looked like Popeye elbows, with those big joints, and his arms would swing low when he walked. He was comical just to look at.

In our working together, he told me a whole lot about himself. He was born and partially raised in Tennessee. His dad was a doctor. His mother died when he was real young, so his dad hired different women to take care of him while he was out seeing about the patients. Smoot was a peculiar kind of kid. If he didn't get along with any of the women his dad hired, he would do things that would give them so much trouble they would quit. During World War I, he was in the army. That would tell you what age he was. Just after the war, he found a job right up in the edge of Oklahoma. In a coal mine. He'd just been working a few days when the miners pulled a strike.

Smoot insisted on entering the mine to work as he had been hired to. Striking miners came after him, and he fought back, using the pick. He attacked several, and not knowing whether or not he might be wanted for murder, he traveled south and spent several years in Mexico. He eventually returned to South Texas to work at cotton gins.

Baird kept up with Smoot for a number of years, then lost track of him, only to rediscover him in Brownfield (near Lubbock) when Smoot was quite elderly. He had married a woman who already had two children, although she and Smoot had never had children of their own, and he seemed quite content. He had lost most of his eyesight, however, and while he did not recall many of the episodes that Baird found so amusing, he did remember Baird as the young man who had given him a Bible with large print. No doubt the gift was balanced by the fact that Baird used humorous "Smoot stories" as rewards for good behavior by eleven-year-old boys in many years of Sunday school classes.

The tedium of long hard days was broken by fires, accidents, problems with machinery, and practical jokes. Frank Smoot was a brilliant student of human nature and the unparalleled author of folklore. Donald Baird began one story:

I got my dad to come to Harlingen the first year I was down there to help gin and he and Smoot were

Gin crew, Producer's Gin, Harlingen, Texas, 1940. Top row, left: C. D. Baird; top row, 2nd from right: Donald Baird; bottom row, left: Frank Smoot. *Courtesy Donald Baird*

a lot alike. The one was doing something to the other one all the time. From the steam engine into the gin there was a belt about 14 inches wide. Of course, it didn't run fast, but it ran fast enough. Smoot got a can, or some kind of a container, of water and set it on that belt. It was supposed to come out and throw water all over my dad. But it turned over and spilled on that belt, and when that water got on the belt it began to slide. It ripped a strip about four inches wide and about twenty feet long off that belt and every time it came around the pulley it'd go wham, wham, knocking off dust and dirt. I can still see Smoot running to get in and shut the engine off. He had real long feet and looked like he was going around sideways to turn into the engine room.

Occasionally Smoot's jokes became less than amusing. Someone at the gin was needed to grease the conveyor to the seed house. "The conveyor carried the seed in and it would pyramid out (of the conveyor) until it would build up, going farther and higher," explained Baird.

The man who greased that conveyor got caught in it one night and they didn't know it until the next day. It had just beat him all to pieces, ground him up. It took some time to get another person to do that. Smoot had to go up and grease the conveyor every time. About once every hour he'd have to go up along a path beaten out along the side of this slope of cotton seed in order to grease it. The gin

finally found another man who wanted the job. Smoot showed him how to go along and grease the conveyor. But, Smoot told me, "I got to thinkin' how much fun it'd be to bury a hose, 'bout a two-inch hose, through the seed, so whenever he'd come along, I could be on the other side of the seed pile and talk to him through that hose." One night he could hear the man, who was superstitious, coming along, whistling and singing pretty loud so he could keep any ghosts away. When the man got even with the hose, Smoot said, "This night I'll meet you in paradise." The man ran outta there. He lived about three blocks from the gin and when he got to the house, he didn't stop at the door. He ran through the door. Folks said he was out of his head, just crazy. Couldn't tell anybody what happened. Smoot said, "I didn't tell anybody what happened. I didn't want 'em gettin' me for it." Said he lived about three days and just died. So Smoot was always telling me somethin' like that, wondering if the Lord would forgive him.

Charlie Hunter described another type of practical joke. He had hired a "Church of Christ preacher" and the man's gin crew to work at one of his gins. The preacher kept his crew busy and happy—apparently by devising practical jokes.

We had four suctions [telescopes], two on each wagon. One afternoon I looked up there on the wagon and this man had him a broomstick or something about that long and he was digging around in the cotton while he was feeding the suction. You see, when they got their wagons emptied, they would bring in another wagon over to the scales and carry it [the empty wagon] to the yard and then pick up another load and bring it under their suction. This preacher had gone down and figured out which wagon this old boy was gonna get, so he wrote on the tag, "Beware of Snakes." That's all he put on there. Now, this old fellow was as scared of snakes as he could be. He was digging around in that cotton like crazy, using 'deep suction' on those snakes. Everybody else knew what was going on but him. I never did have a bit of trouble out of that crew!

L. V. Risinger had his own version of a practical joke:

We used to have a big old depot stove in the shop. And we'd always have a few mice. Well, they'd come out and get under that stove at night in cold weather 'cause it was warm on the concrete. One got to be tame, a great big old male, and he'd come jump up on your leg and get up on your knee and you could feed him various and sundry things. One day we caught him going in a piece of pipe. Dug around in a carbide can and took a pair of gloves and caught him and cut his tail off. From then on we would identify him as Old Bob. Of course, that made him wild for a little while. Finally, he got pretty tame again. Dad was talking to a customer one day, and Old Bob came out from under a cylinder grinder and ran up Dad's leg. This customer jumped about a foot high. "My God, Mr. Risinger, a mouse just ran up your leg!" Dad said, "Yeah, that's Old Bob. He'll be down in a little bit." That old boy said, "Damn!" and out the door he went.

"I think there's quite a lot to be said about the steam engine and cotton ginning," Risinger concluded. "It seems like they just belonged together."

For all its romance, however, the steam engine contained one enormous, inherent problem. As stated succinctly by Risinger, "Once your central power source went down, you were out of business until you got it going again." Any malfunction of the engine stopped the entire plant's productivity until repairs were made. This dependency on a single power source led to a need for diversified power. "Charlie [Hunter] had a good board of directors and he is the first one that I know of who changed from one central power source to dividing it up and having independent drives for everything important."

After more than thirty years of use, the boilers became old and worn out. Hunter explained, "You had to add more machinery to the gin all the time. A 150 horse [power] motor was about as big as you could get then, and we just had to have more horse-power than that." The steam engine produced about 125 horsepower, but, added Risinger, "If that governor was wide open and taking all the steam you had, then that's all it would do." There was no way to increase the power load, and more ginning equipment demanded cheaper and more efficient power. It took Hunter three years to change one gin plant's power from a central source to diversified [electric motor] sources. Two years later, he shut down his second gin plant and converted to diversified sources at one time.

Gin plants at the turn of the century reflected the larger capacities made possible by system ginning, but handpicked seed cotton continued to be taken to the gin in wagon loads. According to O. R. Carey, "When the farmer came to the gin with a one- or two-bale load, he could tell the ginner what his load should make in terms of weight, and it had better be close or the ginner would hear about it!"

As the ginner made his way through the building, inspecting every stage of the system, he carried a "gin stick," a piece of whittled wood one-half inch wide and about eighteen inches long, or an appropriate tree limb, which he used to loosen cotton or to check moving parts without getting his hands caught in the machinery. Hunter became so skilled that he could "walk up to the press, punch the bale with that stick, and tell you how much cotton was in it. That's the way I could tell when I had a bale of cotton."

Since bales were not weighed until after they were wrapped and tied, the ginner had to know when the press box had reached its capacity so that the flow of cotton could be stopped and the bale tied out. A ginner knew the press box was full when he heard the belt to the tramper slipping. Unlike Hunter, who used a stick, some ginners put their fingers through gaps in the press doors to gauge the density. Others could tell by the position of the steel retainer "dogs," which had knobs extending through the door of the press box. According to Hunter, when the press box was full, indicating a weight of five hundred pounds, the ginner would call out, "Bale o' cotton!"

Gin crews worked long hours, often eating meals on the job with no breaks. Twelve-hour shifts—from seven in the morning until seven at night—were usual, and often two crews rotated to keep the gin operating twenty-four hours a day. In a "short year" of less cotton production, one crew might work a sixteen- to eighteen-hour day. There were no wages at time and a half; only straight time was paid, and twenty-five cents per hour was considered a good wage. Crews were made of up neighboring farmers; there were few

Custom gin plant of the southeastern United States in 1900. *Courtesy Library of Congress*

South Plains gin, Coleman County, ca. 1910. *Courtesy Donald Baird*

local blacks and no Hispanic migrant workers in the South Plains during those early years. When Hunter entered military service at the outbreak of World War II, he was earning eighty cents per hour. His wages were ninety dollars per week in the fall and fifty dollars per week in the summer, with a house furnished.

Not only did system ginning push the production of "white gold" further south and west, it initiated a "gin rush." From pipes and fans to gin stands and presses, all of the primary and auxiliary equipment of system ginning "outfits" began to be produced in quantity. For the twenty-year period from 1890 to 1910, technological advances upgraded ginning methods faster than either individual or custom gin plant owners could keep up with them.

Steam engines were the primary sources of power at large plants, and steam tractors were used in place of engines and boilers at smaller plants; internal combustion tractors, burning either gasoline or kerosene, would serve the same purpose a few years later. By 1910, diesel engines had begun to replace steam on a limited basis.

Three pneumatic systems for transferring seed cotton became available. Munger's system brought seed cotton from wagons or storage bins inside the building to the separator, with its screened drum, which served to both clean the cotton and separate it from the air flow. Cotton dropped from the separator into a sealed belt distributing system that carried the cotton to feeders mounted above the gin stands. Another system took cotton to boxes with flexible canvas "legs," which were known as pneumatic elevators. These elevators did not clean, but composed a series of elephant-like trunks that carried seed cotton to the feeders. A valve near the fan intake controlled suction. The third means of transferring seed cotton depended upon a fan invented by Samuel Rembert of Memphis, Tennessee, in 1897. Suction was used to pull seed cotton through a fan casing and then to blow it into the distribution system. (The fan design was later improved by means of an exaggerated cone developed by Gerald Franks at the U.S. Cotton Ginning Research Lab, Stoneville, Mississippi.)[8]

Two types of distribution systems also developed. Munger had designed the separator, known as a "blow box" or "dropper." Its function was twofold: to act as a cleaning device as seed cotton passed through a section of screen that caught trash, and to drop the cotton from the air flow through an outlet and into the distribution system. A belt distributor with spiked teeth carried cotton along a closed wooden conduit to the feeders. Another type of distributor used flexible flaps at close intervals inside the conduit to make small pockets and to create an air seal which helped to control the flow of cotton. By 1888, David Saylor (also "Sailor") of Little Rock, Arkansas, had varied the system by using suction to convey cotton to an elevator placed above "droppers" on top of the gin stands. Air flow was regulated by a valve. When the valve was opened, suction from a fan pulled cotton from the wagons into the system. When it was closed, breaking the suction, cotton fell into the droppers.[9]

Careless feeding of cotton through the telescope

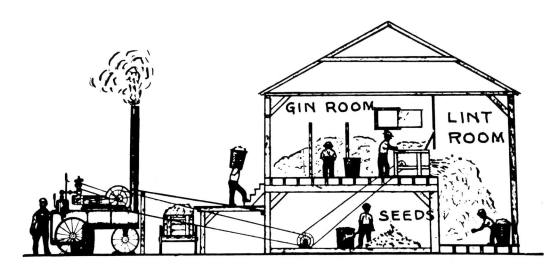

Single stand cotton gin with temporary stalls on the ginning floor; press was in the yard. Steam tractor powered the gin stand with a belt from the flywheel. *From C. A. Bennett,* Saw and Toothed Cotton Ginning Developments *(drawing by Prof. D. A. Tompkins)*

or a blockage in the system could cause excess cotton to collect in the hoppers to the feeders, since the distributor was closed at both ends. Munger's earliest design (1884) had required a man to turn off the suction and stop the flow of cotton. Munger later modified the system to include an extra telescope on the ginning floor, but there was no box or "pen" to contain the cotton that backed up and spilled out of the suction pipe. The excess cotton was fed manually into a hole in the floor or wall and was later retrieved and fed back into the system through the secondary pipe. By 1890, an outlet at one end of the distributor permitted excess cotton to fall into an overflow pen (an open box around three sides of the secondary pipe) that stood at one end of the battery of gin stands. The secondary pipe, or telescope, provided quick reentry of cotton into the system. Bells and shutoffs were used to warn the gin hands of an overflow.[10]

Increased ginning capacity called for more extensive cleaning methods before seed cotton reached the gin stands. Early cleaning methods had included manual sorting or whipping, and after 1860, improvements inside the gin stand deflected leaves, sticks, stems, and hulls. System ginning required a shift to auxiliary means of cleaning because of rougher harvesting methods and bulk handling of seed cotton.

Traps located in the suction line, well before the seed cotton reached the separator, caught rocks, bits of metal, and green bolls.

A seed cotton separator and cleaner was patented in 1877, and a machine for separating bolls and hulls followed in 1891. These machines had carding teeth that held the seed cotton while stripper (non-toothed) and picker (spiked) rollers loosened foreign matter. A screw conveyor removed the trash. In 1894, Henry Rembert of Willis, Texas, received a patent for a lint cleaner that could use either single or double cylinders made of coarse mesh screen (a rotary screen drum) to allow the air flow to remove trash. Seed cotton cleaners were normally positioned ahead of the gin stand, but the placement of this cleaner was unusual in that it received ginned cotton from the lint flue and passed it through to the condenser.[11] Overhead-mounted air line and gravity cleaners became available in 1900. These beater-type cleaners were placed in the suction line that carried seed cotton from wagons or stalls to the separator. Some designs combined the air line cleaner and the separator.

Feeders were of two types also. Invented in 1872, the horizontal or slightly tilted apron feeder contained moving slats which conveyed cotton to a spiked cylinder where it was again cleaned before entering the roll box of the gin stand. These feeders could be moved back onto legs to allow access to the gin stand. A 1909 F. H. Lummus Sons Co. catalogue described the operation of its cleaning feeder in detail. "A large mass of cotton passing tightly between two fluted rollers is held by these rollers firmly and passes slowly down on to the picker roller." The picker roller spun at two hundred revolutions per minute, while the fluted feed rollers turned one to three times per minute, depending on the amount of cotton to be fed into the gin stand. The picker roller was fourteen inches in diameter with six hundred spikes, and "each lock of cotton as it gets within reach of the pickers is beaten many times before it is taken off by the pickers, and then it is driven and beaten against the curved screen . . . before it is discharged into the gin." The feeder was placed above the gin. A conveyor "shoved into and through the line of feeders" carried trash and dirt to one end of the battery of gin stands for disposal.[12]

In 1912, John E. Mitchell, Sr., of St. Louis, Missouri, redesigned the simple horizontal feeder to include extracting capability. Extracting was the removal of coarse foreign matter by means of a toothed carding process instead of screens or grids. Mitchell's feeder extractor led to hundreds of patents granted to him, his sons, and his employees. Mitchell feeder extractors were popular with ginners for many years.[13]

The gin stand itself received technological attention as well. Small hand- or tractor-driven gin stands were available, often for export purposes but also for farm use where production was limited. Still operated by a main belt drive, one style of gin was made completely of wood; another style was made more durable by the use of a cast-iron frame. The number of saws varied from sixty to eighty, and ten-inch diameter saws were the most commonly used. (Available in 1909, twelve-inch diameter saws were preferred by 1920.) Gin stands per battery numbered between three and five.

Gins were distinguished within the industry as "single-rib plain" which had single ginning ribs, and "huller," which had picker rollers and huller ribs. As defined in the 1909 Lummus catalogue, "The Huller Gin differs from the plain gin in having two roll boxes or breasts; the outside roll box into which the cotton is dropped is provided with a spiked picker roll, which loosens up and throws the cotton against the saws, the saws catching the cotton, carrying same into the inside breast, the bolls and hulls being rejected or stopped by projecting prongs on the ribs, drop out to the floor, and the cotton passing into the in-

Battery condenser with two, 20-inch wire drums, double rubber doffing rollers; air discharge, at either end, allowed dust to be expelled through metal flues extending through the roof. *From F. H. Lummus Sons Co. Catalogue, 1899; courtesy Lummus Industries, Inc.*

side breast is ginned in the usual manner."[14] Huller ribs protected the saws from damage and kept large pieces of trash from being ginned with the cotton. Both plain and huller gins used an adjustable seed-board, and both were popular for many years because of the simplicity of their construction and long working life.

One significant modification to the technology was the development of the air blast gin. Eli Whitney had used brushes attached to strips of wood to doff lint caught on the spiked cylinder. On December 5, 1893, one hundred years after Whitney, Robert King of Mansfield, Louisiana, patented a multijet air blast gin. A pipe three or four inches in diameter was mounted behind the ginning ribs and above the saws. A nozzle was set between each pair of saws, and a blast of air from the nozzle would send the lint from the gin stand into the flue. Manufacturing rights were assigned to Kingsley and Douglas of St. Louis, Missouri. In 1895, inventors Lumpkin and Ogden modified the principle to one long nozzle that swept

Gin stand with feeder and condenser. Seed fell through a hole cut into the floor to the screw conveyor underneath. *From F. H. Lummus Sons Co. Catalogue, 1899; courtesy Lummus Industries, Inc.*

the full length of the saw cylinder. Another patent, issued to A. D. Thomas of Little Rock, Arkansas, used a combination of brush and air blast in order to gin damp cotton. In 1911, Frank Phelps, also of Little Rock, improved the ability of the air blast gin to eliminate motes (immature seeds) and trash. The Carver Gin Company manufactured an air blast gin, but more successful was the air blast attachment which could be installed on a regular gin stand by removing the brush and replacing it with the air blast attachment.[15]

The gin stands were linked by flues (or "transitions") to a master condenser. The wooden, rectangular flues were first lined with galvanized metal, then completely replaced by galvanized metal pipes. The master condenser continued to be used instead of individual condensers. Seed disposal was also automated, either blown through pipes or screw-conveyed through wooden conduits beneath the ginning floor. The farmer's planting seed was routed to the customer bin and the rest was routed to a seed hopper or a seed storage house in the gin yard.

The bale press had undergone as many changes as the gin stand. The hand-operated, rope winch press used on the ginning floor had replaced the old wooden yard press, but it, too, would be shortlived. As early as 1870, a steam-powered single box press with an up-packing ram was available. Winship Machine Company of Atlanta, Georgia, manufactured a down-pressing, single box, single screw, iron frame press, and some double screw, single box presses were available. Cotton was placed in the press box at the ginning floor level, but bales were tied out at either raised platform or ginning floor level, depending upon whether the press was up- or down-packing. Iron and steel screws were used, and steam trampers replaced foot power.

Munger had increased baling capacity with his double box press, and it was placed on a turntable set into the ginning floor so that it would revolve. A screw continued to be used for compression, but in 1884, Munger added a steam tramper (or plunger) which had been available as early as 1878. The steam piston tramper eliminated foot tramping, but an operator was needed to rake cotton from the lint slide into the box and even it up, then to turn a rod-controlled valve to start and stop the tramper.

The screw compressed the cotton from beneath the bale box, and the tramper compressed the cotton from above the charging box, but when the tramper was raised to allow more lint into the charging box, the cotton sprang up. Munger added steel retainer "dogs" to hold the cotton down while the

Single box press; the box was 24″ × 54″ and 10′ long; steel screw was 5″ in diameter. *From F. H. Lummus Sons Co. Catalogue, 1899; courtesy Lummus Industries, Inc.*

tramper was raised. Munger's first "dogs" were saw-tooth, or curved, in design. By 1900, he had developed the horizontal press dog with its knob-like end that extended through the press door and became a common feature on various styles and sizes of bale presses.

The wooden bale presses were bottom hinged, opening to the floor so that the bale could be rolled out. By 1930, they began to be side hinged (also developed by Frank Phelps) and constructed of metal. In 1911, two different sizes of bale presses were being made for 500-pound bales. A 750-pound-bale press was designed to help Mississippi cotton growers reduce certain taxes, but the large bale often broke the compresses. Complaints were taken to the New Orleans Cotton Exchange, which called a meeting of cotton gin manufacturers. Since bale sizes varied by manufacturer, the Exchange asked for a standardized press box for bale uniformity. The industry agreed to a single size, twenty-seven by fifty-four inches. In support of this decision, the Exchange agreed to penalize all bales weighing more than 600 pounds or less than 400 pounds.[16]

Winship received a patent in 1893 for a double-

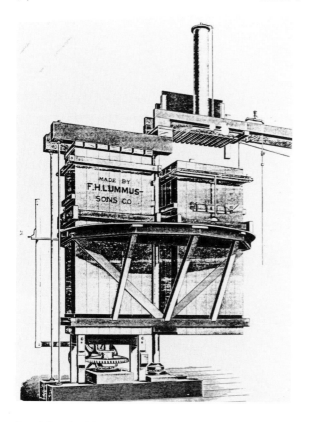

Revolving double box press, 24″ × 54″ × 10′; 5″ diameter screw; steam tramper; box was made of seasoned white oak and straight-grain yellow pine. *From F. H. Lummus Sons Co. Catalogue, 1899; courtesy Lummus Industries, Inc.*

box press on a turntable that provided a platform for lint sliding down from the condenser. The platform was placed level with the press box, and the lint was manually raked into the box. This manual process disappeared as cotton was processed more efficiently through the gin stands and condenser to be fed directly into the charging box.

A round bale press made by Bessonette was sold in 1893. Two hundred and fifty-pound bales stirred interest in higher density bales, but the industry had begun to standardize at five hundred-pound flat bales, and round bales remained in limited use.

Improvements in roller ginning were also taking place during this "gin rush." Patents had been issued during the Civil War and post-war years for improvements to roller gins. Such patents included moving the relative positions of the knives and varying construction of the ginning rollers. A patent granted in 1892 returned to the churka gin but added fan suction. J. Daig of Gainesville, Florida, received a patent in 1895 for using springs to hold the fixed knife against the roller at a constant pressure. Other inven-

tors experimented with adding combs at right angles to the moving knife to stir up the seed cotton for better feeding. Increasing the number of rollers was also tried.

In 1900, J. E. Cheesman formed the Cheesman Cotton Gin Company in New York City to manufacture and sell roller gins, beginning production in 1902. His roller gin modifications reversed the position of the fixed and movable knives from the original McCarthy gin design, added cast iron end frames to the gin stand, and incorporated a small drum cleaning feeder to regulate cotton flow. In July, 1902, thirty-two of these gins were set up at the Valdosta (Georgia) Ginning Company, making it the nation's largest roller ginning plant with a capacity of more than one hundred bales of Sea Island cotton processed per day. Cheesman's advanced design included steel pipes as cores inside the covered, wooden rollers for extended durability.[17] Inventor W. H. Wentworth, from San Antonio, Texas, devised a vertical roller gin. He returned to McCarthy's fixed and moving knives, but used internal and external gears to operate a total of six ginning rollers.

Matthew Prior, of Watertown, Massachusetts, was known throughout the industry for his roller ginning inventions and modifications. He went to the

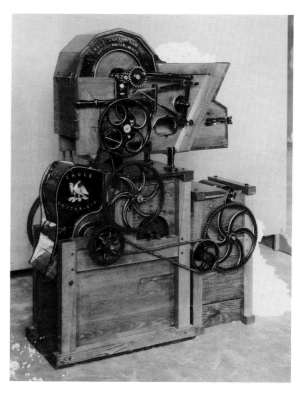

Eagle cotton gin, feeder, and condenser, ca. 1915. *Courtesy Smithsonian Institution*

Complete system outfit, from wagon to press. Eagle Cotton Gin Co. won first prize at the Dallas Exposition and Texas State Fair, October, 1893, for best system gin. *From C. A. Bennett,* Saw and Toothed Cotton Ginning Developments

reverse knife design as early as 1900 and tried out metal ginning rollers and moving knives that were like combs. In 1938, Prior told United States Department of Agriculture ginning expert Charles Bennett that bronze rollers with a slight roughness were the best for enabling the fibers to cling to the roller surfaces, but he had also discovered that laminating grasscloth or haircloth fabric and canvas, pressed into layered strips and wound in spirals around the rollers, had worked very well as a replacement for the usual leather or walrus hide.[18] Laminated canvas and rubber roller covers were preferred after 1938.

System ginning meant system manufacturing, and companies had to expand production or close their doors. The Eagle Cotton Gin Company, as previously described, enjoyed a long, continuous history. After its reorganization in 1877, Eagle specialized in beautifully crafted and finished hand gins, feeders, and condensers made of maple. Eagle shipped to Savannah, New Orleans, and Galveston, and its export trade was primarily to Brazil. In 1885, Eagle, like other companies, decided to produce system gins and manufactured elevators, lint flues, and double-box presses until 1899 when it became part of Continental Gin Company.

The Winship Machine Company of Atlanta, Georgia, began as a small, water-powered factory in 1845 with a capital investment of twenty thousand dollars and twenty employees. The factory moved from its rural location to Atlanta in 1853 and reformed as Joseph Winship and Company. The company made guns and ammunition for the Confederate army during the Civil War. The factory was destroyed by fire when Atlanta was torched in 1864, but the factory was soon rebuilt. Joseph Winship retired in 1869, and his two sons continued the business until 1884, when it was formally incorporated. During its long history, Winship had produced freight cars, cotton gin machinery and presses, steam engines and boilers, cane mills, and syrup kettles.[19]

In order to acquire more business east of the Mississippi River, Robert S. Munger built a new plant in Birmingham in 1890, leaving the Dallas plant intact. He formed business alliances with W. T. Northington—an attorney and brother-in-law of Merrill Pratt, nephew of the founder—and with Daniel Pratt, Merrill Pratt's son. Continental Gin Company records indicate that W. T. Northington, who was president of the Northington-Munger-Pratt Company of Birmingham which had formed in 1892, began to approach others with the idea of a merger during the summer of 1899. Eventually, six companies composed Continental Gin Company: Smith Sons Gin and Machine Company (a Birmingham company that made gins, feeders, and condensers); Winship Machine Company, Atlanta; Munger Improved Cotton Machine Manufacturing Company, Dallas; Daniel Pratt Gin Company, Prattville; Eagle Cotton Gin Company, Bridgewater; and Northington-Munger-Pratt Company of Birmingham. Incorporation papers were drawn up on November 17, 1899, and Robert S. Munger received 8.33 percent of the company's stock as payment for his patents.

In 1901, Continental began to consolidate its manufacturing enterprises. Gin stands continued to be made by the individual companies, but Continental would limit itself to two styles of elevators (the pneumatic elevator with chutes above the feeders and Munger's vacuum box with belt distributor to the feeders), to the Northington-Munger-Pratt condenser and lint flue, and to the feeder made by Smith Sons Gin and Machine Company. Complete system "outfits" for demonstration purposes which had been set up in Dallas and Birmingham were refurbished in order to attract more business.

In 1911, Continental built additional warehouse space and consolidated its manufacturing efforts. The Pratt and Munger gins were Continental's biggest sellers, and the Smith, Winship and Eagle gins were no longer produced except for the export trade. The Smith and Winship factories shifted to Munger gins, and Eagle concentrated on gins for export and a machine used by oil mills to delint cottonseed.[20]

If Continental was growing rapidly, so likewise was one of its chief rivals in the industry, the Lummus Cotton Gin Company.

Franklin H. Lummus was an entrepreneur much like Daniel Pratt and Robert S. Munger. Lummus was born in Massachusetts in 1824, but spent most of his early life in New York City. He and his father formed the New York Car and Steamboat Gas Company in 1857. The sale of petroleum products was too far ahead of its time to succeed, and the younger Lummus and his brother-in-law Augustus Wetmore soon opened a business that manufactured and sold jewelry. Lummus had married and begun a family, but he joined the Union army in 1862 and served until his honorable discharge in October, 1863. As already indicated, cotton remained a powerful economic force in spite of the war, and late in 1863, Lummus and his partners Henry C. Hogden and Joseph Wilde created the New York Cotton Gin Company.

Israel Brown, whose inventions have been men-

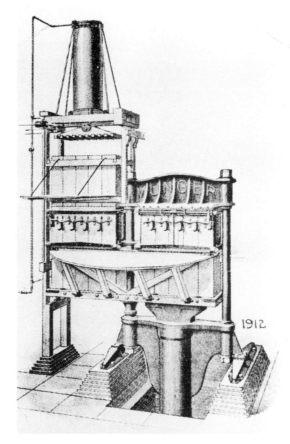

Munger-designed double box ginners compress manufactured between 1897 and 1913. *From C. A. Bennett,* Cotton Ginning Systems in the United States and Auxiliary Developments

tioned earlier, had formed a partnership with Dr. E. T. Taylor, first in Gerard, Alabama, and moving to Columbus, Georgia, in 1849, to manufacture cotton gins. Local businessman Welcome G. Clemens bought Dr. Taylor's portion of the company in 1854, making the new company W. G. Clemens, Brown, and Company. Israel Brown moved to Connecticut during the war and manufactured gins for export to South America under his own company name. Lummus and Brown had become acquainted and conducted business during the war. In 1867, Lummus bought out Brown's share in W. G. Clemens, Brown, and Company. Two years later, Lummus moved to Georgia, settled accounts, reorganized the company, and gave it the name Franklin H. Lummus Company. Sales agents displayed the small gins in hardware stores in Columbus, Georgia, and Montgomery, Alabama, for sale to planters and farmers.

The Columbus factory was too small, and the company moved to Juniper, twenty-five miles east,

Franklin H. Lummus. *From F. H. Lummus Sons Co. Catalogue,* 1909; courtesy Lummus Industries, Inc.

which had sufficient water power from a nearby creek to drive the machinery for mass production. In 1879, E. Frank Lummus joined his father in the company, and in 1882, he received a patent for a lint cleaner. Younger son and brother Louis E. Lummus began to take part in the company in 1887, and in 1891, F. H. Lummus Sons Company was formed. The family-owned company became a corporation in April, 1896, four months after the death of Franklin H. Lummus.

F. H. Lummus Sons Company continued to grow, increasing stock holdings, creating a board of directors, and acquiring land in Columbus for additional facilities. A new manufacturing plant and office were built in 1899, and the company moved from Juniper to Columbus. By 1901, Lummus was turning out about six hundred ten-inch diameter saw gin stands per year. In all, Lummus manufactured five types of gin stands, an elevator distributor, flues, a battery condenser, both simple screw and double box presses

with steam trampers, and screw conveyors for seed handling.[21]

Lummus was a pioneer in ginning research, setting up a model gin plant at the factory in 1907. Lummus was also particularly attracted to the air blast principle for doffing lint from the gin saws. In 1908, Lummus arranged with the Epps Air Blast Gin Company of Sherman, Texas, to manufacture and sell air blast doffing attachments. The brush cylinders used for doffing lint were made of wood and horsehair, and rodents often ate the horsehair, thus unbalancing the wooden cylinder shafts and limiting their effectiveness. In addition, both brush and saw cylinders required separate pulleys. The air blast attachment would make possible a single drive pulley, requiring less horsepower, and would simplify maintenance.[22]

In 1910, Lummus opened a branch office in Dallas and that year changed its name to Lummus Cotton Gin Company. The air blast principle became accepted by ginners, and in 1916, Lummus issued licenses to Continental and to the Stephen D. Murray Company of Dallas to manufacture air blast attachments for their gin stands.

Lummus' research led to recognition for one of its chief engineers, Thaddeus S. Grimes. Among his achievements were improvements to the air blast attachment, the "Waffle Iron Control" which was a mechanism to stop the feeder if the gin breast had to be pulled away from the saws to clear a blockage, the double spiral roller for separating and discharging hulls, a double-box down-packing press, and the use of couplings to connect gin stands to each other to eliminate the line shaft and numerous pulleys and make possible the one story gin.[23]

In spite of occasional lawsuits (Continental lost a patent infringement suit for a cleaning feeder to the Stephen D. Murray Company and inadvertently underwrote the success of one of its competitors), the cotton ginning industry was well on its way toward the fulfillment of its own success story.

No one could have imagined the impact that was about to be caused by a tiny, and prolific, insect.

CHAPTER EIGHT

"The Horse Could See"

If the turn of the century saw a virtual explosion in the technology and mass production of gin machinery, the years between the end of World War I and 1925 brought a multitude of changes in the growing, harvesting, and marketing of cotton.

Boll weevils were first seen in Texas in 1892, having traveled north from Mexico, and they quickly spread across the Cotton Belt. In 1917, the entire crop of Sea Island cotton was ruined by boll weevils, amounting to a loss of thousands of bales and millions of dollars. The long staple cotton industry was decimated.

Thousands of upland cotton crops were destroyed as well, and by the early 1920s, the damage was so severe that one-half million Texas bales were left in the fields. Cotton prices dropped from twenty-three cents to five cents per pound. Emphasis on cotton growing shifted from Central Texas to the High and Rolling Plains regions of Texas and Oklahoma and continued across the South Plains near Lubbock. Since there was no irrigation on the plains, farming was difficult, but the boll weevil had not yet reached that area. The level plain was advantageous to the farmer who, with six mules or a tractor, could manage up to two hundred acres and produce between 80 and 120 bales per season.[1]

Most of Texas, and the South, did not escape the insect's ravaging of the crop. The United States Department of Agriculture estimated a $3 million loss to the helpless southern farmers. The weevil passed through the stages of egg to larva to pupa to adult beetle in 27 days, a significant portion of cotton's 150-day (frostfree) growing cycle. Other pests included the flea hopper, cotton leafworm, cotton bollworm, and pink bollworm. Two methods of dealing with the insects were developed: the plant itself was altered and pesticides were introduced.

As early as 1897, cotton breeding had begun with the work of H. J. Webber for the U. S. Department of Agriculture. During the 1920s, researchers intensified their efforts to create new plant varieties, keeping in mind several criteria. Adaptability to local soil conditions and rainfall patterns was important, regardless of the variety of cotton grown. Early maturity was required because weevils could not breed until the squares had formed. If cotton set its bolls before the weevils had time to develop, much of the crop could be saved. Once the squares were infested, no more bolls would set. Squares punctured by weevils would drop off, and infested bolls would develop poorly, if at all. Any locks within the bolls would be ruined. Texas had the advantage, especially in the South Plains, of long periods of dry weather in which infested squares fell off the plant to be dried in the sun, thus killing the larvae. Any weevils that had survived the winter would destroy the squares of the spring's first planting, but a second crop might be grown after a long, dry interim. Storm resistance was necessary, especially in West Texas where strong winds and early winters could damage a crop. Large bolls made picking cotton faster, easier, and cheaper. Once mechanical harvesting began, different stalk heights were developed. The U.S. Department of Agriculture and university experiment stations (such as Texas Station at Texas A&M University) developed several disease-resistant varieties. Since spinners preferred staple lengths of one inch or more, research included seeking ways to produce longer fibers. Acceptance of a particular variety in a community was desirable because the seed could easily be kept pure for both planting and sale to cottonseed mills. Using gin-run seed, which mixed seed of different varieties, was the farmers' common practice (as opposed to the purchase of new seed from plant breeders or commercial seed houses), and the result was decreasing production and shorter staple length. If the same cotton variety were grown throughout the community, it would generally bring a better price because it could be sold in larger lots of uniform staple and grade.[2]

The decimation of the Sea Island cotton crop in 1917 led to the rapid establishment of American-Egyptian cottons, which were being grown on a limited basis in West Texas, Arizona, and California. The term "Egyptian" is misleading in that the long staple

Front view of system gin; steam power plant is implied. *From F. H. Lummus Sons Co. Catalogue, 1909; courtesy Lummus Industries, Inc.*

variety did not originate in Egypt. Seeds from South America and the West Indies were taken to Africa during the Colonial period, and Peruvian varieties were transplanted along the Lower Nile about 1820. Attempts to grow Egyptian cotton in the Southwest, beginning in 1898, were unsuccessful, but breeders created hybrids that were successful. The first significant American-Egyptian crop appeared in 1918. Two years later, it cost Arizona and California growers four cents per pound to pick Egyptian cotton, because of its small bolls, while upland cotton growers spent only two cents per pound to have their cotton picked. Boll size was important because fifty to sixty bolls would produce a pound of upland cotton, but more than one hundred bolls were needed to produce a pound of American-Egyptian cotton. Seed salvaged from the 1917 crop of Sea Island cotton was planted in 1933, and a commercial crop was ready for sale in 1936, but the newer varieties grown in the Southwest maintained their hold on the market.

Beginning in 1916, the second change in cotton growing attributed to the boll weevil was the use of pesticides. Manually applying a mixture of calcium arsenate, molasses, and water to the tops of the plants with a mop, before the squares formed, proved effective. By far the most widespread practice was dusting the fields with a powder of calcium arsenate. Dusting apparatus varied from hand-held sticks with

bags attached at either end, to hand-held sprayers with long nozzles, to two-row traction dusters with plow handles and a single wheel. Spraying with crop dusters was popular in many areas for speed and range, especially since the best results were obtained when the air was calm and the plants damp or moist, which meant night or early morning applications. Three sprayings were usual, four days apart, when weevils had infested 10–15 percent of the squares.

C. A. Myers described dusting for cotton worms rather than boll weevils in the Beeville, Texas, area in the 1920s. "We would poison cotton from horseback. We'd take a pole twelve to fifteen feet long and lay it across the saddle horn. We'd put about five pounds of Paris Green in flour sacks tied to each end of the pole. We'd mount the horse and ride along the row, and the shaking and bumping of the horse would make the dust settle on the cotton stalks. About four rows at a time could be treated. We always did this at night, often after midnight, when the wind laid and dew would cause the poison to stick." Myers, a youngster of about ten years old, rode along the rows without the benefit of a lantern and frequently in pale moonlight. When asked how he could see where he was going, he laughed and said, "I didn't have to. The horse could see."[3]

Even though Cotton Belt farmers produced an enormous crop of 18,618,000 bales of cotton in 1926,

Rear view of system gin showing lint flue behind gin stands, condenser, and bale press. Large centrifugal fan provided air stream. *From F. H. Lummus Sons Co. Catalogue, 1909; courtesy Lummus Industries, Inc.*

the yield was only 186 pounds of cotton per acre which sold for eleven cents per pound. One-half bale, or 250 pounds, per acre was considered minimum yield to be worth growing cotton at all.[4]

The boll weevil infestation led to other changes as well. In the early 1920s, sharecroppers and tenant farmers, both black and white, began migrating to southern cities, and northern industrial areas drew many workers to the factories. Insects, uncertain rainfall, poor seed, low yields, diminished cotton quality, and fluctuating market prices could not compete with the predictable, even if low, incomes of industry.

Farmers spent more money on harvesting than on any other aspect of the production process because cotton was still picked by hand. "We had a great long sack made out of sailcloth or ducking," said Mrs. Minnie Bains of Brookshire, Texas, "and it had a strap that you put around your shoulders. You buckled some knee pads around your knees so you could get down and crawl if you needed to. Then you'd drag those sacks along the rows. Very few people, when I was coming up, put cotton in a basket to carry it to the gin. You would weigh in at noon, when the sack became heavy, and again later in the evening. Everybody would pick about one hundred pounds before he'd come weigh it in."[5]

If the rows of cotton were long, the farmer would place the wagon midway down the row; if the rows were short, the wagon would be set at row's end. The

scale might be a portable field scale, suspended from a raised wagon tongue, or a large scale on the ground at the barn. Since the sack was six to twelve feet long and was often weighed in the field, "a green boll was placed in the bottom corner of the sack," explained C. A. Myers, "and a piece of wire wrapped around the corner to make a neck and then bent to make a hook. The hook and piece of wire were hung on the scale along with the strap. That made the sack fold and not touch the ground."[6]

Tallies were kept of the amount each worker picked, and he or she was paid accordingly. Workers were known to pick during the morning, collect their earnings, and leave, but most remained throughout the long, hot days. Whether or not an actual contest was held, each worker took satisfaction in trying to pick more than the others. A wagon held about fifteen hundred pounds of seed cotton. Most of the weight came from seed and trash; five hundred pounds was fiber. The farmer always knew just how much cotton, or how many bales, had come from his fields.

Lunches were eaten in the field at midday. The farm owner's wife would ring a bell to call workers to the ends of the rows to get water. "One nice thing about picking cotton," said Mrs. Bains, "was that the farmer had dropped in a few watermelon seeds along in his field and you'd have a cool watermelon to stop and eat as you picked. We did that in Shelby County prior to 1924." Once picking began, men, women, and children worked side by side in the fields. When ginning began, particularly at plantation gins, the men would leave the fields mid-morning after the cotton had had time to dry out from the night's dewfall and go to work in the gins. The day's picking would be finished by women and children, with even very small children picking cotton low to the ground.

"At the end of the day," explained Mrs. Bains, "you'd weigh everything out. If you had enough pickers, you could get the wagon loaded up and ready to go to the gin. If you didn't have enough pickers, they just had to put a tarp over the wagon so the next day's pickings would go into it. It was hard work. But none of us knew any better. Everybody else who lived on the farm was doing it. We didn't think we were having a hard time." After all, cotton was the only cash crop, a family's income for the year.

After most of the picking had been done, the fields were "scrapped" of any remaining seed cotton. "At the end of the season," continued Mrs. Bains, "for most of the people who lived on the farm and helped with the work, there would be a portion of the lint cotton that did not go into the bale and that would be sold, to those who wanted it, to make their quilts and bedding and even mattresses. They'd pay a little bit, and if they didn't need all those things for themselves, individuals would sell them and get their Christmas money."

Picking cotton was slow and tedious. During the early years of the century, it was done by the time-honored method of removing locks of cotton and leaving bolls and burrs on the stalks in order to gather the cleanest possible seed cotton. Some pickers were skilled enough to use both hands to pluck the fibers and leave the burrs on the stalks. Others would hold the boll steady with one hand and pluck the fibers with the other. The burrs had sharp points on them, and fingers and hands were often swollen and bleeding by the end of the day. Within a few years, however, as the work force dwindled, workers began to snap (or "pull") the entire boll with burrs and locks of fibers off the plant. The result was dirtier but faster harvested cotton.

Cotton growers needed a mechanical means to harvest their crops. A steam tractor picking machine was tried as early as 1896, and L. A. Lind of Skidmore, in Bee County, built a two-row mechanical cotton picker in 1912. Such machines were too expensive and too far ahead of their time, however, for general acceptance.

More successful was the simple cotton sled devised

Two-row mechanical cotton picker built by L. A. Lind in 1912. *Courtesy Hidalgo County Historical Museum*

in 1914 by a Lubbock-area farmer who needed to pick his cotton quickly in order to avoid losing the crop to a storm. The first sled was a section of picket fence dragged by mules down the rows to strip off the cotton. In 1926, the South Plains found itself with a huge cotton crop, the few available Mexican migrant workers could not pick the cotton fast enough, and low prices for cotton meant that harvesting had to be economical. Local blacksmiths placed boxes with V-shaped fronts on runners to make a sled that would strip cotton off the stalks. The threat of loss to high winds and early frosts called for emergency measures, and West Texans invented another kind of sled, a box with a groove through the center of the bottom that stripped cotton from the stalk. "I saw my first mechanical stripper in 1934 or 1935," stated L. V. Risinger of Lubbock. "It was a big box on runners, a sled, with fingers in the front, drawn by two horses. As it stripped the cotton off the stalks, you stood there with a rake and kept it pulled to the back of the box."[7] After frost had caused cotton plants to drop their leaves, a farmer with one horse and a sled could harvest as much as four or five acres a day.[8] Another device was that of a team of mules or horses hitched to a wagon with a crude V-shaped attachment or section of fence fastened to the front of the wagon bed. The team was driven through the cotton fields, and both open and green bolls as well as trash were stripped, or rough-harvested, as they passed. A boy drove the team and a man using a pitchfork could rapidly fill the wagon bed. When the wagon was full, the cotton was emptied into a truck and taken to the gin.[9]

Another variation of the sled, mounted on the front of a wagon, was a wooden device with slatted "fingers" that curved upward on the ends to grab the stalks. A later sled was attached to the side of a tractor with a chain conveyor to carry cotton to a hopper next to the driver's seat.

Both hand-snapped and sled-harvested cotton, which had about the same spinning qualities, were generally one to two grades lower than handpicked cotton, but due to a reduction of available labor, early frosts, and low-growing stalks, especially in the South Plains, such mechanical assistance was increasingly necessary. Use of the cotton sled enabled a farmer to raise and harvest between 150 and 200 acres at a cost of two to three dollars per bale. More responsibility fell on the ginner to clean bolls and trash from the seed cotton.

Beginning in the 1920s, county extension agents from land grant colleges such as Texas A&M and Texas Tech, vocational agricultural teachers, local cotton buyers, and U.S. Department of Agriculture experts conducted classes on all aspects of farming cotton, with special emphasis on grading and classing so the grower would have a better idea of the value of his crop. Classes were also offered to ginners who, because of the expense of setting up custom gins, bore the dual burden of making a profit for themselves and their stockholders and turning out the best possible number and quality of bales for the growers who required and paid for their services. Whether the plant was "line" (part of a syndicate) or independent, ginning began to take on the character of big business.

The number of gin plants in Texas had decreased from 4,607 in 1912 to 3,923 in 1925. The fewest gins (3,772) were operating in 1922. Across the Cotton Belt, the number of gin plants had decreased from approximately 28,000 in 1912 to 18,000 in 1925. More than 20 percent of the total number of gin plants were in Texas. The loss in number of gin plants, however, was offset by increased bale capacity at each one. In 1906, 80 percent of the facilities in the United States had fewer than two hundred saws per plant (in Texas, 48 percent); two stands of forty saws each were normal. By 1919, only 53 percent of U.S. gins had less than two hundred saws (16 percent in Texas). Many of the Cotton Belt's larger gin plants were located in Texas and turned out an average of 963 bales yearly between 1914 and 1925 (as opposed to 642 bales average across the Belt). System ginning allowed between three and five gin stands per battery, and the gin stands increased from seventy saws to eighty in the 1920s and ninety by 1940, gradually providing greater bale capacity at fewer gin plants.[10]

Volume of production affected the cost of ginning. Plants that could process between 1,000 and 1,500 bales had an average cost of $6.97 each in the 1924–25 season, while plants with a volume between 3,000 and 3,500 bales had an average cost of $4.58 per bale. Texas gins averaged 963 bales per season, with an average cost of about $5.70 per bale. Other operating costs were affected by the number of gin stands per plant, fuel costs, labor costs, and insurance.[11]

In 1925, a U.S. Department of Agriculture study estimated that over $200 million were invested in U.S. gin plants, and ginning and tying out that year's crop cost about $6.00 per bale.

Charges for ginning Texas cotton were based on the hundredweight of seed cotton (excluding bagging and ties) and varied from 30¢ to 40¢ for picked cotton and from 40¢ to 50¢ for "bollies." (A "bollie" was a partially opened boll struck by frost and then gathered and ginned.) The customary charge for bagging and ties in 1925 was $1.50 per bale "pattern."

Normally, the grower sold his seed to the ginner to pay for ginning fees. Ginners usually bought about 75 percent of the ginned seed from the grower. The ginner then sold the seed to cottonseed mills for a profit of 91¢ per bale after drayage. The remaining 25 percent was returned to the grower for his next year's crop. During the 1920s and 1930s, as more uses were found for cottonseed oil, the oil mills would exchange cottonseed meal for ginned seed. The farmer used the meal for cattle feed, and the mill made its profit from the oil.[12]

Custom ginning had five purposes: to process the seed cotton and turn out the best possible sample, procure and sell bagging and ties, buy and sell seed and any leftover or second-run seed cotton, and occasionally to buy and sell bales of cotton. Every custom ginner was considered a public ginner and was subject to certain statutes. The public ginner had to acquire a license from and file a surety bond with the State Commissioner of Warehouses before beginning operation. The bond was not less than $250 or more than $1,000 per gin plant. Both had to be renewed each year, the license for a fee of $1.00 and the bond for about $3.50. If a grower believed that his cotton had been damaged at the gin, he could file a lawsuit against the ginner, who would then make good the damages out of the bond or repair the damages. If the entire amount of the bond was used up, the ginner had to give a new bond or lose his license. The ginner was also responsible for making certain that the bale would remain covered during compressing and that the bagging would remain in a good condition so that identification markings were visible at all times. Ginners were to attach a metal tag to each bale which would be stamped with the number of

Battery of gin stands showing separator, fan, distributor with spiked belt, feeders, and gin stands; manufactured by Continental Gin Co. under Munger patent in 1910. *Courtesy Continental Eagle Corporation*

the bale (matching that of the ginner's records) and the number of the gin license.

"The settlers from the plantations would vie with each other as [to] which one was going to get to the gin first with the first bale," said Mrs. Bains, "because they would be free from the cost of having to pay to have their bale of cotton ginned. The wagons then would line up just like you line up for gasoline, one behind the other, and wait their turn to get their cotton ginned." The slowness of moving horse- or mule-drawn wagons and later tractor-pulled trailers in and out of the gin yard would lead to yet another revolution in technology.

The farmer would check in at the office to set up his account and then wait in line with the wagon. If his cotton could not be ginned that day, he would leave the wagon in the yard, ride his horse or mule home for the evening, and return the same way the following day. If he lived at a distance, he would remain at the gin yard, eating a cold supper and sleeping under the wagon.

Mrs. Bains added a telling detail:

When they would bring in the wagons, the hands, as we called them, brought with them a little lunch and they would sit out there with their wagons. They'd put some of that lunch material, containers and so forth, in the wagon with the cotton, not thinking anything about what happened to it. If it were glass or a can that they'd been drinking out of, it would shoot through the chute into the gin and would catch on fire. The fire was down inside the cotton bale after it was pressed and brought out, and the person who was putting the bales out for sale would find a hot spot on the side of it, if the fire was way down deep. I believe that the treatment was to cut a little hole in the hottest spot, maybe a triangle or a round hole, and pour kerosene in there through a funnel to put the fire out. Kerosene smothered the fire inside the bale.

During ginning season the entire town lived by whistles. One was used to announce the beginning of the twelve-hour ginning day and to bring forward

Exterior of Farmers Gin Association gin plant at Burton, Texas, built in 1914. *Courtesy Richard Hofmeister, Smithsonian Institution*

Approximate configuration of Farmers Gin Association initial system. *From F. H. Lummus Sons Co. Catalogue, 1913; courtesy Lummus Industries, Inc.*

the first wagon. Another was used for the midday break, and a louder, longer whistle blast was used to call for help in case of fire.

Gins were located in towns with transportation connections, and as seen earlier, the gin was the center of the community. If four or five large gins were clustered together, a trading center formed that drew growers from an eight- to ten-mile radius. Smaller gins served growers from a four- to five-mile radius, depending upon roads and geography.

An example of the custom gin and its relationship to the community was (and is still) found in Burton, Texas. Burton lies in Washington County, the northern part of Stephen F. Austin's original land grant, and was settled primarily by German immigrants. In 1913, the Wendt and Knipstein gins turned out about forty-five hundred bales, and so much cotton was being produced in the area that another gin was needed.

On December 2, 1913, a group of area farmers and ranchers met to organize the Burton Farmers Gin Association. A board of directors was elected, and city residents were permitted membership in the company. Shares were to be issued at fifty dollars each. A second meeting took place on December 15, and a committee was established to obtain pledges to purchase enough shares to equal ten thousand dollars. Stockholders could not acquire more than six shares. At this meeting a constitution was adopted, and annual meetings were set for the second Thursday in January of each year. The members who were present decided to buy lots, construct a gin, and purchase machinery.

In early 1914, the Burton Farmers Gin Association spent $11,800 to construct a two-story gin and cottonseed storage building of galvanized iron. (A larger seed house was added in 1921.) A well was dug to provide water for the boiler, and the steam engine was fueled by some two hundred cords of wood per season until the owners began to use coal in 1919.[13]

The initial ginning system was set up like others of the time. A Tips steam engine powered an eighty-foot-long line shaft on the ground floor, and pulleys operated four and later a fifth gin stand on the second floor. A telescope was used to suction cotton from the wagons and into the air flow and send it to the separator from which it dropped into the distributing system. A spiked belt carried the seed cotton to the feeders and gin stands. A screw conveyor carried seed to a bucket elevator at one end of the battery of gin stands. The chain-driven bucket elevator was a vertical conduit containing buckets or cups for collecting and moving seed into its own dis-

Bucket elevator; at the Farmers Gin in Burton, the elevator is made of wood. *From Lummus Cotton Gin Co. Catalogue, no. 35, ca. 1940; courtesy Lummus Industries, Inc.*

tribution system to the seed house or the customer's seed bin. The ginned lint was pneumatically carried to the battery condenser and double-box bale press.

In 1925, the Burton gin was modernized, and the steam engine was replaced with a Bessemer Model IV, 125-horsepower diesel engine. The Bessemer, a ten-thousand-gallon fuel tank, pillar blocks, a new mechanical room for the engine, and freight charges amounted to $7,800, even with the steam engine traded in—almost the cost of the entire gin plant eleven years before. The Bessemer arrived partly assembled and had to be moved by local residents using jacks and prybars to inch the five-ton engine along a wooden track from a flatcar on the Southern Pacific Railroad siding fifty yards uphill to the concrete pad inside the new mechanical room. The effort required a day and a half, and residents say that the men cheered when the engine was moved onto the pad and bolt placement was a perfect fit.

The noisy engine expelled exhaust through vertical stacks behind the building directly into the air. (Mufflers made from an old boiler were placed under

Bessemer Type IV diesel engine, 1925. *Courtesy Jeff Tinsley, Smithsonian Institution*

the engine room floor, where they remain.) Ten years later, complaints about soot led to the use of exhaust pipes which were laid in the ground, their exposed ends aimed at the railroad right of way. Neighbors claimed that their noise was almost identical to that of a locomotive. The noise of the diesel engine was distinctive, as described by O. R. Carey. "You could hear one of those old gas oilers running for ten miles on a good clear morning about sunup, every time it turned over."[14]

A cooling tower was erected a few yards from the engine room to provide a source of circulating water for the Bessemer. Gin hands could take showers in the wooden room built beneath the metal tank. Starting the Bessemer required two men working for about two hours to prepare the engine. An air compressor powered by a Model T Ford engine was replaced by an electric motor in 1940. Once operational, the engine would continue with little attention for most of the day, being idled down at times of equipment maintenance or lunch.

The Bessemer was used continuously until 1962, when a crosshead failed in one cylinder, freezing the engine after only two bales had been ginned. Since the engine powered the line shaft to which the belts and pulleys were connected, the week's repair time that followed completely stopped all ginning. Later that year, a 125-horsepower Allis Chalmers electric motor was installed, making gin operation easier and more efficient, but the Bessemer was repaired and used as an auxiliary power source.[15] The Burton Farmers Gin remained in continuous operation from its first season in 1914 until its last season in 1974. Even though most of the original equipment was gradually replaced by both new and used equipment, as growing and harvesting conditions changed, the gin remains a remarkable example of sixty years of ginning technology.

Most of the equipment was purchased from the Lummus Cotton Gin Co., and Billy Thompson, executive technical coordinator with Lummus Industries, described the gin plant as it was when it was "mothballed" in 1974 for the next season's cotton.

A second telescope was added to increase seed cotton input and reduce time spent repositioning

Account ledgers for Farmers Gin Association gin at Burton, still readable after sixty years. *Courtesy Richard Hofmeister, Smithsonian Institution*

the long trucks and trailers that replaced the shorter wagons. Seed cotton was moved by air from the truck to the unloading separator located high in the gin building. Suction air was provided by a large centrifugal fan. The seed cotton was discharged from the separator into a hot air system which lowered the moisture content of the cotton and enabled the machinery to produce a cleaner and smoother grade of fiber. The drying air was heated by a large gas burner and was pulled through the burner with a fan. The seed cotton from the separator was blown through a tower drier and then through a Lummus Thermo-Cleaner that, in addition to drying, removed sand and other trash from the cotton. The seed cotton was transported by the same air stream to a Lummus hot air cleaner. A second fan was used to pull the air and trash from the hot air cleaner, known as a push-pull system.

The seed cotton was discharged from the hot air cleaner into a Lummus "Little Giant" stick and green leaf extractor, then to a Lummus hull separator, and into the belt distributor from earlier days. The distributor carried the seed cotton to a battery of five Lummus (L-E-F) extractor feeders over eighty-saw

automatic air blast gin stands with double spiral picker rollers. The ginned seed was carried by screw conveyors to a bucket elevator that lifted the seed to an overhead seed scale where the seed were weighed. From the scale, the seed could be diverted to the seed storage house or into a sterilizer before being conveyed to the customer's seed bin. The sterilizer was required to control the pink bollworm which began to infest cotton crops in large numbers during the 1940s.

The ginned lint was pneumatically conveyed from the gin stands through a lint flue to a lint cleaner manufactured by Moss-Gordin, and from there it was blown into the battery condenser. The lint from the condenser was sent as a batt down the lint slide and into the tramper charging box. The chain-driven tramper (developed by Thaddeus Grimes) pressed the lint into the wooden double box press where steel "dogs" held the cotton in place. While one box was filling, seed cotton in the other was compressed by means of a hydraulic, up-packing ram. The press box doors were bottom hinged, and once the bale was wrapped and tied, it was removed from the press and rolled onto the floor. The finished bale was lifted

Illustration of Lummus Thermo-Cleaner of the type installed at the Farmers Gin Association gin at Burton. *From Lummus Cotton Gin Co. Catalogue, no. 35, ca. 1940; courtesy Lummus Industries, Inc.*

Lummus Hull-Separator and Cleaner of the type installed at the Farmers Gin Association gin at Burton. *From F. H. Lummus Sons Co. Catalogue, no. 28, ca. 1928; courtesy Lummus Industries, Inc.*

by block and tackle onto a scale where it was weighed and tagged.[16]

Bales at the Farmers Gin varied between 319 and 670 pounds, with an average of 550 pounds. It took about 1,350 pounds of handpicked and 1,500 pounds of machine-picked cotton to make a 500-pound bale. (In contrast, 2,250 pounds of stripped cotton made a bale in the South Plains area.) Cotton was hand-

picked in the Burton area until the 1950s, and laborers were paid between one and two cents per pound, while growers earned between ten and thirty-five cents per pound. Ginning charges amounted to $1.70 per hundredweight for picked cotton, $2.40 for any machine-harvested cotton, and $4.25 for bagging, ties, and buckles. By 1971, the price of ginning hand-picked cotton was $2.05, while machine-harvested cotton was $2.75. Bagging and ties had risen to $6.50.

The crew at Burton usually consisted of a manager and four gin hands: two ginners, one press man, and an engineer. If the crew was shorthanded or there was an emergency, women worked side by side with men on the ginning floor, but they normally functioned as bookkeepers, assigning bale numbers, recording weights, and issuing separate receipts for bales and for cottonseed.

Weight determined the ginning fee, which was usually offset by selling the seed back to the gin. The grower was not required to physically "catch" his seed and reweigh it; the value was determined by multiplying 60 or 62 percent times the weight of the seed cot-

Belt distributor, feeder, and 80-saw gin stand with double spiral picker rollers, all Lummus. *Courtesy Jeff Tinsley, Smithsonian Institution*

Lummus bale press; original wooden sills were replaced with steel sills; up-packing press box is bottom hinged. At rear is second box (below tramper charging box) with steel "dogs" in place. Background shows Moss-Gordin lint cleaner, ca. 1960. *Courtesy Jeff Tinsley, Smithsonian Institution*

ton to determine the amount and hundredweight value of the seed. The grower could, however, collect his seed and sell what he did not require for planting or livestock feed directly to an oil mill in Brenham. Brazos Valley Cotton Company was the buyer for most of Burton's cotton.

As illustrated by the South Plains gin receipt on page 90, the grower's transaction with the gin was itemized by each wagon load of cotton. By the time he was in the fifth grade, Donald Baird had become skilled at figuring gin receipts. The receipt was printed with the gin owner's name and the gin's bond number; in this case, his father owned the gin. The cotton grower's name was filled in on the top line, and the landlord's name followed. (The initials on the gin receipt shown stood for W. P. Bratwell.) The date and bale number followed. Baird explained:

After the bale number came the gross weight of the wagon (wagon plus seed cotton). The tare weight was that of the empty wagon. Net weight meant the weight of the seed cotton. We charged thirty cents per hundredweight at the time [1933], and the hundredweight multiplied by 30¢ gave you $4.08 for ginning. We charged $1.00 for bagging and ties, and we hauled the bale to town for 10¢. That gave a total of $5.18 for ginning, wrapping, and hauling the bale to town. The seed weight was 816 pounds, figured on about 60 percent of the weight of the bale. We didn't have seed scales that gave the actual weight until later. For many years we had half-and-half cotton—that is, half seed, half cotton. But after there got to be so many sticks, burrs, and trash in it, we had to go to the bale weight and figure a percentage from that in order to keep the amounts clear. Most accounts were settled at the end of the season, but if the farmer needed money halfway through the season, he could sell his cotton for a certain price and settle up with the gin. If he had more cotton, he could run another tab and settle up later on. These particular farmers took their seed home because they had lots of cows to feed.

Both the cotton grower and the ginner were concerned with the quality of cotton. Classing cotton to determine its quality and therefore its value was a skill practiced by factors and buyers and often a

C. D. BAIRD GIN

BONDED GIN NO. 3146

Dressy, Texas

Mr. *Frank Garner*

Landlord *W P B*

Date *9 — 26*, 193*3*

Do Not Lose This Bill

Bale No. *578*			
Gross Weight	2	4	2	0
Tare	1	0	6	0
Net	1	3	6	0
Ginning at per Cwt.			3	0
Bagging and Ties		4	0	8
Hauled to Town		1	1	0
Total		5	1	8
Net Weight of Seed		8	1	6
Disposition ½ Rent Carried Home				
Sud. Home				
Sold at $ _____ per ton				
Less Ginning and Wrapping				
Check for Balance				

By Cash 3 5 0 0

By Check 1 8 7 4

Total $ 5 3 7 4

$ 50.90

Farmer's ginning account slip issued by the C. D. Baird Gin, September 26, 1933. *Courtesy Donald Baird*

mystery to the grower. He knew his variety of plant and could estimate the number of bales he would have, but the value of his crop was determined by others. The purpose of classing was to match bales of similar grade, staple, color, and character in lots for better representation of the quality of the crop within the area and to enable the spinner to meet his own milling requirements. Each bale was sampled and classified by grade, staple length, and character.

Grade referred to the color and smoothness of the fibers and the amount of trash content in the bale. Color was determined by the amount of rainfall and could be snowy white, spotted, tinged yellow, or gray, all of which would affect the brightness of the fabric. The quality of smoothness was affected by the ginning process. High moisture content would make fibers rough or matted and reduce their value. Less trash content meant cleaner fibers.

In 1909, the U.S. Department of Agriculture established nine standards for grading upland cotton: middling fair, strict good middling, good middling, strict middling, middling, strict low middling, low middling, strict good ordinary, and good ordinary. White grades of cotton that fell into these categories, especially if the staple length was one inch or greater, received the highest prices. There were five additional white grades, five tinged grades, and three grades each for yellow- or blue-stained cotton. In 1918, the U.S. Department of Agriculture established staple standards. Longer fibers were stronger and preferred by the mills. A weak, immature fiber would make small neps (knots) and fail to absorb as much dye, thus reducing the quality of the fabric. Character referred to general smoothness, cleanliness, and preparation for market.[17]

During the 1930s, farmers had difficulty paying their ginning fees. If the farmer could not pay them, the ginner sold the cotton for the farmer, settled the account, and gave the farmer a check for the balance. The ginner would take the bales to a "cotton yard" where a public weighmaster would weigh each bale and issue a receipt for the bale to indicate its weight and to show that it had been delivered by the ginner.

The farmer could sell his own cotton if he wanted to. According to Donald Baird: "The farmer would go to the cotton yard, get his sample, and carry it up the street to the cotton buyers. Most of the bigger merchants in town would buy cotton, and straight cotton buyers would come into town and be there the whole season. They would pay the farmer according to however the cotton classed out and for the weight of the bale."

In the early days samples were rough cut from a bale for the buyer's inspection. Bales sampled several times and left exposed to the elements could quickly depreciate in value. The U.S. Department of Agriculture standardized grading procedures beginning in 1958. As a bale was being pressed, three lint samples of about a handful each were taken from the bale. In order to be representative, one sample came from each side of the bale and one from the middle. Each sample was wrapped in brown paper, tied with string, tagged with the grower's identification, and sent by the ginner or the compress to U.S. Department of Agriculture cotton classing offices. (In Texas, they were located in Austin, Waco, Dallas, or Lubbock.) The classing office returned a sample card to the grower that included the gin's license number, the warehouse bale number, and the grade.

Because cotton would not perish like food crops and there was always a market available, cotton could be stored for long periods of time. Once the quality of the bale was established, it might be sold through a cotton merchant or a marketing cooperative to the spinner and temporarily stored in a warehouse or shipped directly to market. In many cases, however, bales were stored in government-approved warehouses and the grower could immediately borrow money based on the value of his cotton.

Frankie Jaster operated a government-approved warehouse only a few blocks from the Farmers Gin in Burton. To avoid problems relating to confusion about ownership, the grower brought his own bales in wagons to the warehouse. Jaster weighed the bale and took samples from the sides if the grower wanted them for a local buyer and usually charged $1.50 for this service. After receiving, weighing, and tagging each bale, he issued a receipt to establish ownership. Jaster, who was bonded, could store the bales up to two years. "Sample tags and receipts were important," he stated. "They could be used to borrow money from the bank. If stolen, they could be used to secure a fraudulent loan!"[18]

Using stored cotton as collateral, the grower could obtain a loan from the federal government in the fall which would come due in the summer. According to Jaster, "The government released bales in July. The farmer could redeem his cotton at that time by paying back the loan, but that seldom happened. The government usually claimed the cotton. Both the farmer and the government speculated. Cotton might be worth more—or less—when it was released in July."

The government worked through buyers like Brazos Valley Cotton Company, Allenberg, and Anderson, Clayton and Company, and when the bales were sold, Jaster was responsible for "out handling" the bales on two-wheeled hand trucks to the Southern Pacific Railroad dock a few yards from the warehouse.

The delicate and intricate business of ginning, selling, and storing cotton was inseparable from the fluctuating baseline of production. Down from the thousands of bales processed by the Burton gin in the early years, only eighteen were ginned in 1973, and sixteen the following year. The Farmers Gin Association was optimistic, however, and in November, 1974, the equipment was lubricated, belts were loosened, and records were left in place for the next season. No more cotton was ginned, however, and an entirely unexpected future awaited that gin plant.

If the Farmers Gin at Burton remained frozen in time, changes were taking place elsewhere that would catapult ginning into the realms of industry and agribusiness.

CHAPTER NINE

The Gin at Kickapoo

To reach the Stanford gin on the Kickapoo was to travel east of Burton and backward in time. Turning left off a rusty trestle bridge, one took a steep angling road downhill and into the heart of the Trinity River valley where cotton fields that had once covered one thousand acres disappeared into the tree lines. The road passed through dense stands of pine and oak, sweet gum and dogwood, wound through a thicket that dripped Spanish moss, and straightened near a broad pasture with a dairy building on the right. Like a slow-moving southern stream, the road meandered across a railroad track and curved to the left, toward the foothills on the north side of Kickapoo Creek.

The WBT&S railroad track lay parallel to the farm road and in front of a string of half a dozen frame houses whose porches faced the track. The WBT&S ran from Livingston (eleven miles east of the farm) to Trinity, Groveton, Camden, and points north. The WBT&S stood for Waco, Beaumont, Trinity and Sabine, although the line never went as far as Beaumont. Folks in East Texas called it the "Wobblety, Bobblety, Turnover and Stop." The track crossed Kickapoo Creek by means of a small trestle bridge and disappeared into the forest; the farm road curved to the right, crossed the creek, and swept uphill toward Onalaska.

Nestled in that curve stood a general store, a couple of barns, a blacksmith's shop, and the cotton gin. Lewis S. Stanford owned and ran the gin, which remained in continuous operation from 1917 through 1968, for thirty-five of those fifty-one years.

"My daddy was sawmillin' over in Trinity," Stanford explained. "He came to Onalaska in 1911 and bought a farm." Samuel Tyler Stanford, the son of a Confederate soldier who had ridden from Appomattox to the small town of Carlisle, Texas, to start over after the war, was born in Trinity County in 1876 and spent most of his life there before moving to Polk County. Samuel Stanford and three stockholders established the Onalaska Livestock Company to raise cattle and cotton and to build a sawmill and the gin.

The first gin was built in 1912 next to a sawmill pond to get water for the boiler. My daddy ran it there until 1917. That was when he put the boiler on a flatcar and moved it to Kickapoo, to the center of the farm. The boiler was moved with a stump puller and winch, by mule team to and from the flatcar, and from the flatcar to the gin building. A peckerwood sawmill stood next to the gin until 1933. We used the same belt from the sawmill to drive the gin pulley. This way we didn't have to burn valuable timber as fuel for the boiler. The belt was sixty feet long, fourteen inches wide, and one-half inch thick. I probably put enough new string laces on that belt to make one whole cowhide.[1]

The gin operated from August through December with most activity in October, and the sawmill was activated whenever there was a need for lumber for the owners or their neighbors during the rest of the year. A gristmill on the ground floor of the gin operated each Saturday year-round from 1917 through 1968.

As more families moved into the Trinity River valley and fenced off their farms, the open range along the river bottom quickly diminished. Within a few years of settling on Kickapoo Creek, the Onalaska Livestock Company was forced to sell three hundred head of cattle. In a twist of fate, this trend would be reversed in the late 1940s.

A small community grew up across the road from the gin until there were thirty families living and working on the farm. A one-room schoolhouse was built next to the general store, and in 1924, a young woman named Bessie Mae Clarke was hired to teach the tenants' children. Three years later, that schoolhouse was modified to become the home of newlyweds Bessie Mae and Lewis Stanford.

During ginning season, the farm crew became a labor force for the gin. One man was needed to work the telescope inside the wagons full of seed cotton; another oversaw the gin stands; the blacksmith and another hand ran the press. Lewis himself weighed in the cotton and kept the books. The tenants were paid with "Kickapoo checks," coin-sized brass pieces with a value stamped on one side and "Onalaska Livestock Company" stamped on the other. The "checks" were good at the farm commissary and at a mercantile store in Onalaska.

Samuel Stanford held two big barbeques for his tenants each summer. The first was held on June 19, commemorating the day in 1865 when Negro slaves in Texas had received word of their emancipation. The other barbeque was held on July 4. He cooked three beeves and six to twelve goats for each celebration. The cooking was done in a pit near the Kickapoo, and food was spread out on tables along the creek bank. Eating, singing, dancing, and storytelling lasted until the food was gone, and the moon was high, and the gin shone like a mirror in the dark shadows of the valley. Lewis was sawing timber when he learned of his mother's death in 1932. His father died the following year. No more barbeques were held, and the sawmill was dismantled. The farm's primary focus became cotton.

The steam-driven gin at Kickapoo was of two-story construction, with the stands and bale press on the ginning floor and the line shaft and pulleys underneath. In 1928, the gin was converted to diesel power, using a two-cylinder Fairbanks-Morse engine to operate two Lummus gin stands. Like most ginners, Stanford was faced with the dilemma of turning out the best samples possible at the greatest cost effec-

Catalogue illustration of a three-cylinder diesel engine. *From Continental Cotton Ginning Machinery Catalogue, no. 165-A, ca. 1933; courtesy Continental Eagle Corporation*

tiveness for his gin. That meant upgrading machinery whenever possible, adapting instead of replacing the entire system. Over the years he chose new equipment carefully, always considering the moisture content and cleanliness of his cotton, which was still picked by hand.

Single-story gin outfit. Overflow, Thermo-Cleaner, and seed scale are of particular interest. *From Lummus Cotton Gin Co. Catalogue, no. 35, ca. 1940; courtesy Lummus Industries*

As system gin manufacturers expanded their product lines, ginners had more equipment than ever to
choose from. Turn-of-the-century systems included
pneumatic handling of seed cotton by telescope from
the wagon to the separator, a spiked belt distributor,
chutes or droppers to flat feeders and into sixty- or
seventy-saw gin stands, rectangular flues through
which lint blew to a master condenser, a steam-driven
tramper over the cotton box, and an up-packing
screw press for the bale box. The Murray patent cotton elevator could be substituted for the belt distributor. Screw conveying systems removed seed from
under the ginning floor and carried it to both the
seed house and the customer bin. Some gin compresses began to be manufactured and sold, although
most flat bales were taken to large compress and warehouse facilities in centralized rural areas and less often
to port cities.

By 1930, all gin manufacturers were turning out
similar systems. One story installations were favored
for new gin plants, but equipment had to be usable
in the older buildings, many of which remained
throughout the Cotton Belt. A plantation, single-
gin outfit consisted of a pneumatic elevator, feeder,
plain or huller rib gin stands, condenser, and single
box press. Newer plants, however, were increasingly
designed for bulk handling of seed cotton.

Two types of cleaners came into popular use.

Revolving drum separator to be placed above conveyor
distributor. *From Continental Cotton Ginning Machinery
Catalogue, no. 165-A, ca. 1933; courtesy Continental Eagle Corporation*

Beater cleaners requiring an air-sealed construction
were placed in the air line through which seed cotton passed from the bins or telescopes to the sepa-
rators. Later units combined the air line cleaner and
separator. By 1911, overhead bulk cleaners were placed
outside the air line. Known as gravity cleaners, they
did not depend upon the air flow but instead used
revolving cylinders to clean trash from the seed cotton. The air line cleaner had its cleaning cylinders
parallel with the air current, but the popularity of
gravity cleaners brought about the improvement of
the air line cleaner by placing its cylinders at a right
angle to the air current.[2]

In 1918, an overhead bulk cleaner with a boll
breaker was invented and used in Mississippi, and in
1927, the Gullett Gin Company devised a gravity
cleaner with boll breaker, in both horizontal and inclined units. Continental advertised a cotton cleaner
with boll breaker and cleaner separator. Inside the
separator, loose dirt and trash were removed from the
seed cotton that then passed through a vacuum feeder
to a breaker bar where unopened bolls were broken
into bits. The cotton moved under four rollers,
passed over a screen for additional cleaning, and was
discharged into the distributor. Trash fell through the
screen to a conveyor for removal from the system.[3]

Bulk cleaning meant bulk feeding into the gin
stands. Flat and small drum feeders were replaced by
large single drum feeders connected to a pneumati-

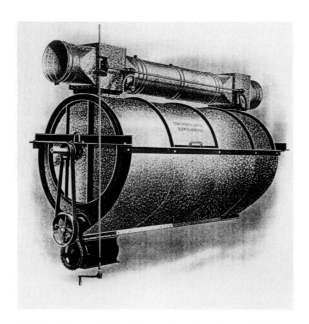

Air line cleaner designed to trap rocks and metal objects
before they reach the elevator. *From Continental Cotton Ginning Machinery Catalogue, no. 165-A, ca. 1933; courtesy Continental Eagle Corporation*

Seventy-saw, air blast gin with huller feature. *From Lummus Cotton Gin Co. Catalogue, no. 1612, ca. 1910; courtesy Lummus Industries*

cally fed dropper. A float in the upper part of the roll box remained in contact with the seed cotton by means of a spring. Pressure against the float was determined by the tightness or looseness of the roll, and the movement of the spring along a lever that controlled the float adjusted the rate of feed. If the roll were too tight, the float would lift and thus reduce the amount of feed; if it were too loose, the float would drop and increase the amount of feed. If the breast of the gin had to be raised for inspection, to dump hulls, or to clear a chokage, often caused by damp hulls, the feeder would automatically shut off; once the breast was lowered, the feed would begin again.[4] The Stephen D. Murray Company made a popular big drum feeder, and the John E. Mitchell Company added extracting features to its feeder to remove large trash.

Common features on seventy- and eighty-saw gin stands were twelve-inch diameter saws, automatic feed controls, and direct connect couplings for air blast gin stands. Lummus added double picker rolls, one spiked cylinder placed on top of the other, to separate cotton locks from burrs. A seedboard kept the seed roll in place in order to be picked up by the saws, and burrs, hulls, and trash fell to the bottom to be removed by the conveyor. Continental gin stands incorporated an independent saw and brush drive capa-

bility. This meant that the saw cylinders and brushes were driven from opposite ends of the gin stand, reducing belt slippage and increasing efficiency.[5]

Burr machines were developed in the mid-1920s. The Hancock Picker was a vertical burr extractor that used belts of carding cloth to hold locks of cotton while stems, hulls, and burrs were stripped and brushed. The trash was carried away by screw conveyor while the seed cotton continued toward the gin stand. The Streun Big Bur extractor made by Hardwicke-Etter of Sherman, Texas, was a horizontal machine that used stripper and doffer cylinders to remove foreign matter from the seed cotton.[6]

Lint flues, which had been rectangular wooden conduits, were first lined with and then replaced by galvanized iron. Individual condensers, which had once been set behind the gin stands, were replaced by a single battery condenser over the lint slide at the press. Single-box screw presses continued to be manufactured, but double-box presses were becoming more popular. Belt-driven and steam-powered trampers were available. Chain-driven and hydraulic models were also in use. Hydraulic rams were replacing screws for greater bale densities.

In July 1930, Congress passed an act to establish

Master condenser with down discharge; some units discharged up. *From Lummus Cotton Gin Co. Bulletin no. 660, ca. 1940; courtesy Lummus Industries, Inc.*

Tower drier, invented by Charles A. Bennett, became a necessary feature of every gin. *From Lummus Cotton Gin Co. Bulletin no. 635, ca. 1940; courtesy Lummus Industries, Inc.*

the Regional Research Ginning Laboratories at Stoneville, Mississippi; Mesilla Park, New Mexico; Clemson, South Carolina; and Chickasha, Oklahoma, for the U.S. Department of Agriculture. Research had begun in 1926 to explore drying methods to reduce losses from ginning moist, and especially machine-picked, cotton. Charles A. Bennett, assigned to the Delta Station at Tallulah, Louisiana, experimented with previous horizontal and vertical tray driers, but his tower drier, first used in Stoneville on the crop of 1932, became the "Government Tower Drier." It was initially used with a steam coil heater, but experiments included natural gas burners, fuel oil, and heat from internal combustion engines. The twenty-two-foot-high tower had thirteen shelves (or floors). Cotton from the telescope moved through the separator and was routed by an unloading fan through a pipe and into the drier where it tumbled down the shelves to an outlet at the bottom and continued its path to the gin stands. The tower drier was produced by gin manufacturers in full and shorter heights for different installations.

The Great Depression affected the grower, the ginner, and the gin manufacturer alike. Cotton prices

had always fluctuated. From an all-time low in 1898 when a crop of eleven million bales had sold for less than five cents per pound, the price of cotton rose to a high of thirty-eight cents per pound for an eleven million bale crop in 1919. In 1926, the enormous crop of eighteen million bales sold for about eleven cents per pound. In 1931, the crop of fifteen and one-half million bales fell to five cents per pound. The cotton industry came to a halt.[7]

The Bankhead Bill of 1936 reduced cotton acreage in an effort to stabilize production and raise prices, and Stanford's allotment was seven hundred acres. His worst year was 1933, when it took all seven hundred acres to produce one bale of cotton. The U.S. Department of Agriculture issued stamps to farmers based upon their allotment. The allotment, established by the local USDA board, was based upon average yield. The grower could not sell his cotton without the stamps, and if he grew more than he was allotted, he could not sell the extra amount. The stamps came in sheets with the grower's identification number on one end, but the stamps were in five pound increments, and when the ginner tore them off the sheet, there was no way to know whose they were. Ginners were required to collect the stamps from the growers and mail them in to the USDA offices. Donald Baird's father was a Coleman County ginner who preferred to drive two hundred miles to Dallas to deliver the stamps rather than trusting them to the mail, but the box full of stamps "was like so much confetti," Baird explained. When his father reached the USDA office in Dallas, he set the box on a table and told the clerk, "You count it!" The use of stamps to try to keep the growers and ginners "honest" was quickly suspended.[8]

During the Depression, ginners made do with the equipment they had, and gin manufacturers turned to pursuits such as making steel buildings for gin plants, a few cotton driers, and even road grading equipment to keep their workers employed. Harvesting and ginning cost the grower almost as much money as the cotton would bring when sold.[9]

The National Industrial Recovery Act of 1932 required gin manufacturers to organize formally into an industry, eliminating competitive prices and sales terms in keeping with the new practices demanded of other industries, but this enforced economic rigidity was dropped as soon as the economy began to improve. In the meantime, manufacturers remained optimistic. Continental, which set up both brush and air blast gins at its Birmingham factory for demonstration purposes, displayed its equipment at the Ginners Convention in Dallas for the first time in 1935.

Lummus, known for its active research department, continued to exhibit its new developments at the convention.

The 1938–39 season brought both a shortage of cotton and low prices, and the impending war required a restructuring of manufacturing processes and tools for production of war materiel. Continental competed for and was awarded contracts by the Navy to manufacture gun mounts and gun shields. Additional contracts were awarded for five-inch gun shields, 100-pound chemical bombs, sighting systems, fragmentation bombs, rockets, and other items. Continental won production awards, including the Navy "E" pennant, from the Navy Department's Bureau of Ordnance.

Lummus was equally involved in the war effort, manufacturing power-driven magnetic cable reels and stern towing chocks for mine sweepers, bow plates, deck and pilot house assemblies, ammunition racks for submarine patrol vessels, a mine release device for mines placed by parachute, and high explosive shells. Lummus was awarded the Army-Navy "E" Award for production excellence.

While both companies' manufacturing was necessarily devoted to the war effort, their design teams continued to work on improvements to gin stands and to auxiliary drying and cleaning machinery. After the war it took several years for manufacturers to return to standard production and for growers to acquire the capital to spend for new equipment, but increased reliance on machine harvesting would make this new equipment necessary for the cotton growers' survival.

Cotton production played an important role during World War II. A bulletin published by the Texas Agricultural Experiment Station at College Station in 1942 stated that there was a greater need for cotton (2.5 million tons) than for rubber (1 million tons) and that it required at least 250 pounds of cotton per soldier to equip the army. In this sense, of course, cotton uses varied from clothing and bandages to food, paint, and ammunition.

There was no shortage of cotton, but the bulletin urged growing varieties of longer-than-average staple length ($^{15}/_{16}$ as opposed to ⅞ inches) for the best spinning varieties without loss of yield. Spinning qualities were especially important because domestic textile mills were not buying a sufficient quantity of Texas cotton in proportion to the amount produced. The strength of the fibers was averaged between a mix of good and poor varieties, rather than on a uniform strength from a single variety. Since Texas (and other states) had lost many of its foreign markets due to the war, domestic markets had to be found and the strength of the fibers (which determined spinning qualities and therefore price) taken into consideration more than ever before.

The bulletin also stressed the need for a pricing structure based on uniform quality of the fiber rather than on "hog round" or "point buying." Well before the outbreak of the war, the loan value of cotton was set by the USDA classing office in each area. If a buyer offered a grower so many "points" over the loan value, the grower could sell it to the buyer. If not, the grower could sell the cotton to the government. The 1942 bulletin stated rather bluntly:

> The interests of merchants in quality may be quite different from those of the growers and those of the manufacturers. The merchants' stock in trade is that of knowing the quality of cotton produced in the various areas of the cotton belt and that of knowing the quality of cotton demanded by the various mills. Merchants are vitally interested in maintaining a margin between buying and selling prices that will yield a profit over their operating costs. It does not follow that the merchants are particularly concerned about the maintenance of a price system in the farmers' market recognizing in full the quality demands of the mills. The prevalence of "point buying" throughout the cotton belt is evidence to the contrary. "Point buying" fails in large measure to take care of differences in the quality of specific bales, as represented by grade and staple length. Producers of high quality cotton are underpaid; producers of low quality cotton are overpaid. This failure of the local market to recognize quality is most discouraging to the grower who might wish to improve the quality of his cotton. "Point buying" succeeds in taking care of differences in average quality among the different local markets [and] discourages individual effort to improve quality.

The solution was for a community to concentrate on growing a single variety for "even running lots as to staple length and spinning quality" and to "facilitate good ginning."[10] Frederick Law Olmsted would certainly have appreciated this approach.

In conclusion, the bulletin applauded the low cost of cotton production in Texas as a distinct advantage to growers. Rainfall affected the amount of hoeing and cultivating necessary to control weeds, while soils, topography, climate, and natural ground cover affected the type of machinery that could be used for harvesting. A family on the High Plains, where an annual rainfall of twenty inches was average, could manage two hundred acres with two-row tractor equipment and produce seventy-five bales with less time spent in the fields at a cost of about five cents per pound of lint (based on prevailing prices from 1933 to 1938). By contrast, in Northeast Texas, which closely resembled other parts of the Cotton Belt with its timbered areas, smaller fields, and higher average rainfall of forty-five inches, one-row and part-row horse-drawn equipment was commonly used. More weed control was required, leading to more chopping and hoeing in the fields, and the cost of producing one pound of lint rose to thirteen cents. The answer to the problem of cost productivity was to be found in greater mechanization. Two- and four-row tractor equipment was needed, and once wartime restrictions were lifted, large-scale mechanical harvesting could begin.

The shortage of labor during the war called more and more for hand-snapped and machine-stripped cotton. Dirt in cotton lowered its grade and placed more responsibility than ever on the ginner to provide an acceptable sample. Deems and McDaniel of Continental developed an impact cleaner to remove the increased amounts of hulls, leaves, and other trash. As described in a 1952 Continental sales catalogue, "This machine was composed of a series of cylinders using discs, spaced sufficiently apart to permit the hulls to pass through, and a series of spiked drums above the disc cylinders. The cotton passing

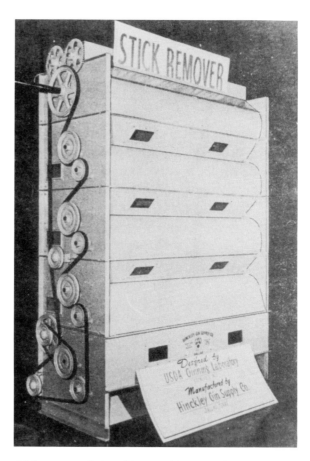

Stick remover designed by Gerald N. Franks. *From C. A. Bennett,* Cotton Ginning Systems in the United States and Auxiliary Developments

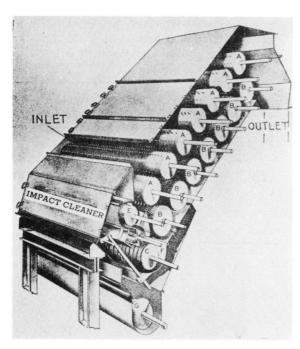

Deems-McDaniel Impact Cleaner using a combination of spiked drums, serrated disks, reclaimer saws, a reclaimer brush, return roller, and hull pan with trash conveyor at the bottom. *From C. A. Bennett,* Cotton Ginning Systems in the United States and Auxiliary Developments

through the machine was thrown back and forth between the series of cylinders, loosening the hulls which, along with the dirt, dropped through the space between the discs. Surprisingly, this machine also removed a large amount of motes which heretofore had been removed largely by the gin."[11]

Continental's Eugene H. Brooks, of their Dallas facility, devised a lint cleaner to eliminate motes and any leaf or pepper trash that had slipped through the gin stand. The lint cleaner, which had its own condenser, was positioned behind the battery of gin stands. "This machine removed the trash from the lint as it passed from the gins to the press, and on all except especially clean picked cotton, this machine increased the value of a bale of cotton from $10.00 to $20.00 per bale."[12]

A ninety-saw gin stand with changes in the frame, roll box, and moting system, designed by Continental in 1949, was first marketed in 1951 and was highly successful. Gerald N. Franks of the U.S. Department of Agriculture Ginning Laboratory at Stoneville, Mississippi, received a patent in January, 1952, for a stick remover. The device looked similar to a tower drier, but was wider and not as high. It used a kicker roller to send cotton downward past a series of saws and brushes that would sling off sticks into a large trash hopper for removal and then discharge the seed cotton toward the feeders.[13]

Lummus had been equally active during these years. The popular automatic huller gin, developed by Thaddeus Grimes in 1917, had a double spiral roller that separated the hulls and discharged them automatically. This feature was important to the ginner because of adaptations to the cotton plant to make it storm-proof (that is, bolls were less easily broken off the stalks by high winds and rain) and because of the increased amounts of trash from hand-snapped and machine-stripped cotton. During the late 1930s, Lummus developed and patented a double moting eighty-saw gin stand. The double moting system removed motes (immature seed bearing immature fibers) and trash from areas above and below the air blast nozzle. A twelve-inch canvas belt extending the length of the battery of gin stands carried away motes from above the nozzle, and a hull conveyor beneath the gin stands carried away motes and trash from the area below the nozzle. Lummus also manufactured an extractor feeder, a cleaning feeder, gravity (the Trashmaster) and air line cleaners, the Thermo-Cleaner (for drying and conditioning cotton), an all-metal condenser, single- and double-box presses with chain tramper, both metal bucket and spiral (auger) elevators, a tower drier, a hot air furnace and fan assembly powered by gas, a seed scale, and a gin compress that would turn out eight 400-pound bales per hour. During the war, Lummus concentrated on improvements to its air blast gins, and by 1948, its engineers had developed a multijet nozzle that used separate air jets to doff lint from individual gin saws. As mechanical harvesting placed greater burdens on the gin manufacturers to provide machines with greater capacity, ninety-saw gins came onto the market in 1951. Lummus made improvements to the roll box design and moting system. The two end saws were removed to allow room for a special drive arrangement for the picker rollers, and the "Super 88-Saw Gin," which could turn out seven bales per hour, replaced the ninety-saw gin through the 1950s. The "Little Giant" stick machine, using Lummus' sling-off principle, was developed in response to the ginners' need to remove stick and green leaf trash.

In spite of the advances in technology, in many areas, particularly where rainfall was high and fields were small, time-honored practices of planting, chop-

ping, and picking cotton changed slowly. C. A. Myers of Beeville described the slow evolution of planting customs in his area. "They would open a furrow and drop cotton seed by hand and cover it with a double shovel [pulled by a horse or mule]. Later they got a walking planter and one man with a team of two mules would open the furrow and cover it. As I recall, my dad had a breaking plow and four mules to pull it. Some folks had a walking cultivator or a riding cultivator. Eventually we had iron wheel tractors."[14]

Iva Cabrera was the fourth of thirteen children and a member of the only Mexican-American family living in the Trinity River valley during the war.

A few months out of the year we went to school in Cold Springs; the rest of the time we were in the fields. Mother, who was always pregnant, worked alongside Daddy. At noon, Mother went home and made dinner and brought it back to the fields. We sat on the ground to eat, rested, and went back to chopping cotton. When the plants were up six inches or so, we'd leave two or three stalks of cotton, chop weeds off each side, chop in the middle between clumps of cotton, and clean those weeds out. We'd go down one row and up the other, chopping with hoes. We went back to the house late in the day and did our chores. When it was time to pick cotton, we'd work morning till night, dragging our sacks down the rows. We'd take our sacks to the wagon, where they were weighed. When the wagon was filled, Daddy would take it to the gin in Camilla. We had to pick the bolls before it rained so they wouldn't be knocked to the ground and gotten muddy. Later we'd go back through and pick scraps of cotton off the stickers from the bolls. Dad would get one bale; our boss would get the other. We worked on halves, bought groceries on credit. We had no money at the end of the year; we worked for groceries. I got my first shoes when I was in the sixth grade.[15]

Beginning with a shortage of labor during World War II, a variety of factors began to assail the role of domestic cotton in the marketplace. Synthetic fibers such as rayon and nylon, first manufactured in 1925, became abundant during the war. Cotton entering the market from Brazil, Egypt, and India increased in availability while U.S. cotton production dropped. To help U.S. growers compete successfully in both domestic and foreign markets, the agricultural experiment stations began to encourage increased mechanization, using their research laboratories to develop new harvesting methods as seen in the 1942 bulletin. Manufacturers of farm implements

Turn-of-the-century, single-row, horse-drawn cotton planter. *Courtesy* The McGregor Mirror

also sought new ways to mechanize planting, cultivating, and harvesting cotton.

Lewis Stanford continued to use tenant labor until 1942, but most tenants left for the higher-paying jobs in the cities. Even with some tenants remaining as day workers, Stanford had no choice but to begin mechanizing. That year he bought two tractors with cultivating equipment. The first Farmall tractors, which had detachable equipment, had been used in the Corpus Christi area beginning about 1925. Horse- or mule-drawn attachments remained in use through the Depression when many farmers could not afford the Farmall. After 1940, the Farmall and other general purpose tractors began to be used across the Cotton Belt with greater frequency for plowing, planting, and cultivating.[16]

Once the cotton seed had germinated, the new shoots had to be thinned, leaving two or three in clusters about twelve inches apart. Weeds had to be continually removed from the clusters by plowing in between the rows and chopping out smaller weeds between the clusters with hoes. Cultivating equipment, from sweeps to shovels to prongs, broke up the soil and pulled up grass and weeds, but had to be used half a dozen times through the season.

Stanford's new tractors could reach two rows, and he added four-row cultivators, so that ten rows in all could be worked at one time. Thinning the plants and chopping was done with hoes when he had sufficient labor, but cultivating equipment soon eliminated most manual tasks. He preferred a butane burner for clearing grass from the cotton stalks. Such flame cultivating was practiced in some areas. Fed by butane or propane gas, a series of four to eight nozzles placed on the ground shot flames across the row, burning grass and weeds, but the fire was not hot enough to damage the cotton stalks. Herbicides would later be used to kill weeds both before and after the plant had emerged.

Dusters, mounted on and powered by tractors, were available for spraying calcium arsenate in areas infested with boll weevils. Manual and mule-drawn

Turn-of-the-century, horse-drawn, cotton stalk knocker. *Courtesy Mrs. Sadie Hoel; copy from Institute of Texan Cultures*

sprayers were gradually discontinued, and airplane dusting grew in popularity. But if planting and cultivating could be managed by tractor attachments, the difficulties of picking the cotton remained.

Samuel S. Rembert and Jedediah Prescott had received a patent for a cotton picker in September, 1850. With its picking cylinders and disks, it was an early spindle picker. A thresher type picker had been tried in 1886, but it cut off the whole plant, attempting to thresh the cotton as if it were grain, and was not successful.

Thomas B. Hyde of Taylor, Texas, invented a pneumatic harvester in the 1890s that inventors experimented with into the mid-1920s. Four or more hoses were attached to a suction fan, and the end of the hose was held against the cotton boll to pull the lint off the burr. It was supposed to be able to pick one thousand pounds of seed cotton per day. Unfortunately, this picking machine did not eliminate hand labor, since the hoses had to be placed against individual bolls, and it also suctioned a great deal of trash in with the cotton.[17]

The first stripper harvesters were developed in the 1870s but did not become popular until the 1920s in West Texas. Stripping had already begun with the

sleds built and used in large numbers in West Texas, especially after the huge crop of 1926. The sleds were most effective after the first frost when cotton plants had dropped their leaves, but sledding picked up both open and unopened bolls. Even so, four or five acres could be picked in a day, at a cost of about $2.75 per bale, and sleds cost between $9 and $27.

The success of the simple sleds led to experimentation by Deere and Company and by the Texas Agricultural Experiment Station at Texas A&M University. Deere made mule-drawn strippers and both one- and two-row tractor pulled strippers. They cost about $185 each and were intended to strip up to one hundred acres per season. The Depression halted further developments, since labor-saving implements took needed jobs from workers, and few were sold until the war years. By 1948, there had been a reversal in the trend, and some six thousand strippers appeared in Texas and Oklahoma. In 1947 alone, as much as 15 percent of the cotton in the South Plains was picked by stripper harvesters.[18]

The first patent for a stripper harvester had been issued to John Hughes of North Carolina in March, 1871, and a stripper that attempted to "comb" the boll off the plant had been tried in Texas in 1872. Revolv-

Pneumatic harvester invented by Thomas B. Hyde. Hoses pulled fibers out of the burrs but also "harvested" a great deal of trash. *Courtesy The Texas Collection, Baylor University, Waco, Texas*

Farmall stripper harvester and wagon. *Courtesy Fred Elliot, Texas A&M Agricultural Extension Service*

ing spiked rolls were attempted in 1874. In 1943, a tractor-mounted stripper with dual rollers and nylon bristles appeared, but self-propelled harvesters did not come into common use until the early 1950s.

The stripper harvester worked like the sled in that it pulled the boll off the plant, usually in one pass through the field. As the stripper moved along the rows, the plants slipped between rollers or brushes that revolved and pulled the bolls, plus leaves and twigs, into the machine. Some used finger-type projections instead of rollers or brushes to catch the bolls. Strippers were most effective in the broad fields of the Texas and Oklahoma plains, where the plants were smaller and closer to the ground.

The disadvantage to stripper harvesting was the amount of trash to be cleaned in the ginning process, but for large areas the quickness of harvesting was an advantage since a stripper could cover between twenty and thirty acres per day.

The spindle picker remained a dormant technology after 1850, but Angus Campbell, of the Deering Harvester Company, perfected the principles of spindle picking during the 1890s. In 1912, he and Theodore H. Price constructed the Price-Campbell experimental harvester. It left cotton unpicked and/or damaged the bolls and was not successful. The International Harvester Company and independent inven-

Two-row spindle picker. *Courtesy Stephen C. Britton*

Mechanical cotton picker being demonstrated in Wharton County in 1917. *Courtesy Wharton County Historical Museum, Wharton, Texas*

Dumping cotton from spindle picker into wagon. *Courtesy Texas A&M Agricultural Extension Service*

Green boll separator and basket mounted on a stripper, November 1962. *Courtesy Fred Elliot, Texas A&M Agricultural Extension Service*

tors John and Mack Rust continued experiments, developing a one-row picker that became available in 1941. Only a few were sold, but after the war ended, between fifteen hundred and two thousand spindle pickers began to be used on cotton farms across the Cotton Belt, primarily in the Mississippi Delta and San Joaquin Valley of California. Only about sixty were in use in Texas in 1948, but alterations in the plant structure to make it taller and thinner plus defoliation with calcium cyanamid made spindle pickers more popular.

Spindle pickers pulled locks of cotton from the bolls by means of grooved or barbed spindles that revolved as they reached deeply into the plant. The rapidly turning spindles added moisture to the cotton to make it stick to the barbs. Rubber doffers loosened the cotton which was then blown into a steel basket. Spindle pickers worked best in areas where cotton plants grew tall prior to defoliation.

The disadvantages of the spindle picker were that it covered only five to fifteen acres per day and had to be used two or three times during a season.

While mechanical harvesting aided the grower in many ways, it was not universally practical. Farmers who produced only three or four bales could ill afford the expensive machines. An International Harvester Company picker of the type used most often in West Texas cost almost $6,000 in 1948, and if it were mounted onto a Farmall tractor, the cost rose to $7,600, out of the question for a grower with fewer than thirty acres. In contrast, a John Deere stripper sold for $900. Cooperative ventures were formed by

groups of growers to purchase machines for "custom harvesting," and itinerant harvesting crews filled the needs of some areas, but the stripping and spindle picking machines were practical only for areas that had room for the expansion of cotton acreage.[19]

Besides the additional trash that had to be cleaned from seed cotton, mechanical harvesting created other problems for the ginner. In West Texas, the naturally low relative humidity combined with heat from extra cleaning cycles produced static electricity. For many years steam or mist was added to the cleaning feeders and air blast fans, and steam spray or wetting agent solutions were added, through nozzles, as cotton moved from the lint slide into the bale press. A moisture control system to furnish humid air to feeders was developed, and antistatic chemicals became popular.

Where spindle pickers were used, the additional moisture had to be removed from the cotton by cleaning and drying, and while a humidification system was unnecessary, measuring the amount of moisture in the cotton became essential. Moisture content from 6½ to 8 percent was considered optimum for preventing breakage to the fibers.

Both portable and laboratory moisture meters

with wet and dry bulb thermometers were developed to measure the difference in relative humidity of air in the cotton and percentage of actual moisture content. A later improvement also measured resiliency of lint as an indicator of moisture content.

The tower drier quickly became an integral part of the ginning outfit. The driers varied from four to six feet wide and seventeen to twenty feet high, and the number of shelves ranged from sixteen to twenty-four. A butane, propane, or natural gas burner provided the heat that was blown by a fan into the drier. Because moisture content in cotton could be anywhere between 12 percent and less than 4 percent, care had to be taken not to over- or under-heat the cotton in the driers. Seed cotton spent only a few seconds inside the drier and was allowed to cool before continuing through the system, and each drier could process several bales per hour.

In 1953, Lewis Stanford began to machine-pick cotton and required more ginning machinery: lint and impact cleaners, a burr machine, a drier, and a new condenser. The original Lummus gin stands were replaced with Continental units. Fourteen electric motors were needed to take the place of the diesel engine. He had already bought a seed sterilizer in 1948 when a pink bollworm quarantine was placed on East Texas cotton. The sterilizer burned butane and tumbled seed like a concrete mixer through the seed line. The butane killed the larvae but did not damage the seed. One afternoon, a strong northwest wind blew sparks from a trash pit into cotton bales waiting on the press platform, and butane fueled the resulting fire that destroyed sixty bales and the platform. Stanford never rebuilt the platform, and he refused to relight the burner. Instead, he hired a bulldozer and dug a pit eighty feet by forty feet by twelve feet near the creek bank. He had the seed blown into the hole, spread nitrogen fertilizer on it, wet it, and kept the whole pit as compost—for twenty years—so that it would kill the bollworm larvae.

Fires had always been a problem at gin plants, and beginning in 1954, fire code restrictions required by insurance underwriters initiated changes in the layout of the physical plant. Minimums of forty feet between buildings, forty feet from buildings to bale storage, and one hundred feet to incinerators were necessary for the lowest insurance rates. For open cotton storage, gin buildings could not be closer than two hundred feet, and incinerators had to be built at least five hundred feet away.[20] Buildings needed to be placed conveniently near to roads and rail lines; the layout generally included the gin house, an office, a cotton storage house with an unloading shed, a seed

Elevated seed bin with dump doors in cyclone style. *From Lummus Cotton Gin Company Catalogue no. 35, ca. 1940; courtesy Lummus Industries, Inc.*

house with overhead conveyor from the gin plant, and an elevated seed bin with dump doors so that the grower could easily recover his seed. In areas where burrs were used for fertilizer, metal burr hoppers with cyclones mounted above and dump doors for trucks were new additions to the gin yard. Truck scales were placed either adjacent to the office or beneath the suction telescope. In many cases, especially if a gin served a large area, the trailers themselves were used for storage and parked under sheds in order to reduce the amount of moisture collected in the open beds. If the trailers were left outside, they were covered with tarpaulins, but the cotton could not be worked until mid-morning in order for dew to have time to evaporate and the cotton to dry.

One noticeable addition to the gin yard was the "cyclone." A cyclone was a metal cylinder ending in a cone-shaped hopper bottom. Trash was pneumatically transferred from the gin to the top of the cyclone to pass through fans with perforated cones to kill the bollworm larvae. Centrifugal force sent trash swirling into the conical hopper; air escaped through the central part of the cylinder. Large and small diameter cyclones were used, depending upon the amount of trash or bollworm infestation, and smaller cyclones were often used in conjunction with incinerators.

Machine harvesting, which brought dirtier cotton into the ginning system, produced dust and fine trash that escaped through dust flues and conveying systems. Because townships began to crowd around the gins, the dust led to many complaints, just as there had been complaints about soot from steam engines and noise from diesel engines. As more gin plants converted to electric power, these annoyances disappeared, but the problem of increased amounts of dust and trash remained. In addition, quarantines because of pink bollworm infestations required treatment of the trash before it could be taken from the gin yard. Dust, fire, and the spreading of insects and plant diseases mandated that the trash be disposed of by conveying or blowing trash into cyclone collectors, subsequently hauled or blown into an incinerator, allowed to form a compost pit, or collected in a dust pile near the gin building. The composting of gin trash was often successful when the pit was large and sufficient moisture was available for chemical reactions. Because composted gin trash was free of cotton diseases and weed seeds, it was considered safe to return to the fields. In the mid-1950s, however, scientists in the Texas State Department of Health, U.S. Department of Health, Education, and Welfare, the Bureau of Mines of the U.S. Department of the Interior, and the U.S. Department of Agriculture conducted a detailed study that resulted in recommended usage of cyclone trash collectors.

New buildings were one or one and one-half stories. Equipment mounted firmly to concrete floors vibrated less and lasted longer. Most structures were of brick or galvanized steel, and new buildings had fewer roof offsets, leading to simpler and less expensive construction. Bale presses, which required so much of the building's height, were more often up-packing, with the hydraulic ram contained in a pit, or the single-story down-packing type. A two-story press could be used in one and one-half story buildings with a raised platform of steel or concrete that left room underneath for a pump, a work bench, and space for storage of tools and spare parts such as belts. Line shafts were gone, except in the older buildings, and electricity replaced steam and diesel engines. The advantage of diversified power was that part of the equipment could be serviced while other parts remained in operation.

One improvement brought about by mechanical harvesting was the green boll trap. Stripper harvesting caught green, or immature, bolls along with open bolls and locks. Green bolls were broken up by cleaners, but the damp fiber and soft seeds often entered the gin stands and collected on the saw teeth so tightly that they could not be doffed. Eventually the entire seed roll would be too clogged to revolve, and the gin stand would have to be stopped and the saw teeth manually cleaned. Placed either in the suction line from the wagon or at the discharge from the tower drier, green boll traps prevented their entering the gin stand. Since green bolls were heavier than mature bolls, they could be separated by a change in air velocity that allowed them to drop into a chamber for removal. Centrifugal force, in another style of trap, sent the bolls through a duct; at a sharp turn, the lighter bolls would continue and the heavier ones fall into a collection chamber.[21]

The gin stands themselves were redesigned with larger capacities. In 1961, Continental made a gin and feeder unit with 119 saws of sixteen-inch diameter that could turn out six bales per hour. Its even larger 141-saw gin could process between eight and ten bales per hour. Gordin made gins of 75 or 140 saws of sixteen-inch diameter. Murray sold a gin with 80 or 90 saws of eighteen-inch diameter. Lummus increased its saws to 88 but kept the standard twelve-inch diameter, choosing to increase the capacities of its gin stands more gradually.

Brush gins were manufactured by Continental, Gordin, and Hardwicke-Etter, while air blast gins were manufactured by Continental, Lummus, Hardwicke-Etter, and Murray. All of these companies also made lint cleaners, and the popular Moss-Gordin lint cleaner remained in use in gin plants for many years.

Post–World War II changes in ginning were also reflected in the development of long-staple hybrid cottons and advances in roller ginning. Even though Sea Island cotton reemerged in the 1930s with modest success, it was abandoned again during the war. Egyptian cottons were introduced into the Southwest in 1898, but did not adapt on their own. In 1902, USDA scientist Kearney traveled to Egypt where he studied the cotton-growing culture of the Nile Valley. In 1908, two Mit Afifi varieties appeared: Somerton and Yuma. The Somerton was a late-appearing plant with too much accompanying vegetation. The Yuma, however, was more successful. A few hundred acres were planted in the Imperial Valley of California and the Salt River valley of Arizona in 1912. Approximately 16,000 bales of Yuma cotton were produced five years later.

Yuma cotton was very fine and had a staple length of about $1\frac{7}{16}$ inches. To maintain its spinning qualities, Yuma cotton had to be roller ginned. Unlike the increasingly complicated saw gin outfits, roller ginning at the time was relatively simple, consisting of a cleaner feeder with a spiked belt that conveyed handpicked cotton to the roller. Dirtier cotton was sent through a cleaner with a three-cylinder picker roller and then to an inclined shaker before it was fed to the gin.[22]

Pima cotton, which had been found as an individual plant in a field of Yuma cotton in 1910 and received great attention by breeders, became commercially available in 1918. Its staple was finer, lighter in color, and longer (1%$_{16}$ inches) than Yuma. This variety was immediately successful; more than ninety-two thousand bales reached the market in 1920. It was adopted by seed breeders and growers alike and became the parent plant for American Pima and other long-staple varieties grown today.

Roller ginning improvements had been slow in coming and were generally expensive, considering the unstable production of long staple cotton. After 1930, however, modifications to the old-fashioned McCarthy style gins began to be made. Some of these improvements consisted of replacing plain with ball bearings and making sturdier frames for the gin stands. During the war years production increased, the old McCarthy gins wore out, and new roller gins were developed. Nearly 74,000 bales of long-staple cotton were produced in 1942, but two years later the number of bales fell to 8,600, and in 1949, only about 4,000 bales reached the market. Production increased to over 60,000 bales in 1950 due to expanded planting in Arizona, New Mexico, and Texas; it rose to 93,000 in 1952, and eventually leveled off at about 60,000 bales.

Growers continued to handpick Pima cotton, and ginners treated it more gently than they would upland varieties, but a similar ginning system developed. The long-staple cotton was suction fed from the wagons, passed through extractor cleaners and the three- or four-cylinder cleaner, and continued to the separator or dropper. It then collected on the upper floor and was placed manually in chutes so that it could drop into the battery of between twelve and thirty-six roller gins below. After ginning, the lint fell onto the floor and was carried by hand to a single box bale press.

The roller gins that were produced during the 1940s had frames made of cast iron or steel; ball and roller bearings with better lubrication methods resulted in more dependable operation; roller and crank speeds were increased. Roller lengths were available in forty- and fifty-four-inch sizes. The new gin plants were usually of two stories, with the gins on the ground floor and the separator and cleaner on the upper floor.

After 1950, roller gin plants took on the appearance of saw gin establishments. One or one and one-half story, all steel buildings replaced the old wooden or brick two-story structures, and all machinery was placed on ground level concrete floors. Electric motors at each gin stand took the place of line shafts, and a system outfit closely resembled that of a saw gin: pneumatic suction from a telescope; cleaning, extracting and drying units; cleaning feeders above each gin stand; belts or flues to convey the lint to a condenser; a double-box press; augers for seed removal.

After machine harvesting began in the 1950s, the problems of over-drying because of additional cleaning and of static electricity had to be addressed. Scientists at the Southwestern Cotton Ginning Laboratory at Mesilla Park, New Mexico, devised a steam line inside the roller gin that was successful, and antistatic agents brushed onto the roller also proved beneficial.[23]

Pima cotton and its hybrids were taken to compresses and marketed in the same ways that upland varieties were. Lewis Stanford, for example, loaded the cotton into WBT&S boxcars on the siding near the gin. His cotton was delivered to the Moody Cotton Compress Company, port side at Galveston. In 1948, when the rail line was discontinued, Stanford bought two trucks, a short-bed or "bobtail" to take the seed to mills in Hearne, Waco, or Houston, and a Dodge tractor with a flatbed trailer that would carry fifty-three bales at one time.

Charging farmers two dollars per bale, Stanford drove the cotton to the docks at the Houston Ship Channel. Anderson, Clayton and Company of Houston and Kehoe of New Orleans were his usual brokers. They cut samples from each bale, and Stanford took the samples to the Cotton Exchange Building in Houston where buyers classed the cotton and set the prices. Once the prices were agreed upon, the broker paid Stanford and he, in keeping with a century-old tradition, acted as broker for the farmers. Some would come to the gin office and pick up their checks, and all accounts with the gin would be settled. In many cases, Stanford simply mailed the checks to the farmers. After 1958, samples were cut and tagged at the gin and mailed to the U.S. Department of Agriculture office in Austin for classing and pricing. The USDA-issued "green cards," which set the grade and value of the cotton, were sent to the ginners who could hold on to the cards until ginning fees were paid or could sell the cotton to recover those fees. Whether the cotton was sold by the ginner or the farmer, the buyer paid for the cotton according to the class and value indicated on the green card, a definite improvement over the "point buying" or "hog round" method of selling cotton.

Later, the ginner carried the cotton to the local compress which performed the services of paperwork, sampling, and weighing. The compress issued the warehouse receipt and sent the cotton sample to the classing office.

Other traditions were fading as well. Stanford had already begun gradually reducing his cotton acreage from its 700-acre allotment and increasing his pasturage for cattle. Beginning in 1966, cotton growers were permitted to move their allotments to other areas, since the allotment was tied to production rather than to a specific piece of land, and Stanford made arrangements to sell his remaining 500-acre allotment. The allotment program was abolished in 1978.

Additional difficulties began to accumulate. The primary problems with growing cotton in East Texas were insect infestation and too much dampness in the cotton, requiring more cleaning and drying equipment at the gin. He could not get laborers to chop, hoe, or pick cotton, and machine harvested cotton was not satisfactory. The spindles pressed down on the already damp cotton, crimping it, and even though he began to defoliate in order to minimize leaves and stems, he was nevertheless penalized in the grading system. The flooding of the Trinity River made cotton farming a nightmare of risk and expense, and Stanford began to plant more soybeans, hay, and milo. The era of large-scale cotton farming in the Trinity River valley was drawing to a close.

As a member of the soil conservation district, Stanford was also appointed to the Trinity River Authority, which was established as a state agency to oversee irrigation and conservation in the Trinity River watershed. He recognized that a dam and lake were needed to control the flow of the Trinity in frequent flood and occasional drought. An engineering study showed that the logical site for the placement of the dam was at the lowest and widest point along the river, in the heart of the Trinity River valley, between the wooded walls of the foothills.

The Trinity River Authority bought the gin from Stanford, along with his rich river bottomland, and allowed him the use of the gin until he was forced to dismantle it. He sold some of the equipment to other gins, and the remainder he hauled by truck to the top of the hill above Kickapoo Creek to be stored in an old dogtrot house. He left the seed hopper, however.

One warm afternoon in the spring of 1969, he found a use for some concrete blocks which were lying beneath the seed hopper. He drove down to the valley and loaded them onto his truck. When he reached the bridge across the Kickapoo, he looked into his rearview mirror and saw water swirling into the "bottom." The valley filled so quickly that he knew this would be his only load. He could never go back.

Lewis Stanford can now look out across Lake Livingston from his back yard on the high ground. The seed house has vanished, knocked down by the waves, but he knows where it stood. The cotton field and the gin house may be gone, but the fishing is good.

CHAPTER TEN

From Modules to Memories

September. A time for hopes, prayers, and endless hours of hard, gritty work.

The long season of clearing, planting, plowing, and protecting acres of cotton is over. With the harvest comes the beginning of a new season, a time of commercial enterprise and, with luck, prosperity.

Deep in the cloud-covered bowl of the Brazos River valley, a Mexican-American laborer sniffs rain and watches a spindle picker making its way slowly along the rows of stalky plants bursting with snowy fibers. If the rain will keep heading east toward the Navasota and Trinity rivers, this last field will be emptied from the steel basket of the spindle picker, compressed into a module, and taken to the gin in a matter of hours.

Between the paved roadway and the rutted turnrows stands the module builder, an enormous red steel box. Perched in a cab that overlooks the interior, an operator controls a tramping device that compresses seed cotton into a module that resembles a huge loaf of bread. When the module is complete, the laborer will use a tractor to pull the steel box forward, leaving the "loaf" beside the road. The module will then be covered with a tarpaulin. Today there will be no copper stencils and india ink or cattle brands; identification of the grower and of the field will be sprayed onto the sides of the module with a special paint that will not damage the cotton.

At the moment, however, a driver is backing a module mover up to another "loaf." From the cab of the truck, the driver maneuvers controls that will tilt the specially designed trailer to slide under the end of the module and pull it onto the bed of the trailer with a series of moving chains. When the module is in place, the driver will lower the trailer to a flattened position and haul it to the gin.

At the gin, he will offload the module by reversing the chains and slowly pulling the trailer out from under the module. He may leave the module on the ground for later processing, or he may back the trailer into the drive-through and deposit the cotton beneath the suction telescope.

The bulk handling of seed cotton, which was first developed for the gin, has now extended to the field. As summarized by ginner Donald Baird, "The ginning industry has changed according to the demands of the farmer, who wanted his cotton ginned as soon as it could be. Back in the beginning, they would bring in cotton in a wagon, unload it into a basket and set it up on the ginning floor, then carry it in and put it into the bin. The ginning system grew with air unloading for the wagons and automatic feeders for the gin stands, but the farmer soon began to harvest cotton faster than it could be ginned. The gins built cotton houses that would hold several bales for each farmer. A farmer could have anywhere from three to thirty or forty bales in stalls that would be ginned later. This relieved a lot of pressure on the gin because cotton could be ginned during rainy or bad days when it couldn't be harvested.

"The gins began to put in drying systems so the farmer could harvest his cotton when there was a little more dew on it or it was a little bit damper. That would gin and dry it at the same time.

"Still, the farmer was harvesting more cotton, faster, all the time. The module system was developed so the farmer could unload into it and press it in the field. Some farmers I know of have harvested their whole crop before they ever sent a bale to the gin."[1]

By 1968, when Lewis Stanford was "floated out" by Lake Livingston, cotton harvests were once again surpassing gin capacities. The largest gin plant at the time, located in California, produced forty bales per hour. Most gins turned out considerably fewer. Greater mechanization in the field and in the gin plant was making large-scale cotton production by fewer growers economically feasible, but a time/production gap between harvesting and ginning led to the use of large numbers of trailers that had to be stored in limited shed space or in open yards.

Donald Baird explained:

Back in the late twenties we had a small cotton house that would hold one bale per stall and which

This turbo-charged, four-row spindle picker can harvest more than seven bales of cotton per hour. *Courtesy National Cotton Council*

This module, or "loaf," is left in place on the turnrow and will be moved at a later time. *Courtesy Stephen C. Britton*

Module mover pulling cotton onto the flatbed trailer by a series of moving chains. *Courtesy Stephen C. Britton*

we would use for a farmer who wanted to catch two or three bales of seed for planting. He would bring some in and put it at the cotton house, and then we would gin three or four bales at the same time so he would get purer seed from his own cotton.

But beginning in the thirties, the farmer would come in and say, "How long is it going to be before I can get my wagon? How long before I can get my trailer back? I need it."

The farmer would have trailers that would hold five or six bales and maybe he would send five or six of those trailers to the gin at the same time. He would be waiting with his stripper, waiting for his trailers to come back from the gin.

They would bring in several bales, or several trailers holding five bales, and it was easier if we could run four or five trailers together at the same time and gin straight through. That way we would have one remnant where we might have five remnants if they brought them in one at a time. That worked fine, but the farmer who had just brought in a load didn't want us to gin all these together, he wanted us to gin his in line when the time came. There was always a lot of argument and fussing about who was ahead and who was next in line.

They ticketed the trailers, but that didn't relieve

the problem. A farmer might have two and a half bales on his trailer. If a man's ticket number was coming up next and he was standing out in the yard waiting for his trailer, he wouldn't let you pull one from the back to get another half bale off of it to gin with the other two and a half because he wanted his to go in line. Naturally, he wanted to get his seed and his business taken care of at one time, but the main problem was to get the trailer back. He needed it out in the field. They finally solved that problem with the modules.

In 1971, Lambert Wilkes, under the auspices of Texas A&M Agricultural Extension Service and Cotton Incorporated, a research division of the National Cotton Council, authored the module concept. To find out how large a module he could build, he experimented with a small hay ricker. Cotton from a harvester was unloaded into the ricker and stored on a turnrow, permitting continuous harvesting in lower rainfall areas. In high rainfall areas, however, water on the ground would soak through the cotton and ruin it with mildew. He devised a high-density package stored on a pallet to isolate it from the ground. The first module consisted of about

Modules can be deposited at the gin yard for later processing or can be placed directly under the suction telescope. *Courtesy Stephen C. Britton*

three bales, and Wilkes gradually made the modules longer and higher.

The steel module builder is a self-contained unit with a cab and hydraulic tramper. Holding up to fifteen thousand pounds of seed cotton, the module builder forms a "loaf" eight feet high by eight feet wide by thirty-two feet long that equals between ten and twelve bales. The module can be built directly onto the ground or on metal or wooden pallets. Pallets were popular at first, but growers have learned to build modules on well-drained areas in the field and now tend to place the modules on the turnrow instead of on pallets. With good drainage, even in areas of high rainfall, only the bottom six inches of seed cotton will be affected. Coolness of the ground will prevent fires. When the module is formed, rear doors on the steel box are opened and the module builder, which has adjustable wheels, is simply driven forward by a tractor. The module, with sides tapering in six inches at the top, is covered by a synthetic tarpaulin. If the module gets wet from the top (from rainfall) or is put up wet (i.e., has a moisture content

of 15 to 16 percent), spontaneous combustion can occur. (Heat and moisture, combined with the density of the module, will cause the organic matter such as burrs and stems to decay, this creating methane gas and even more heat. Eventually, the fibers will catch fire, before the organic matter does, from spontaneous combustion.) Once the tarpaulin is in place, the owner's initials and/or field identification are spray-painted on. Harvesters empty basketloads of seed cotton into the builder and begin another module.

Once the module is formed, it has to be moved to the gin. Wilkes borrowed a haystack mover at first, but it was not heavy enough. He worked directly with a manufacturer to make a module mover sturdy enough to load and carry the densely compacted cotton to the gin. The flatbed trailer design proved the most workable and is usually termed a module mover or hauler.

Wilkes began his experiments in the Rio Grande valley and moved across the state to the South Plains in order to adapt his system to varying rainfall conditions. Modules first gained popularity in Califor-

Spindle picker unloading seed cotton into module builder. *Courtesy Stephen C. Britton*

nia due to very large harvests, and soon growers in Arizona and Mississippi accepted bulk handling of seed cotton in the field. Modules began to be used in the South Plains in the 1970s and in the Brazos River valley a decade later.[2]

Before modules became widely used, other methods were employed for transferring cotton quickly from the field into the ginning system. According to A. L. Vandergriff, ginning industry consultant, inventor, and at different times president of Continental Gin Company (1959–1965) and executive vice president of Lummus Cotton Gin Company (1947–1959), cotton was unloaded by means of a dumping system. "Cotton would come to the gin in pairs of trailers thirty feet long and ten feet wide, tied together. That's the way the tractors were pulling them through the cotton fields. We'd run those two trailers onto a platform, tie them down, turn them wrong side up and dump them into a pit, and feed out of that pit into the gin automatically. That was the beginning [of the concept] of the module feeder."[3]

Whether from trailers or modules, older gins still use telescopes to introduce seed cotton into the gin-

ning system, but sophisticated module feeders are preferred at large installations. Module truck drivers offload the cotton into a dispersing and feeding system that consists of conveyors made of flat wire belting or chains. The module feeding system, like other parts of the gin plant, is either remote controlled from a bank of television monitors and a space-age console or by a simpler station of push buttons. Large gin plants are now so fully automated that few employees are needed to operate a battery of more than twenty gin stands that can each process up to fifteen bales per hour. Depending upon the number of gin stands, the entire system may turn out more than sixty bales per hour.

Regardless of the age or technological sophistication of the machinery in a gin plant, the purpose remains the same as in Eli Whitney's day: to separate seeds from fibers so that cotton can be spun into textiles. Robert Munger's developments of air conveying and automation of ginning for bulk handling of seed cotton are principles inherent in ginning systems today. But whether the gin plant is the most modern or a combination of old and new equipment, the pro-

Hydraulic tramper compresses up to 15,000 pounds of seed cotton in the module. *Courtesy Stephen C. Britton*

cess of cleaning, drying, ginning, and packaging cotton for sale and shipment to market has changed very little in the last century.

Ginning systems vary according to whether the cotton has been spindle- or stripper-harvested, thus determining the types of cleaning equipment needed, and according to the amount of moisture content in the cotton, thus determining the amount of drying needed. (A very high moisture content will affect the ability of the saws to separate fibers from seeds. A low moisture content can lead to over-drying, making the fibers brittle, weak, and difficult to spin.) The overall condition of the cotton affects classing, and therefore the value, of the finished bale.

Seed cotton may be suction fed from trailers or modules by telescopes or conveyed into the gin plant by a module feeder, but in either case it is drawn into the air stream. A rock and green boll trap is placed between the telescope and the separator, or between the discharge from the module feeder and the first tower drier. The trap is placed in the air line to catch stones and green bolls, and magnets are used to catch any bits of metal that might create sparks and cause a fire.[4]

The cotton passes through the trap and into a separator which stops the flow of cotton through the

Rear doors of module builder open to allow it to be pulled away, thus leaving behind the familiar loaf." *Courtesy Stephen C. Britton*

Brazos River Valley gin; one module waits on the ground, covered by a tarpaulin and painted with field identification; another module lies on the trailer of the module mover; a third is in place beneath the suction telescope. *Courtesy Stephen C. Britton*

Lummus Industries, Inc.'s "Mole" module feeder. *Courtesy Lummus Industries, Inc.*

Modern gin plant continues to follow Munger's system design with separator, distributor, feeders, and gin stands. *Courtesy Continental Eagle Corporation*

air stream. The separator may be a spiked drum or a series of three spiked cylinders, proving the adaptability of Whitney's original concept. The cotton drops by gravity past a vacuum wheel and into a feed control hopper. Rollers inside the hopper control the rate at which the cotton is fed into the conditioning system, and rate of feed is electronically determined by the ginner. (An air line cleaner is often placed before the feed control for stripped cotton.)

The first element of the conditioning system is a tower drier, which may consist of between eleven and twenty-four shelves, and through which cotton moves from top to bottom along the surfaces of the shelves by means of heated air. (Heaters may be gas- or oil-powered, and centrifugal fans are used to generate the air stream for moving and drying seed cotton. Ginning experts refer to push-pull systems where cotton is pushed through a gas-fired heater into the top of the tower drier, and pulled through an oil-fired heater from the tower drier and sent to the separator.)[5]

After initial drying, seed cotton then passes through machines designed to clean as much trash as possible from the cotton before it reaches the gin stand. The first cleaner is usually a cylinder cleaner ("hot air" or "inclined") that can be horizontal or angled at about 30 degrees. Cylinder cleaners have six to seven spiked cylinders that revolve at about 400 revolutions per minute. Seed cotton passes beneath the cylinders where it is scrubbed over grid rods or screens and agitated, and foreign matter falls through spaces between the rods and into the trash conveying system. Two cleaners may be used in a parallel, or split-stream, arrangement for greater seed cotton handling capacity. Cylinder cleaners are also needed to break up wads of cotton and to prepare it for additional drying and cleaning.

The seed cotton is then fed to an extractor cleaner usually referred to as a stick and green leaf machine. If the cotton is relatively dry, it may pass from the tower drier directly into the extractor cleaner. If the

Modern gin plant showing condenser, lint slide, tramper, and double box press. *Courtesy Continental Eagle Corporation*

Well-known "government" tower drier, elevated due to lack of floor space. Overflow pen is in foreground. *Courtesy Stephen C. Britton*

seed cotton has a moisture content greater than 10 or 12 percent, two stages of drying may be necessary before it reaches extracting machines. This extra drying is needed because the high temperatures required for a single stage of drying would damage the fibers. A dual system allows for some cooling in between stages so that the fibers are dried only to the optimum 6 to 8 percent. A second or even third drying and cleaning system are identical to the first. Trash from the inclined cleaner is picked up by the pull fan and discharged to cyclones outside the building. A trash fan blows sticks and burrs to a box built for this purpose outside the gin plant.

The stick machine is used to remove large bits of trash picked up by mechanical harvesting. Inside the machine, highspeed saws use centrifugal force to sling off trash, while grid bars or wire brushes placed around the saw cylinder keep as much of the seed cotton as possible adhering to the saw cylinder. One, two, or more sling-off cylinders may be used. Some seed cotton is invariably flung off with the trash, however, and reclaimer saws, which turn more slowly than the cleaning saws and have more grid bars, catch the cotton and return it to the main cotton flow airstream.

Once the coarse matter has been removed, the seed cotton enters a conveyor distributor to the gin stands. Excess cotton falls into the overflow hopper

Uncontained trash pile behind a Fort Bend County gin plant. *Courtesy Stephen C. Britton*

Modern gin plant combining old and new features; console makes it possible for fewer gin hands to control more equipment. *Courtesy Mr. and Mrs. Michael Moore; Stephen C. Britton, photographer*

at one end of the battery of gin stands, and a separator above the conveyor distributor returns overflow cotton to the distributor. (At older gin plants, cotton is returned to the air stream by means of a telescope.) Feeders may contain extractors and/or cylinders for cleaning, but their primary purpose is to supply seed cotton continuously to the ginning saws. Inside the gin stand, rotating saws pass between stationary ginning ribs. The edges of the teeth are parallel to the rib and pull rather than cut the fibers away from the seeds.[6] Saws catch the cotton and pull it past huller ribs that deflect hulls and sticks. In some gin stands, the seeds fall between huller and ginning ribs to a conveyor and are carried away; in others, a tube in the roll box augers the seeds away. The fibers caught on the saw teeth pass behind the ginning ribs where motes and trash are cast off by centrifugal force. Most gin stands today have returned to the brush method of removing lint from saw teeth because the earlier disadvantages to saw and brush gins have been eliminated. The bristles are nylon instead of horsehair, discouraging rodents from eating

them, and the steel drums that hold the brushes are designed to maintain an even balance for smoother operation as they remove lint from the saw teeth. Ginners had objected to the problem of lint, or "green cotton," blocking the air blast nozzles and causing fires, and the air blast principle is seldom used today. Both twelve- and sixteen-inch diameter saws are available, and the number of saws varies between 158 and 161 in a single unit. In more graphic terms, the eighty-saw gin stand of the 1930s could turn out one and one-fourth bales per hour; contemporary gins can produce thirty bales per hour.

As the brushes remove lint from the saw teeth, they act as a fan to create an air stream that blows the lint into a duct that will transfer it to one, two, or more lint cleaners. Ginned lint collects on a condenser drum where it forms a batt. The batt is fed to a saw cylinder that normally turns at 1,000 revolutions per minute, and saws move the lint over grid bars that eliminate any leftover motes or small "pin" trash. The lint cleaner combs and blends lightly spotted cotton to a white grade. Lint is then blown

through a flue to the battery condenser where it collects around a screen drum. The lint attached to the drum is doffed by steel rollers and sent down the slide into the charging box of the bale press.

Presses come in various sizes and types. A down-packing hydraulic press allows the press to sit on a floor-level slab. The boxes are turned from the self-contained unit rather than from a turntable in the floor, similar to Robert Munger's original press design. Turntable presses, however, are available with up-packing rams. Some presses have the familiar steel press dogs, but others have electronic signals from a bale weight indicator that tell the press operator when a bale is complete. The tramper, which may be chain or hydraulically driven, then stops automatically until the press has been turned. Perhaps the most remarkable changes have been in the removal of the doors and the faster, automatic strapping of the bales. In 1972, the ginning industry agreed to adopt the universal density press, which standardized bales at 20 inches wide by 54 inches long by 28 inches thick with a density of twenty-eight pounds per cubic foot, in order to avoid penalties set by export shippers. (Non-universal density bales still have to be compressed for shipping.) Jute and burlap are

Batt of lint leaves condenser and slides along chute to tramper charging box. *Courtesy Stephen C. Britton*

Hydraulic ram holds bale in place for wrapping and tying. *Courtesy Stephen C. Britton*

Bale being rolled out of press for weighing. *Courtesy Stephen C. Britton*

still used but have been largely replaced by synthetic bagging; steel bands and buckles are used on jute or burlap, but wire ties are used on synthetic bagging. Bale weights average five hundred pounds.

For many years, A. L. Vandergriff explained, "The whole capacity of the gin plant was bottlenecked by how fast you could package the cotton. The government [U.S. Department of Agriculture] marketing system required that you put twenty-one pounds of tare [wrapping, ties, and buckles] on a bale. If you didn't have twenty-one pounds of tare, they deducted that much from your cotton anyway. I had to automate the press in order to get the gin capacity that I wanted and that the industry had to have. About twenty bales an hour was what you could gin by hand, strapping it and wrapping it. My approach was to strap the bale naked and to strap it automatically. For a while we strapped bales with cardboard instead of the regular jute bagging in order to keep the material out of the slots of the press. We were faced with the problem that we couldn't merchandise that cotton except direct to the mill because it couldn't go through normal trade channels. The

USDA had not relaxed the requirement about wrapping. I went to work with the National Cotton Council and we set up a bale packaging committee [Joint Industry Bale Packaging Committee] and worked toward getting rid of tare weight and back to net weight trading so that we could sell cotton based on the net weight of the package." The frequency of sampling resulted in cuts in the bales that made them unacceptable at the mills. Vandergriff and members of the committee were eventually successful in having the packaging rules changed. Polypropylene and polyethylene bagging solved the packaging problem. "It's beautiful. It [the bale] sits outside, sealed, and doesn't have to be warehoused." Vandergriff was told that synthetic bagging would cause the cotton to mildew. "I said, you've got to prove that to me. So I put up two hundred bales and sent them to a mill and left them for a year. Nothing happened. They were perfect." Vandergriff, who has twenty-five patents, devised an automatic bale packager as early as 1971. Presses were designed to strap the bale naked. A conveying system carried the bale to a machine that would automatically sample, wrap, and tag it.

Bales being loaded onto a truck for delivery to a compress. *Courtesy Stephen C. Britton*

The bale was then weighed and transported to a storage area.

Automation in gin plants requires sophisticated controls systems. Computers monitor everything from air temperature to rate of feed at the gin stands to weight of a bale. Filters keep the air almost dust free, and noise is kept to a minimum. Even more modest gin plants use small computers to exchange information, keep accounting records, follow the ups and downs of the stock market, and predict the timing of boll weevil emergence in the spring for environmentally sound methods of insect control.

The slow but steady growth of the American-Egyptian, plus foreign, long-staple cottons required continued improvements in roller ginning technology, even though the McCarthy principles remained consistently in use. A. L. Vandergriff explained:

> The McCarthy roller gin has a stationary knife that runs tightly against the roller, and it has the reciprocating knife that moves up and down, and between the strokes of the reciprocating knife the cotton is pushed against the surface of that roller. It picks up the fibers and pulls them under the stationary knife. A blade comes up and pushes the seed off. It's that simple a process. For years they [researchers] had worked on a method to strip those seed[s] with some rotating member, but they had all overlooked one important factor, in that the reciprocating knife moves past the pinch point of the stationary knife

Roller gin using a combination of the ancient churka rollers and McCarthy fixed and moving knives to process long-staple varieties. *Courtesy Continental Eagle Corporation*

Sample of cotton showing U.S. Department of Agriculture sample identification card. *Courtesy National Cotton Council*

half the distance of the length of the staple of the cotton.

That overlap had not been taken into consideration previously, and seed was often pushed off the blade with lint still on it. "So I determined what diameter roller I would have to have for one-inch cotton to push that seed half the length of the staple to turn it loose." Vandergriff's modification proved highly successful.

Vandergriff, Wilkes, and others continue experiments with roller gins as more long staple cotton varieties such as Supima and Acala are grown successfully. Varieties with staple lengths that vary from 1⅜ inch to 1⁹⁄₁₆ inch are being grown in the El Paso, Texas, area, and in parts of New Mexico, Arizona, and California. Over six hundred thousand bales were produced in 1989, which meant a production of over eight hundred pounds of long staple cotton per acre.[7] Roller gin plants are virtually identical to saw gin plants, except for the use of rotary and stationary knives instead of saws, pneumatic doffing of lint inside the gin stands, and a preference for air flow rather than saws inside the lint cleaners.

The classing system for determining the value of cotton is based on staple length, grade, and Micronaire reading. Staple length is dependent upon variety of cotton planted and overall growing conditions and is less important than grade in placing a value on the cotton. Grade, however, is based on a subjective, visual determination of trash content, color, and sample preparation which is often made instantly.[8] Cotton classers can select from thirty-eight grades and one below grade code, and staple lengths for upland cotton range from below ¹³⁄₁₆ inch to 1½ inch in length. The Micronaire, an instrument invented in 1947, is used to measure the fineness of the fibers in micrograms per inch. High Volume Instrument (HVI) classing is increasingly favored by textile manufacturers because it standardizes characteristics that allow them to save costs in achieving particular yarn quality and to use electronic quality control methods. HVI classing gives readings in strength, uniformity of fiber, staple length, color, trash, Micronaire, and in the future, degree of fiber maturity. All of these features affect spinning, dyeing, and durability.[9] Cotton classing offices are centrally located by regions. The compress sends a sample to the U.S. Department of Agriculture classing office which, in turn, issues a card bearing the gin number, warehouse bale number, grade, staple, color, trash content, strength of fiber, and Micronaire reading, and a warehouse receipt is still a negotiable instrument.[10]

Since the turn of the century there has been a decided alteration in ginning as an enterprise. A gin plant that might have cost between seven and eleven thousand dollars in 1914 could cost between two and ten million dollars in 1990. In 1914, Texas had 4,694 gins; in 1989, there were 526. Over 17 million acres were planted in cotton in 1926; by 1988, cotton acreage had dropped to 5.6 million. A little over 6 million bales of cotton were produced in 1949, and 5 million bales were harvested in 1988.[11] The 1990 crop in Texas produced 4.7 million bales, worth an average of three hundred dollars each.[12] Cotton yields of less than 200 pounds per acre in the years from 1870 to 1920 became 427 pounds per acre by 1959 and 605 pounds per acre by 1988. The trend is clearly toward a reduction in total acreage but with an increased amount of lint per acre, and while the number of gin plants has decreased, the capacity of the remaining gins has increased.

Gin manufacturers have made increased capacity at fewer gin plants possible by making equipment larger and more efficient, and a similar trend toward consolidation has affected the manufacturer as well as the ginner. Gullett, Hardwicke-Etter, Murray, Mitchell, Moss-Gordin, and others have become historical entities. A few pieces of equipment exist in very old gin plants, and parts for them are still available, but the original companies have become parts of Continental Eagle Corporation or Lummus Industries. Small companies such as Consolidated Cotton Gin Company keep the free-enterprise system active, and peripheral industries from moisture meters to module builders are highly competitive. As always, the ginner's investment in new equipment is determined by his needs, his budget, and the reputation and service of the manufacturer.

Another important trend has also taken place in terms of the ginner's ability to influence his industry. Plantation gin owners like Jared and Leonard Groce, Samuel Goodman, and Hermann Focke were at the mercy of weather, geographical isolation, a market over which they had no control, and rapidly advancing technology. Today's ginner, who is often a grower as well, is no longer isolated by his rural status. He uses contemporary communication tools, belongs to professional organizations such as coop-

eratives and attends conventions, takes action for or against decisions by legislatures and public utilities, works with agencies to resolve safety, insurance, and environmental concerns, and forms a link between inventors, researchers, and manufacturers. He is part of a larger network, organized under the umbrella of the 1939-founded National Cotton Council which sponsors plant, insect and technological research, advertising and promotion, formal trade agreements, legislation for labor reform, ceilings for pricing structures, letters of credit, and programs for energy efficiency. The ginner has always been part of an intricate, worldwide industry. Now, at last, he has a voice in determining its impact on his livelihood and his life.

Many are relieved and thankful that times have changed. Gone are the days when a grower brought his mule-drawn wagon to the gin and took his place in a line that might extend a mile or more down the road. He checked in at the gin office, set up his account for ginning fees and amount of seed to be sold and returned, and received an identification tag for his wagon. Before truck scales were installed, he estimated from experience the number of bales he had, but he could not fairly judge the grade and had no idea what his cotton would bring until he established a price with a cotton buyer. He waited at the gin yard, visiting with neighbors, or took in the sights in town. He might run through his list of purchases, planning surprises for his wife and children at home even as he tried not to smell the aroma of a fine boarding house meal which he could not afford. At the end of the day, he returned to the gin yard. If his cotton and seed were not ready, he camped in the yard, sleeping under the wagon, or rode his horse or mule home and returned the next morning. If they were ready, he sold the cotton, settled his account with the ginner, collected his seed, made his purchases, and headed home. The business of half a year's work was conducted in a day, or less, and the joys or disappointments might linger for another year. Or a lifetime.

Cotton rewarded or disappointed with equal ferocity. Futures expanded or shriveled, and lives changed accordingly. When cotton production ceased to be economically viable, and the old gin houses were abandoned, many communities were happy to see them go. Reminders of a painful past—poverty, fires, injuries, deaths—all centered on that gin house and its machinery. Not objects of sentiment or romanticized symbols of a lost past, they were torn down, as often as not, to make room for new buildings. Or weeds. Their passing was not mourned.

But as technological advances in breeding, culti-

Old-fashioned mule gin near Franklin, Alabama. *Courtesy E. W. Russell, photographer, Library of Congress (HABS)*

vating, harvesting, and ginning cotton continue, the distance between the future and the past grows wider. For example, in only one generation, handpicked cotton has become an image relegated to history, not that anyone would wish to return to the back-breaking work and hard times that went with it. More important is the gradual loss of the machinists and ginners who lived the stories, based on hard times, ingenuity, and practical jokes, that have since become folklore. More important is a well-preserved, hand-made, wooden machine lying in parts that no one is certain how to reconstruct. And equally important is a fine old building, protected from vandalism by a chain link fence but sitting idle, nothing more than a storage facility for jumbled machinery parts. Without care, these become irreplaceable losses for which future generations will hold us accountable.

There are rays of hope. The Goodman gin remains on the Texas Tech campus in Lubbock, ready for re-searchers and preservationists. A turn-of-the-century Gullett gin will be restored and placed in its original building at the Governor Bill and Vara Daniel His-

toric Village that originated in Liberty County and was donated to the Strecker Museum on the Baylor University campus in Waco. Museum officials plan a full restoration of the gin plant to working status.

Perhaps the most ambitious project is that of Op-eration Restoration in Burton, Washington County. A grass-roots, non-profit organization purchased the Farmers Association Gin in 1986. Because of its remarkable state of preservation, including all of the gin association's records, the gin plant has received support in terms of donated services and matching grant funding from major universities, state and na-tional historical commissions, manufacturers, and the Smithsonian Institution. Once the gin is operational, a master plan calls for educational tours and park fa-cilities. The Farmers Association Gin at Burton will take its place with the restored and operational West-ville gin at Lumpkin, Georgia, the 1890 gin plant at the Georgia Agrirama in Tifton, Georgia, and others. The Donigan Gin at Brookshire, Texas, is seeing new life as the Cotton Gin Restaurant. The Liles cotton gin in New Summerfield, Texas, is a combined greenhouse and antique shop. The Old South and its agrarian culture have faded into the past, but the art of its technology remains. Without doubt, Eli Whitney, Hodgen Holmes, Fones McCarthy, and Robert Munger would find satisfaction, and perhaps a bit of amusement, in the enduring success of their inventions.

Out in the Brazos River valley, the farm laborer, caught between the uncertainties of nature and the demands of high-tech agribusiness, is not as concerned with the scope of a $20 billion industry that furnishes products from clothing and linens to food, medical supplies, and book bindings as he is with the weather and the price cotton will bring per pound.

As dark gray clouds scud across the valley, he smells rain and prays for a fast wind. Hoping for a little luck, he settles his straw hat on his head, rolls up his sleeves, and returns to the tractor. He pulls the module builder forward to another place on the turnrow and watches the harvester approach, ready to empty another basketload of cotton into the steel box. Like thousands of other laborers, growers, ginners, cottonseed and textile mill owners, his life and his livelihood depend upon the brilliant blooming, rapid harvesting, and thorough ginning of this prehistoric plant.

As it is with the indestructible *Gossypium,* the end of one season inevitably marks the beginning of the next.

Notes

CHAPTER 1

1. Paul A. Fryxell, *The Natural History of the Cotton Tribe*, p. 201.
2. Ibid., p. 168.
3. Natural Fibers Economic Research, *A Chronological History of Cotton*, pp. 2–4.
4. C. F. Lewis and T. R. Richmond, "Cotton as a Crop," *Cotton: Principles and Practices,* ed. Fred C. Elliot, p. 4.
5. Sidney Ratner, James H. Soltow, and Richard Sylla, *The Evolution of the American Economy*, pp. 18–19.
6. Judith Mara Gutman, *The Colonial Venture*, p. 18.
7. Michael D. Coe, *The Maya*, p. 156.
8. Ratner, Soltow, and Sylla, *Evolution*, pp. 15–16.
9. Jack P. Greene, ed., *Settlements to Society*, 1607–1763, pp. 129–39.
10. Ratner, Soltow, and Sylla, *Evolution*, p. 43.
11. Louis B. Wright, *The Cultural Life of the American Colonies*, pp. 12–13.
12. Lewis and Richmond, "Cotton as a Crop," p. 5.
13. Bertha S. Dodge, *Cotton: The Plant That Would Be King*, p. 22.
14. Lewis and Richmond, "Cotton as a Crop," pp. 5–6.
15. Robert Sobel and David B. Sicilia, *The Entrepreneurs: An American Adventure*, pp. 147–48.
16. Charles A. Bennett, *Cotton Ginning Systems in the United States and Auxiliary Developments*, Dallas: The Cotton Ginners' Journal and the Cotton Gin and Oil Mill Press, 1962, p. 1.
17. Charles A. Bennett, *Roller Cotton Ginning Developments*, Dallas: The Cotton Ginners' Journal and the Cotton Gin and Oil Mill Press, n.d. [ca. 1959], p. 1.
18. V. L. Stedronsky, "Development of the Cotton Gin," *Handbook for Cotton Ginners*, Agriculture Handbook no. 260, p. 1.
19. Bennett, *Roller Ginning*, p. 4.

CHAPTER 2

1. Constance M. Green, *Eli Whitney and the Birth of American Technology*, p. 24.
2. Stuart Bruchey, ed., *Cotton and the Growth of the American Economy: 1790–1860*, p. 60.
3. Ibid., pp. 60–61.
4. Whitney's spike gin patent, as cited in Charles A. Bennett, *Saw and Toothed Cotton Ginning Developments*, pp. 65–75. Long description, Oct. 28, 1793, notarized by Elizur Goodrich.
5. Short description of the gin as cited in Bruchey, *Cotton and the American Economy*, p. 59.
6. Ibid.
7. Charles A. Bennett, *Roller Cotton Ginning Developments*.

Dallas: The Cotton Ginners' Journal and the Cotton and Oil Mill Press, n.d. (ca. 1959), pp. 3–5.
8. Green, *Eli Whitney*, p. 43.
9. Ibid., p. 51.
10. F. L. Lewton, "Historical Notes on the Cotton Gin," *The Smithsonian Report for 1937, Publication 3478*, p. 551.
11. Green, *Eli Whitney*, pp. 58–59.
12. Lewton, "Historical Notes," p. 551.
13. Ibid., pp. 558–59.
14. Green, *Eli Whitney*, p. 67.
15. Eli Whitney, letter to his father dated September 11, 1793, as cited in Bruchey, *Cotton and the American Economy*, p. 61.
16. Bennett, *Saw and Toothed Ginning*, Dallas: The Cotton Ginners' Journal and the Cotton Gin and Oil Mill Press, n.d. (ca. 1960), pp. 17–20.

CHAPTER 3

1. Rosa Groce Bertleth, "Jared Ellison Groce," *Southwestern Historical Quarterly* 20 (Apr., 1917): 358–68.
2. T. R. Fehrenbach, *Lone Star*, p. 140.
3. Elizabeth Silverthorne, *Plantation Life in Texas*, p. 13.
4. Raymond E. White, "Cotton Ginning in Texas to 1861," *Southwestern Historical Quarterly* 61 (Oct., 1957): 259–62.
5. Keith Guthrie, *Texas' Forgotten Ports*, p. 141.
6. Noah Smithwick, *The Evolution of a State or Recollections of Old Texas Days*, p. 16.
7. Silverthorne, *Plantation Life*, pp. 106–109.
8. Ibid., p. 117.
9. Charles A. Bennett, *Cotton Ginning Systems in the United States and Auxiliary Developments*, p. 1.
10. White, "Cotton Ginning in Texas," p. 260.
11. Algernon L. Smith, *Continental Gin Company and Its Fifty-Two Years of Service*, p. 9.
12. Bennett, *Auxiliary Developments*, p. 2.
13. White, "Cotton Ginning in Texas," p. 261.
14. Bennett, *Auxiliary Developments*, pp. 2–3.
15. White, "Cotton Ginning in Texas," p. 262.
16. David G. McComb, *Houston: A History*, pp. 22–23.
17. Silverthorne, *Plantation Life*, pp. 121–24.

CHAPTER 4

1. Mildred W. Abshier, "How Cotton and the Cotton Gin Came to Texas," *Cotton Gins of Waller County, Texas, 1825–1976*, p. 3.
2. Harold D. Woodman, *King Cotton and His Retainers*, p. 9.
3. Ibid., pp. 10–14.
4. Ibid., pp. 20–25.

5. David G. McComb, *Houston: A History*, pp. 19–20.

6. William Ransom Hogan, *The Texas Republic, a Social and Economic History*, p. 102.

7. James Montgomery, *The Cotton Manufacture of the United States Contrasted and Compared with That of Great Britain*, pp. 170–94.

8. Keith Guthrie, *Texas' Forgotten Ports*, p. 142.

9. Hogan, *The Texas Republic*, p. 18.

10. Ibid., p. 19.

11. Raymond E. White, "Cotton Ginning in Texas to 1861," *Southwestern Historical Quarterly* 61 (Oct., 1957): 263.

12. McComb, *Houston: A History*, p. 20.

13. Ibid., p. 202 (n. 37).

14. Marie Phelps McAshan, *On the Corner of Main and Texas: A Houston Legacy*, p. 36.

15. White, "Cotton Ginning in Texas to 1861," p. 266.

16. Ibid., p. 267.

17. Ibid., p. 268.

18. Algernon L. Smith, *Story of the Continental Gin Company, 1900–1952*, pp. 17–19.

19. Merrill E. Pratt, Address presented to the Newcomen Society of North America, Birmingham, Alabama, Dec. 13, 1949.

20. Samuel P. Gates, Memorandum to A. L. Smith, Oct. 25, 1955, pp. 1–4.

21. "How the Cotton Ginning Industry Came to Bridgewater, Mass.," typed manuscript, Continental Eagle Corporation (ca. 1915), pp. 5–9.

22. John A. Streun, "History of Early Cotton Gin Inventions," Continental Eagle Corporation, p. 4.

23. Ibid., p. 4.

24. Larry N. Jones, telephone interview with author, Feb. 12, 1990.

25. Charles A. Bennett, *Saw and Toothed Cotton Ginning Developments*, p. 13.

26. Vernon P. Moore, "Development of the Saw Gin," *Cotton Ginners Handbook*, Agriculture Handbook no. 503, 1977, p. 2.

27. Bennett, *Saw and Toothed Ginning*, pp. 23–27.

28. Algernon L. Smith, untitled typed manuscript, Continental Eagle Corporation, p. 13.

29. "Columbian Spinster," *Textile World* (Feb., 1938): 74. (The article was furnished by Smithsonian Institution.)

30. Charles A. Bennett, *Roller Cotton Ginning Developments*, pp. 3–7.

31. Ibid., pp. 8–9.

32. Ibid., p. 11.

CHAPTER 5

1. Elizabeth Silverthorne, *Plantation Life in Texas*, p. 67.

2. Michael Mullin, ed., *American Negro Slavery: A Documentary History*, pp. 20–21.

3. Silverthorne, *Plantation Life*, p. 80.

4. Terry G. Jordan, *German Seed in Texas Soil*, pp. 131–33.

5. Ibid., p. 172.

6. Frederick Law Olmsted, *A Journey Through Texas*, p. 141.

7. Jordan, *German Seed*, p. 175.

8. Olmsted, *Journey*, pp. 182–83.

9. Olmsted, *Journey*, pp. 205–209.

10. Charles A. Bennett, *Saw and Toothed Cotton Ginning Developments*, p. 29.

11. Ibid., p. 30.

12. Charles A. Bennett, *Cotton Ginning Systems in the United States and Auxiliary Developments*, pp. 11–12.

13. "Star Cotton Press Advertisement," *The Texas Almanac – 1857*, Facsimile Edition 1966, A. H. Belo Corporation, n.p.

14. Olmsted, *Journey*, p. 511.

15. Bennett, *Saw and Toothed Ginning*, pp. 30–31.

16. Harold D. Woodman, *King Cotton and His Retainers*, pp. 206–209.

17. Ibid., pp. 213–14.

18. Ibid., pp. 210–27.

19. T. R. Fehrenbach, *Lone Star*, pp. 359–60.

20. Tom Lea, *The King Ranch*, pp. 42–52.

21. Ibid., pp. 182–86.

22. Fehrenbach, *Lone Star*, pp. 365–67.

23. John T. Schlebecker, *Whereby We Thrive, a History of American Farming, 1607–1972*, p. 157.

24. Woodman, *King Cotton*, pp. 236–40.

25. Gilbert C. Fite, *Cotton Fields No More, Southern Agriculture 1865–1980*, pp. 4–5.

CHAPTER 6

1. Alfred M. Pendleton and Edward H. Bush, "Old Gin Dates Back to 1874 or '75," *The Cotton Gin and Oil Mill Press*, (Mar. 27, 1954): 18.

2. Ibid.

3. "Old Gin Moves West," *The Cotton Gin and Oil Mill Press*, (May 27, 1961): 10, 55.

4. T. R. Fehrenbach, *Lone Star*, pp. 419–20.

5. Hyman, Harold M., *Oleander Odyssey: The Kempners of Galveston, Texas, 1854–1980s*, pp. 28–29.

6. Harold D. Woodman, *King Cotton and His Retainers*, pp. 252–73.

7. Fehrenbach, *Lone Star*, pp. 603–604.

8. David G. McComb, *Houston: A History*, pp. 26–27.

9. Ibid., p. 28.

10. David G. McComb, *Galveston: A History*, p. 47.

11. Julius W. Jockusch, Jr., "A Cargo of Cotton That Made History," *Dallas Morning News*, Mar. 4, 1928.

12. T. Lindsay Baker, "The Greek Engineer at the Compress," *Eagle-News* (Cleburne, Texas), Jan. 19, 1989, p. 9.

13. Patricia Ward Wallace, *Our Land, Our Lives*, pp. 94–96.

14. Ibid., p. 95.

15. Charles A. Bennett, *Cotton Ginning Systems in the United States and Auxiliary Developments*, pp. 31–45.

16. Algernon L. Smith, *Continental Gin Company and Its Fifty-Two Years of Service*, p. 13.

17. Ibid., pp. 9–14.

18. Thomas B. Chatham, telephone interview with author, Mar. 27, 1991.

19. Smith, *Continental Gin Company*, pp. 55–56.

20. Bennett, *Auxiliary Developments*, p. 23.

CHAPTER 7

1. Alfred M. Pendleton and Beverly G. Reeves, "The Hermann Focke Gin," *The Cotton Gin and Oil Mill Press* (July 13, 1968): 11–12.

2. "Early Gin Made Duval Co. Big Cotton Center in '80s," *Duval County Facts*, A. M. Pendleton's personal papers.

3. "History of First Gin on South Plains," Whitener Fans, Inc., Lubbock, Texas, The Southwest Collection, Texas Tech University, Lubbock.

4. L. V. Risinger, interview with author, Lubbock, Tex., Apr. 7, 1989, and references following.

5. Charlie F. Hunter, interview with author, Lubbock, Tex., Apr. 7, 1989, and references following.

6. O. R. Carey, interview with author, Lubbock, Tex., Apr. 7, 1989, and references following.

7. Donald Baird, interview with author, San Antonio, Tex., Jan. 30, 1991, and references following.

8. Charles A. Bennett, *Cotton Ginning Systems in the United States and Auxiliary Developments,* pp. 19–20.

9. Charles A. Bennett, *Saw and Toothed Cotton Ginning Developments,* p. 10.

10. Bennett, *Auxiliary Developments,* p. 23.

11. Ibid, pp. 53, 72.

12. F. H. Lummus Sons Co. Catalogue, 1909, p. 16.

13. Bennett, *Auxiliary Developments,* pp. 38, 45.

14. F. H. Lummus Sons Co. Catalogue, 1909, p. 32.

15. Bennett, *Saw and Toothed Ginning,* p. 48. Other sources state that King was from St. Louis, Missouri.

16. Algernon L. Smith, *Story of the Continental Gin Company, 1900–1952* p. 48.

17. Charles Bennett, *Roller Cotton Ginning Developments,* pp. 19–21.

18. Ibid, p. 24.

19. Algernon L. Smith, *Continental Gin Company and Its Fifty-Two Years of Service,* pp. 21–25.

20. Ibid, pp. 37–47.

21. *The Lummus Combination Cotton Gins and Other Ginning Machinery,* F. H. Lummus Sons Catalogue, Jan. 1, 1899.

22. "History of Lummus Gin Company," typed manuscript, Lummus Industries, Inc., p. 12.

23. "History," Lummus Industries, Inc., pp. 14–15.

CHAPTER 8

1. Victor H. Schoffelmayer, *Southwest Trails to New Horizons,* p. 101.

2. E. R. Alexander, "Cotton Enterprise," *Southern Field-Crop Enterprises,* pp. 8–13.

3. C. A. Myers, interview with the author, Beeville, Tex., Feb. 13, 1991.

4. Alexander, "Cotton Enterprise," p. 3. That record crop was grown on 47,653,000 acres.

5. Mrs. Minnie S. Bains, interview with author, Brookshire, Tex., Sept. 1, 1990, and references following.

6. C. A. Myers, correspondence with author, Feb. 13, 1991.

7. Risinger, interview, and references following.

8. Gilbert C. Fite, "Recent Progress in the Mechanization of Cotton Production in the United States," *Agricultural History* 24:1–4 (Jan., 1950), pp. 19–28.

9. Schoffelmayer, *Southwest Trails,* pp. 102–103.

10. James S. Hathcock, *Practices and Costs of Cotton-Gin Operation in North-Central Texas, 1924–1925,* pp. 2–3.

11. Ibid, pp. 3–4.

12. Donald Baird, interview with author, San Antonio, Tex., Jan. 30, 1991, and references following.

13. Annie Maud Knittel Avis, "Burton Farmers Gin," pp. 1–2.

14. O. R. Carey, interview with author, Lubbock, Tex., Apr. 7, 1989, and references following.

15. Douglas Ratchford, "Bessemer Model IV at the Burton Cotton Gin," *Gas Engines Magazine* (Jan., 1990): 24–26.

16. Billy Thompson, interview with author, Burton, Tex., Apr. 21, 1990, and correspondence with author, May 29, 1990.

17. Alexander, "Cotton Enterprise," pp. 56–58.

18. Frankie Jaster, interview with author, Burton, Tex., Nov. 18, 1988, and references following.

CHAPTER 9

1. Lewis Stanford, interview with author, Livingston, Tex., July 18, 1987, and references following.

2. Charles A. Bennett, *Cotton Ginning Systems in the United States and Auxiliary Developments,* pp. 46–47.

3. *Continental Cotton Ginning Machinery,* Catalogue no. 143, p. 34.

4. *The Lummus Cotton Gin Co.,* Catalogue no. 1612, p. 20.

5. *Continental,* Catalogue no. 143, p. 21.

6. Bennett, *Auxiliary Developments,* p. 53.

7. Upshur, Vincent, "Cotton Prices Are Compared," *Fort Worth Star-Telegram,* Aug. 11, 1931.

8. Donald Baird, interview with author, San Antonio, Tex., May 18, 1991.

9. Algernon L. Smith, *Continental Gin Company and Its Fifty-Two Years of Service,* pp. 77–78.

10. "Gearing Texas Cotton to War Needs," Texas Agricultural Experiment Station, Bulletin no. 624, (Nov., 1942): 4–6, 18–19.

11. Smith, *Continental Gin Company,* p. 94.

12. Ibid, p. 95.

13. Bennett, *Auxiliary Developments,* pp. 49–51.

14. C. A. Myers, correspondence with author, Feb. 13, 1991.

15. Iva Cabrera, interview with author, Houston, Tex., Mar. 27, 1991.

16. Gilbert C. Fite, "Recent Progress in the Mechanization of Cotton Production in the United States," *Agricultural History* 24:1–4 (Jan., 1950): 20–21.

17. Ibid, p. 24.

18. Ibid, pp. 24–25.

19. Ibid, p. 27.

20. Agricultural Engineering Research Branch, Agricultural Research Service *Modernizing Cotton Gins,* Agriculture Handbook no. 99, Aug., 1956, p. 4.

21. *Handbook for Cotton Ginners,* Feb., 1964, pp. 98–99.

22. Agricultural Research Service, *Roller Ginning American-Egyptian Cotton in the Southwest,* Jan., 1964, p. 2.

23. *Roller Ginning American-Egyptian Cotton,* pp. 3–22.

CHAPTER 10

1. Donald Baird, interview with author, San Antonio, Tex., Jan. 30, 1991, and references following.

2. Lambert Wilkes, telephone interview with author, Mar. 19, 1990.

3. A. L. Vandergriff, interview with author, Lubbock, Tex., Apr. 7, 1988, and references following.

4. Calvin B. Parnell, Jr., "Cotton Ginning Systems," typed manuscript, Texas Agricultural Extension Service, ca. 1975, pp. 1–13.

5. Billy Thompson, transcript of speech given to Lummus company employees, Oct. 31, 1988.

6. W. Stanley Anthony, "Relative Cleaning Effectiveness of Various Gin Machines," *The Cotton Gin and Oil Mill Press* (May 4, 1991): 10–11.

7. "1989 Pima Production More Than Doubles," *The Cotton Gin and Oil Mill Press* (May 5, 1990): 14.

8. Donald Van Doorn, "Modern Gins and True Fiber Quality," transcript of speech, Jan. 6, 1986.

9. Carl G. Anderson, Jr., "HVI Classing Improves Quality of Texas Cotton," typed manuscript, Texas Agricultural Extension Service, Oct., 1990.

10. Joe Owens, interview with author, Waco, Tex., Sept. 8, 1987.

11. Larry Nelson, "Transition to 1990: A Decade of Progress and Promise," *The Cotton Gin and Oil Mill Press* (May 5, 1990): 7.

12. "Farm Bill Could Increase Plantings but Drop Prices in Texas," *The Cotton Gin and Oil Mill Press* (Dec. 1, 1990): 10.

Bibliography

INTERVIEWS

Bains, Minnie S. Interview with author. Brookshire, Texas, September 1, 1990.

Baird, Donald. Interview with author. San Antonio, Texas, January 30, May 18, 1991.

Cabrera, Iva. Telephone interview with author. March 27, 1991.

Carey, O. R., Jr. Interview with author. Lubbock, Texas, April 7, 1989.

Chatham, Thomas B. Telephone interview with author. March 27, 1991.

Hunter, Charlie F. Interview with author. Lubbock, Texas, April 7, 1989.

Jaster, Frankie. Interview with author. Burton, Texas, November 18, 1988.

Jones, Larry N. Telephone interview with author, February 12, 1990.

Myers, C. A. Interview with author. Beeville, Texas, February 13, 1991. Correspondence with author, February 13, 1991.

Owens, Joe. Interview with author. Moody, Texas, September 8, 1987.

Risinger, L. V. Interview with author. Lubbock, Texas, April 7, 1989.

Stanford, Lewis. Interview with author. Livingston, Texas, July 18, 1987.

Thompson, Billy. Interview with author. Burton, Texas, April 21, 1990. Correspondence with author, May 29, 1990.

Vandergriff, A. L. Interview with author. Lubbock, Texas, April 7, 1988.

Wilkes, Lambert. Telephone interview with author. March 19, 1990.

ARCHIVAL MATERIALS
(LISTED CHRONOLOGICALLY)

Continental Eagle Corporation

Manuscript copies of correspondence between Daniel Pratt and D. G. Olmsted (Eureka Gin Co.), 1861 and 1867.

Drawing: Elevation of the Ginners Compress, July 5, 1900.

Continental Direct Connected Outfits with Air Blast Gins. Bulletin no. 107-A, ca. 1915.

"How the Cotton Ginning Industry Came to Bridgewater, Mass." Typed manuscript, ca. 1915.

Repair Parts of Munger Gins. Bulletin no. 123-A (Third Edition), July, 1921. Courtesy A. O. "Bill" Kressenberg.

Continental Cotton Ginning Machinery. Catalogue no. 143, 1927.

Continental Cotton Ginning Machinery. Catalogue no. 165-A, ca. 1933.

Smith, Algernon L. "Sixty Years Experience with Cotton Gins." Typed manuscript, 1948.

———. *Continental Gin Company and Its Fifty-Two Years of Service.* Birmingham: Continental Gin Co., 1952.

———. *Story of the Continental Gin Company, 1900–1952.* Birmingham: Continental Gin Co., 1952.

———. Untitled typed manuscript, n.d.

"Historical Information about Daniel Pratt." Typed manuscript, n.d.

Richardson, T. C. "His Majesty Gossypium." *Farm and Ranch,* January 18, 1930.

Streun, John A. "History of Early Cotton Gin Inventions." Typed manuscript, ca. 1939.

Pratt, Merrill E. "Daniel Pratt, Alabama's First Industrialist." Address presented to the Newcomen Society in North America, Birmingham, Alabama, December 13, 1949.

Gates, Samuel P. "Memorandum to A. L. Smith." Typed manuscript, October 25, 1955.

"History of Gullet Gins." Catalogue page, n.d.

Redden, Willie. "Creating an Industry." Typed manuscript, 1989.

Various product brochures.

Lummus Industries, Inc.

The Lummus Combination Cotton Gins and Other Ginning Machinery. F. H. Lummus and Sons Catalogue, January 1, 1899.

F. H. Lummus Sons Co. Catalogue, 1909.

The Lummus Cotton Gin Co. Catalogue 1612, ca. 1910.

Drawing: Elevation for Farmers Gin Association, Burton, Texas, February 28, 1923.

Lummus Cotton Gin Co. Cotton Ginning Machinery. Catalogue 28, ca. 1928.

Lummus Cotton Gin Co. Catalogue 35, ca. 1940.

"World War II." Printed Company History, pp. 55–60.

Various brochures: Steel Buildings, no. 610; L-E-F Feeder, no. 622; Hull Separator, no. 627; Tower Drier, no. 635; Condensers, no. 660.

"History of Lummus Gin Company." Typed manuscript, n.d.

"History of the Lummus Super 88-Saw Gin." Typed manuscript, February 8, 1962.

Van Doorn, Donald W. "What Is New From Lummus." Typed manuscript, January 6, 1985.

"Modern Gins and True Fiber Quality." Typed manuscript, January 6, 1986.

Thompson, Billy. Speech given to Lummus company employees. Typed manuscript, October 31, 1988.

Various product brochures.

PUBLIC AGENCY MATERIALS

Texas Agricultural Extension Service,
The Texas A&M University System, College Station, Texas

Alexander, U. U., *et al. Keys to Profitable Cotton Production in the Rolling Plains.* Bulletin B-1455, 8/83 Revision.

Anderson, Carl G., Jr. "HVI Classing Improves Quality of Texas Cotton." Typed manuscript. Texas Agricultural Extension Service, Texas A&M University, College Station, October, 1990.

Ashlock, Lanny, and Robert B. Metzer. *Keys to Profitable Cotton Production in the Coastal Bend.* Bulletin B-1200, 1/79 Revision.

Blalock, James, and Robert B. Metzer. *Cotton Production in the Blackland Prairie and Grand Prairie.* Bulletin B-1628, 5/89 Revision.

Boring, Emory P., III, J. E. Slosser, and Robert J. Fewin. *Windbreak Management to Reduce Overwintering Boll Weevil Habitat.* Bulletin L-2135, 4/85 Revision.

Gaines, J. C. *Cotton Insects.* Bulletin B-933, 7/65 Reprint.

"Gearing Texas Cotton to War Needs." Texas Agricultural Experiment Station, Bulletin no. 624 (November, 1942): 4–6, 18–19.

Metzer, Robert B. *High Quality Cotton Planting Seed—A Guide to Production and Handling.* Bulletin L-1423, 4/76 Revision.

Metzer, Robert B., James R. Supak, and Roy E. Childers. *Keys to High Quality Lint and Seed With A Cotton Module Builder.* Bulletin L-2078, 4/83 Revision.

Metzer, Robert B., and James R. Supak. *Cotton Harvest-Aid Chemicals.* Bulletin B-1593, 12/87 Revision.

Parker, Roy D., and Randy L. Zrubek. *Management of Cotton Insects in the Southern, Eastern and Blackland Areas of Texas.* Bulletin B-1204, 2/89 Revision.

Parnell, Calvin B., Jr. "Cotton Ginning Systems." Typed manuscript. College Station: Texas Agricultural Extension Service, ca. 1975.

Pennington, Dale, and Robert B. Metzer. *Keys to Profitable Cotton Production in the Lower Rio Grande Valley.* Bulletin MP-1290, 8/76 Revision.

Stichler, Charles, Charles T. Allen, Robert B. Metzer, and Carl Anderson. *Pima Cotton Production Guide.* Bulletin L-2241, 7/87.

Supak, James R., and Robert B. Metzer. *Keys to Profitable Cotton Production in the High Plains.* Bulletin MP-1311, 1/77.

Walla, Walter J., and Luther S. Bird. *The Cotton Seedling Disease Complex and Its Control.* Bulletin L-2002, 12/81.

Weaver, Dave. *1988 Suggestions for Weed Control with Chemicals in Cotton.* Supplement to Bulletin MP-1059.

U.S. Department of Agriculture Publications
Agricultural Research Service.

Agricultural Engineering Research Branch, Agricultural Research Service. *Modernizing Cotton Gins.* USDA: Washington, D.C., Agriculture Handbook no. 99, August, 1956.

Agricultural Research Service. *Roller Ginning American-Egyptian Cotton in the Southwest.* USDA: Washington, D. C., Agriculture Handbook no. 257, January, 1964.

———. *Handbook for Cotton Ginners.* USDA: Washington, D.C., Agriculture Handbook no. 260, February, 1964.

———. *Cotton Ginners Handbook.* USDA: Washington, D.C., Agriculture Handbook no. 503, July, 1977.

Hathcock, James S. *Practices and Costs of Cotton-Gin Operation In North-Central Texas, 1924–25.* USDA: Washington, D.C., Technical Bulletin no. 13, July, 1927.

Pendleton, Alfred M., and Vernon P. Moore. *Ginning Cotton to Preserve Fiber Quality.* Federal Extension Service, USDA: Washington, D.C., September, 1967.

BOOKS AND ARTICLES

Abshier, Mildred W. "How Cotton and the Cotton Gin Came to Texas." *Cotton Gins of Waller County, Texas, 1825–1976,* Waller County Historical Commission, 1981.

Agee, James, and Walker Evans. *Let Us Now Praise Famous Men.* Boston: Houghton Mifflin Company, 1969.

Alexander, E. R. "Cotton Enterprise." In *Southern Field-Crop Enterprises.* Chicago and Philadelphia: J. B. Lippincott Co., 1937, pp. 1–60.

Anthony, W. Stanley. "Relative Cleaning Effectiveness of Various Gin Machines." *The Cotton Gin and Oil Mill Press* (May 4, 1991): 10–11.

Avis, Annie Maud Knittel. "Burton Farmers Gin." Typed manuscript, Burton, Texas, 1987.

Baker, Gladys L. "Agriculture." *Dictionary of American History, Revised Edition.* New York: Charles Scribner's Sons, 1976, 1:36–47.

Baker, T. Lindsay. *Building the Lone Star.* College Station: Texas A&M University Press, 1986.

———. "The Greek Engineer at the Compress." *Eagle News* (Cleburne, Texas), January 19, 1989.

Bennett, Charles A. *Cotton Ginning Systems in the United States and Auxiliary Developments.* Dallas: The Cotton Ginners' Journal and The Cotton Gin and Oil Mill Press, 1962.

———. "Getting More from Ginning Machinery." *Cotton Ginners' Journal and Yearbook* 24, no. 1 (March, 1956): 20.

———. *Roller Cotton Ginning Developments.* Dallas: The Cotton Ginners' Journal and The Cotton Gin and Oil Mill Press, n.d. (ca. 1959).

———. *Saw and Toothed Cotton Ginning Developments.* Dallas: The Cotton Ginners' Journal and The Cotton Gin and Oil Mill Press, n.d. (ca. 1960).

———. "The World's Two Types of Gins." Rpt. *The Cotton Gin and Oil Mill Press,* August 11, 1956.

Bertleth, Rosa Groce. "Jared Ellison Groce." *Southwestern Historical Quarterly* 20, no. 4 (April, 1917): 358–68.

Bolton, Herbert E. *Texas in the Middle Eighteenth Century.* Austin: University of Texas Press in Cooperation with the Texas State Historical Association, 1970.

Britton, Karen. "Operation Restoration." *Cotton Gin and Oil Mill Press* (January 14, 1989): 6–8.

Bruchey, Stuart, editor. *Cotton and the Growth of the American Economy: 1790–1860.* New York: Harcourt, Brace & World, 1967.

Buyers Guide to U.S. Cotton 1988. Memphis: Cotton Council International and National Cotton Council of America, 1988.

Carter, Hodding, and Anthony Ragusin. *Gulf Coast Country.* New York: Duell, Sloan & Pearce, 1951.

Cash, W. J. *The Mind of the South.* New York: Vintage Books, 1961.

Clay, W. J. *Agricultural and Statistical Report 1905.* Austin: State Printing Company, 1905.

Clinton, Catherine. *The Plantation Mistress.* New York: Pantheon Books, 1982.

Coe, Michael D. *The Maya.* New York: Thames and Hudson, 1987.

"Columbian Spinster." *Textile World* (February, 1938): 74.

Dethloff, Henry C., and Irvin M. May, Jr. *Southwestern Agriculture, Pre-Columbian to Modern.* College Station: Texas A&M University Press, 1982.

Dodge, Bertha S. *Cotton: The Plant That Would Be King.* Austin: University of Texas Press, 1984.

"Early Gin Made Duval Co. Big Cotton Center in '80s." *Duval County Facts,* A. M. Pendleton's personal papers, n.d.

Economic Services. *Economic Outlook for U.S. Cotton 1988.* Memphis: National Cotton Council of America, March, 1988.

Edwards, Jay. "Pipe Creek's Cotton Gin and Grist Mill." *History of Bandera County Texas.* Bandera County History Book Committee, 1986.

Elliot, Fred C., Marvin Hoover, and Walter K. Porter, Jr. *Cotton: Principles and Practices.* Ames: Iowa State University Press, 1968.

Fairservis, Walter A., Jr. *Costumes of the East.* Riverside, Conn.: Chatham Press, 1971.

Farber, James. *Texas, C.S.A.* New York: Jackson Co., 1947.

"Farm Bill Could Increase Plantings but Drop Prices in Texas." *The Cotton Gin and Oil Mill Press* (December 1, 1990): 10.

Fehrenbach, T. R. *Lone Star.* New York: Collier Books, 1985.

Fite, Gilbert C. *Cotton Fields No More, Southern Agriculture 1865–1980.* Lexington: University Press of Kentucky, 1984.

———. "Recent Progress in the Mechanization of Cotton Production in the United States." *Agricultural History* 24, nos. 1–4 (January, 1950): 19–28.

Fryxell, Paul A. *The Natural History of the Cotton Tribe.* College Station: Texas A&M University Press, 1979.

Gambrell, Herbert, and Virginia Gambrell. *A Pic-*

torial History of Texas. New York: E. P. Dutton & Co., 1960.

Green, Constance M. *Eli Whitney and the Birth of American Technology.* Boston: Little, Brown & Co., 1956.

Greene, Jack P., editor. *Settlements to Society, 1607–1763.* New York: W. W. Norton & Co., 1975.

Guthrie, Keith. *Texas' Forgotten Ports.* Austin: Eakin Press, 1988.

Gutman, Judith Mara. *The Colonial Venture.* New York: Basic Books, 1966.

Henson, Margaret Swett. *Samuel May Williams, Early Texas Entrepreneur.* College Station: Texas A&M University Press, 1976.

"History of First Gin on South Plains," Whitener Fans, Inc., Lubbock, Texas, The Southwest Collection, Texas Tech University, Lubbock, n.d.

Hodge, Frederick W., and Theodore H. Lewis. *Spanish Explorers in the Southern United States, 1528–1543.* New York: Barnes & Noble, 1959.

Hogan, William Ransom. *The Texas Republic: A Social and Economic History.* Austin: University of Texas Press, 1986.

Horwitz, Elinor Lander. *On The Land: American Agriculture from Past to Present.* New York: Atheneum, 1980.

Houston: A Nation's Capitol 1837–1839. Houston: Harris County Historical Society, 1985.

Hughes, Harold D., and Darrel S. Metcalfe. *Crop Production.* New York: Macmillan Company, 1972.

Hyman, Harold M. *Oleander Odyssey: The Kempners of Galveston, Texas, 1854–1980s.* College Station: Texas A&M University Press, 1990.

Industrial Texas 1913. Fort Worth: Texas Commercial Secretaries and Business Men's Association.

Jackson, Donald. *Voyages of the Steamboat Yellow Stone.* New York: Ticknor & Fields, 1985.

Jockusch, Julius W., Jr. "A Cargo of Cotton That Made History." *Dallas Morning News,* March 4, 1928.

Jordan, Terry G. *German Seed in Texas Soil.* Austin: University of Texas Press, 1975.

Kytle, Jack, and Luther Clark, editors. *Alabama, A Guide to the Deep South.* Compiled by Workers of the Alabama Writers' Program of the Work Projects Administration. New York: Hastings House, 1941.

Lea, Tom. *The King Ranch.* Vol. 1. Boston: Little, Brown & Co., 1957.

Lewis, C. F., and T. R. Richmond. "Cotton as a Crop." In *Cotton: Principles and Practices.* Edited by Fred C. Elliot, Marvin Hoover, and Walter K. Porter, Jr. Ames: Iowa State University Press, 1968.

Lewton, F. L. "Historical Notes on the Cotton Gin." *The Smithsonian Report for 1937, Publication 3478.* Washington: U.S. Government Printing Office, 1938, pp. 549–63.

Lich, Glen E. *The German Texans.* San Antonio: University of Texas Institute of Texan Cultures at San Antonio, 1981.

McAshan, Marie Phelps. *On the Corner of Main and Texas: A Houston Legacy.* Edited by Mary Jo Bell. Houston: Hutchins House, 1985.

McComb, David G. *Galveston: A History.* Austin: University of Texas Press, 1986.

———. *Houston: A History.* Austin: University of Texas Press, 1981.

McGovern, George, editor. *Agricultural Thought in the Twentieth Century.* New York: Bobbs-Merrill Co., 1967.

Miller, J. Innes. *The Spice Trade of the Roman Empire, 29 B.C.–A.D. 641.* London: Oxford University Press, 1969.

Montgomery, James. *The Cotton Manufacture of the United States Contrasted and Compared with That of Great Britain, 1840.* New York: Burt Franklin, 1970.

Moore, Vernon P. "Development of the Saw Gin." *Cotton Ginners Handbook #503.* Agricultural Research Service. Washington: U.S. Department of Agriculture, 1977, p. 2.

Muir, Andrew Forest, editor. *Texas in 1837.* Austin: University of Texas Press, 1988.

Mullin, Michael, editor. *American Negro Slavery: A Documentary History.* Columbia: University of South Carolina Press, 1976.

Myers, Gustavus. *History of the Great American Fortunes.* New York: Random House, 1937.

Natural Fibers Economic Research. *A Chronological History of Cotton.* Austin: University of Texas, September, 1975.

———. *150 Years of Cotton in Texas.* Austin: University of Texas, December, 1974.

Nelson, Larry. "Transition to 1990: A Decade of Progress and Promise." *The Cotton Gin and Oil Mill Press* (May 5, 1990): 7.

"1989 Pima Production More Than Doubles." *The Cotton Gin and Oil Mill Press* (May 5, 1990): 14.

"Old Gin Moves West." *The Cotton Gin and Oil Mill Press* (May 27, 1961): 10, 55.

Olmsted, Frederick Law. *A Journey through Texas.* Austin: University of Texas Press, 1986.

Pass, Fred. "Like Cotton Industry, Old Gin to Move West." *The Dallas Morning News,* May 1, 1961.

Paulsen, Gary. *Farm: A History and Celebration of the American Farmer.* Englewood Cliffs, N.J.: Prentice-Hall, 1977.

Pendleton, Alfred M. "The Ginner–Key Influence in Efficient Cotton Mechanization." *The Cotton Gin and Oil Mill Press* (February 16, 1963): 16.

———. "Ginning Cotton in the Blacklands–Understand the Importance of Moisture and Trash on Quality." *The Cotton Ginners' Journal and Yearbook,* 1968, p. 20.

———. "The Good Old Days." *The Cotton Ginners' Journal and Yearbook* 24, no. 1 (March, 1956): 40.

———. "Something to Think About." *Extension Service Review.* U.S. Department of Agriculture, vol. 35, no. 10 (October, 1964): 178.

Pendleton, Alfred M., and Beverly G. Reeves. "The Hermann Focke Gin." *The Cotton Gin and Oil Mill Press* (July 13, 1968): 11–12.

Pendleton, Alfred M., and Edward H. Bush. "Old Gin Dates Back to 1874 or '75." *The Cotton Gin and Oil Mill Press* (March 27, 1954): 18.

Pratt, Minnie E. "Four Autaugans and Their Place in Alabama History." Historical Information about Daniel Pratt (typed manuscript). Continental Gin Company, April 22, 1966, p. 6.

Ramsdell, Charles W. *Reconstruction in Texas.* Third Edition. Austin: University of Texas Press, 1970.

Ratchford, Douglas. "Bessemer Model IV at the Burton Cotton Gin." *Gas Engines Magazine* (January, 1990): 24–26.

Ratner, Sidney, James H. Soltow, and Richard Sylla. *The Evolution of the American Economy.* New York: Basic Books, 1979.

Record of the National Cotton Council: The First Forty Years, 1939–1979. Memphis: National Cotton Council of America, ca. 1979.

Reuben, Richard. "1896 Steam Powered Cotton Gin." Unpublished research report. Tifton: Georgia Agrirama Development Authority, 1977.

Richardson, Rubert N., Ernest Wallace, and Adrian N. Anderson. *Texas: The Lone Star State.* Fourth Edition. Englewood Cliffs, N.J.: Prentice-Hall, 1981.

Schlebecker, John T. *Whereby We Thrive, a History of American Farming, 1607–1972.* Ames: Iowa State University Press, 1975.

Schoffelmayer, Victor H. *Southwest Trails to New Horizons.* San Antonio: Naylor Co., 1960.

Shenker, Israel. "A Painter with Heart, in the Guise of a Misanthrope." *Smithsonian Magazine* (October, 1988): 58–69.

Siegel, Stanley E. *Houston: A Chronicle of the Supercity on Buffalo Bayou.* Produced in Cooperation with the Harris County Historical Society. Woodland Hills, Calif.: Windsor Publications, 1983.

Silverthorne, Elizabeth. *Plantation Life in Texas.* College Station: Texas A&M University Press, 1986.

Smith, Algernon L. *Continental Gin Company and Its Fifty-Two Years of Service.* Birmingham: Continental Gin Co., 1952.

———. *Story of the Continental Gin Company, 1900–1952.* Birmingham: Continental Gin Co., 1952.

Smithwick, Noah. *The Evolution of a State or Recollections of Old Texas Days.* Austin: University of Texas Press, 1984.

Sobel, Robert, and David B. Sicilia. *The Entrepreneurs: An American Adventure.* Boston: Houghton Mifflin Company, 1986.

Stadiem, William. *A Class by Themselves: The Untold Story of the Great Southern Families.* New York: Crown Publishers, 1980.

"Star Cotton Press, Advertisement." *The Texas Almanac–1857.* Facsimile Edition 1966, A. H. Belo Corporation, n.p.

Stedronsky, V. L. "Extra Long Staple Cotton and Roller Ginning." *The Cotton Ginners' Journal and Yearbook* 24, no. 1 (March, 1956): 37.

Steinberg, Alfred. *The First Ten–The Founding Presidents and Their Administrations.* Garden City, N.Y.: Doubleday & Company, 1967.

Teas, Thomas S. *A Trading Trip to Natchez and New Orleans, 1822: Diary of Thomas S. Teas.* Contributed by Edward Teas. Edited by Julia Ideson and Sanford W. Higginbotham. Rpt. from *Journal of Southern History* 7, no. 3 (August, 1941).

Upshur, Vincent. "Cotton Prices are Compared." *Fort Worth Star Telegram,* August 11, 1931.

Wallace, Patricia Ward. *Our Land, Our Lives.* Norfolk/Virginia Beach, Va.: Donning Co., Publishers, 1986.

Webb, Walter Prescott. *The Great Plains.* New York: Grosset & Dunlap, 1931.

White, John C. "A Prospectus on Texas Cotton." *The Cotton Ginners' Journal and Yearbook* 24, no. 1 (March, 1956): 49.

White, Raymond E. "Cotton Ginning in Texas to 1861." *Southwest Historical Quarterly* 61, no. 2 (October, 1957): 257–69.

Woodman, Harold D. *King Cotton and His Retainers.* Lexington, Ky.: University of Kentucky Press, 1968.

Wright, Louis B. *The Cultural Life of the American Colonies.* New York: Harper & Row, Publishers, 1962.

Wright, Louis B., Michael Blow, *et al. The American Heritage History of the Thirteen Colonies.* American Heritage Publishing Co., 1967.

Index

Bale o' Cotton was composed into type on a Compugraphic digital phototypesetter in ten point Galliard with two points of spacing between the lines. Galliard italic was selected for display. The book was designed by Susan Pearce, typeset by Metricomp, Inc., and printed offset by Hart Graphics, Inc. The books were bound by John H. Dekker & Sons, Inc. The paper on which this book is printed carries acid-free characteristics for an effective life of at least three hundred years.

TEXAS A&M UNIVERSITY PRESS
COLLEGE STATION